BEGINNING AGAIN

1

By Leonard Woolf

History and Politics
INTERNATIONAL GOVERNMENT
EMPIRE AND COMMERCE IN AFRICA
CO-OPERATION AND THE FUTURE OF INDUSTRY
SOCIALISM AND CO-OPERATION
FEAR AND POLITICS
IMPERIALISM AND CIVILIZATION
AFTER THE DELUGE VOL. I
AFTER THE DELUGE VOL. II
QUACK, QUACK!
PRINCIPIA POLITICA
BARBARIANS AT THE GATE
THE WAR FOR PEACE

Criticism
HUNTING THE HIGHBROW
ESSAYS ON LITERATURE, HISTORY AND POLITICS

Fiction
THE VILLAGE IN THE JUNGLE
STORIES OF THE EAST
THE WISE VIRGINS

Drama
THE HOTEL

Autobiography
SOWING: AN AUTOBIOGRAPHY OF THE YEARS 1880 TO 1904
GROWING: AN AUTOBIOGRAPHY OF THE YEARS 1904 TO 1911
BEGINNING AGAIN: AN AUTOBIOGRAPHY OF THE YEARS 1911 TO 1918
DOWNHILL ALL THE WAY: AN AUTOBIOGRAPHY OF THE YEARS 1919 TO 1939
THE JOURNEY NOT THE ARRIVAL MATTERS:
AN AUTOBIOGRAPHY OF THE YEARS 1939 TO 1969

A CALENDAR OF CONSOLATION: A COMFORTING
THOUGHT FOR EVERY DAY IN THE YEAR

BEGINNING AGAIN

AN AUTOBIOGRAPHY
OF THE YEARS 1911 TO 1918

Leonard Woolf

HBJ

A Harvest Book
HARCOURT BRACE JOVANOVICH
NEW YORK AND LONDON

Printed in the United States of America

Library of Congress Cataloging in Publication Data
Woolf, Leonard Sidney, 1880-1969.
   Beginning again.
   (A Harvest book ; HB 321)
   Continuation of Growing; an autobiography of the years 1904
to 1911.
   Continued by Downhill all the way; an autobiography of the
years 1919 to 1939.
   Includes index.
   1. Woolf, Leonard Sidney, 1880-1969. I. Title.
JA94.W6A26   1975   320'.092'4   [B]   75-9848
ISBN 0-15-611680-4

First Harvest edition 1972

A B C D E F G H I J

To Trekkie

CONTENTS

ILLUSTRATIONS

Sein Blick ist vom Vorübergehen der Stäbe
so müd geworden, dasz er nichts mehr hält.
Ihm ist, als ob es tausend Stäbe gäbe
und hinter tausend Stäben keine Welt.

His gaze from going through the bars has
grown so weary that it can take in nothing
more. For him it is as though there were a
thousand bars and behind the thousand bars
no world.

RILKE: *Der Panther*

FOREWORD

In writing this third volume of my autobiography I have often been haunted by the lines from Rilke's superb poem 'Der Panther' which I have had printed at the beginning of this book. This volume is the record of my life during the first great war and all through the war one felt that one was behind bars, and now recalling those years it seems to me that one was looking at the world and one's own life through bars. But then another thought, a terrible doubt, came to me. There are other bars, permanent bars of the cage of one's life, through which one has always and will always gaze at the world. The bars of one's birth and family and ancestors, of one's school and college, of one's own secret and sinuous psychology. Has not my mind, my soul, if I have a soul, for the last 82 years been pacing up and down like the panther, backwards and forwards, behind these bars and gazing through them until, so weary, I have seen, not the world or life, but only the bars—a thousand bars and behind the thousand bars no world?

I have to thank the Public Trustee and The Society of Authors for allowing me to quote Bernard Shaw's letter.

Part One

LONDON AND MARRIAGE, 1911 AND 1912

On Wednesday, May 24, 1911, I left Ceylon on leave after my six and a half years there as a civil servant. My leave was for one year. I sailed in the *Staffordshire* with my sister Bella, who had married R. H. Lock, the Assistant Director of the Peradeniya Botanical Gardens. Seventeen days later, on Saturday, June 10, we arrived in Marseille. It was a dull and rather dreary voyage. I like all voyages out, for you sail into the future, the unknown, into a widening horizon. And so all return journeys are somewhat depressing, even if you are on a year's leave and terribly eager to arrive and be once more home. You are going back to what you know—the horizon narrows. I feel that somehow my youth ended on Wednesday, May 24, 1911—though I was already 31, I was a young man when I left Colombo, but slightly middle-aged when I reached Marseille.

It was, of course, very strange and exciting to walk up the Marseille street. What astonished and entranced us most in our first view of Europe was the shops full of every kind of chocolate creams; we ate them steadily on the long train journey to Paris. I remember nothing of the France and Europe of my journey home except the chocolate creams. When we got off the boat at Folkestone, my brothers, Herbert and Edgar, were there to meet us—they had become strangers to me in six and a half years. And when we got into a taxi at Charing Cross and drove into Trafalgar Square, I felt at once, in the rhythm of the streets, that I had come back to a new world. The world of the four-wheeler and the hansom cab, which I had left in 1904, no longer existed. I felt for the moment like a relic from a slower age, for the life into which I was plunging out of Charing Cross railway station had a tempo clearly faster and noisier than what I was accustomed to. I faced it with caution and reserve and some depression.

We drove out to Putney in a London summer afternoon of perfect sunshine—1911 was one of those rare years, an unending summer of the snakeless meadow—in 1911 a summer which began in early spring and gently died away only in late autumn. In 1904 when I landed in Colombo and walked round to the Secretariat, to report my arrival, through the sun and sights and sounds and smells of Asia, I felt, as I wrote in *Growing*, as if my whole past life in London and Cambridge had suddenly vanished, fading away into unreality. And yet Colombo and myself walking in its dusty streets were not entirely real; then and all through my years in Ceylon I felt a certain unreality, theatricality, as if out of the corner of my eye I observed myself acting a part. The curious thing about my return to England was that, driving out from Charing Cross to Putney through the mechanized, bricked up sunshine of this London summer, I felt almost exactly what I had felt seven years ago in Colombo. My life in Ceylon, in Jaffna, Kandy, and Hambantota, suddenly vanished into unreality; but London and myself driving through its ugly streets did not acquire any reassuring reality. Out of the corner of my eye I seemed to observe myself once more acting a part in the same complicated play in front of a new backcloth and with different actors and a different audience.

I was born an introspective intellectual, and the man or woman who is by nature addicted to introspection gets into the habit, after the age of 15 or 16, of feeling himself, often intensely, as 'I' and yet at the same time of seeing himself

16

out of the corner of his eye as a 'not I', a stranger acting a part upon a stage. I always feel, from moment to moment, that my life and the life around me is immediately and extraordinarily real, concrete, and yet at the same time there is something absurdly unreal about it, because, knowing too well what I am really like inside, I cannot avoid continually watching myself playing a part upon a stage. This is the result of observing oneself objectively. It has a curious psychological effect; it helps one, I think, to bear with some equanimity both the ills one has and the ills one knows not of. If you begin to regard yourself objectively, you begin to find that what matters so violently to you subjectively hardly matters at all to the objective you.

Thus it was that driving out to Putney on Sunday, June 11, 1911, about 4 p.m. in the Fulham Road I suddenly once more became aware of a kind of split in my personality, of the I, the real I, sitting in the taxi talking to my sister Bella and my brothers, Herbert and Edgar, and of that other I who had already begun to play a new part in Scene I, Act I, of a quite new play. Today, 51 years later, in June, 1962, I am still playing my part in that play.

When we reached our destination, the house in Colinette Road, Putney, the mixture of reality and unreality, of familiarity and strangeness, was bewildering. This was the same house to which my mother with her nine children had migrated nearly 20 years before, when owing to my father's death we became overnight comparatively poor. It was the house from which, seven years before, I had set out for Ceylon. On the surface very little had changed in the house, the garden, and its inhabitants—except age. The furniture in the house, the pear tree in the garden, my mother, my brothers and sisters, and I myself were all 20 years older. There we all were, the ten of us, all together round the same dinner table as we had been seven years ago and 17 years ago.

Only the cat and the dog were missing, dead, and Agnes the parlourmaid who after 25 years 'service' had retired. I felt a slight feeling of claustrophobia. After the unending jungle, the great lagoons, the enormous sea pounding on the shore below my bungalow, the large open windowless rooms in Hambantota, I felt the walls of the Putney dining-room pressing in upon me, the low ceiling pressing down on me, the past and 20 years closing in on me. I went to bed somewhat depressed.

During the next few days slight depression continued, for the return is nearly always an anticlimax. But I decided, with some misgiving—for I did not know what I should find there—to plunge straight back into the life of Cambridge which I had left seven years ago. Three days after my arrival in Putney I took the train to Cambridge to stay with Lytton Strachey, who was living there in rooms on King's Parade. It was a formidable plunge. I dined at the high table in Trinity, and went to see McTaggart and Bertrand Russell, and played bowls on the Fellows Bowling Green with G. H. Hardy, who was a remarkable mathematician, became Professor at Oxford, and was one of the strangest and most charming of men. I saw my brother Cecil, who was at Trinity and later became a Fellow, and Walter Lamb, who became Secretary of the Royal Academy, and Francis Birrell. On Saturday evening I dined with Lytton and Rupert Brooke and we went on to a meeting of the Society. I had heard from Lytton a good deal about Rupert when he came up to King's from Rugby and was elected to the Society. He was 23 when I first met him on that June evening in 1911, the year in which his book of poems was published. In the narrow circle of Cambridge he had already a considerable reputation—for beauty, character, intellect, and poetry. His looks were stunning—it is the only appropriate adjective. When I first saw him, I thought to myself: 'That is exactly

what Adonis must have looked like in the eyes of Aphrodite.'
The well-known photograph of him by Schell in 1913, which
is the frontispiece of his posthumous book, *1914 and Other
Poems*, neither flatters nor libels him. It is almost incredible,
but he really did look like that. The photograph, of course,
does not show his colouring—the red-gold of his hair and
the brilliant complexion. It was the sexual dream face not
only for every goddess, but for every sea-girl wreathed with
seaweed red and brown and, alas, for all the damp souls of
housemaids sprouting despondently at area gates.

Rupert had immense charm when he wanted to be charming, and he was inclined to exploit his charm so that he
seemed to be sometimes too much the professional charmer.
He had a very pronounced streak of hardness, even cruelty,
in his character, and his attitude to all other males within a
short radius of any attractive female was ridiculously jealous
—the attitude of the farmyard cock among the hens. I never
knew him at all well, though I used to see him fairly often
when he was in England between 1911 and 1914. Before his
quarrel with Lytton he was friendly both to me and to
Virginia. He had a considerable respect for her, I think. He
once stayed with her in Firle over a weekend and on Sunday
morning they went and sat in Firle Park. He began to write
a poem, his method being to put the last word of each line
of rhyming quatrains down the sheet of paper and then
complete the lines and so the poem. At one moment he said:
'Virginia, what is the brightest thing you can think of?' 'A
leaf with the light on it,' was Virginia's instant reply, and it
completed the poem.

In the short time between my meeting him and his death,
Rupert quarrelled violently with Lytton and nearly all his
Cambridge friends, and though we were uninvolved in and,
indeed, ignorant of the quarrel, he included Virginia and me
to some extent in his hostility. In 1915, just before he went

out to the Dardanelles and died in the Aegean, walking down Holborn one morning we met him by chance. We stopped to talk and for the first moment there was hostility and even anger in his look and voice. But almost immediately they seemed to evaporate, and he was suddenly friendly and charming and we went into a near-by restaurant and had lunch. He was gay and affectionate, just as he had been that first evening at dinner in Cambridge.

Lytton and Rupert, Bertie Russell and Hardy, Sheppard[1] and Goldie[2] at the Society on Saturday evening—all this was a wonderful plunge direct from the three years in Hambantota. In the train back to London, I came to the surface once more a little out of breath and slightly dizzy. At the same time I felt the warmth of a kind of reassurance. I had enjoyed my week-end. There was Cambridge and Lytton and Bertie Russell and Goldie, the Society and the Great Court of Trinity, and Hardy and bowls—all the eternal truths and values of my youth—going on just as I had left them seven years ago. Though I was fresh from the sands of Jaffna and Hambantota and from the Kiplingesque, Anglo-Indian society of Ceylon, I found that I was still a native of Trinity and King's, a Cambridge intellectual. My seven years in Ceylon had added a touch to my reserve and aloofness, but I had no difficulty in taking up the thread of friendship or conversation with Lytton and the others where I had left them in 1904.

When I got back from Cambridge, I pursued energetically the pleasures of London life and old friendships. I went to see Leopold Campbell[3], who was now a clergyman, and Harry Gray[4], who was now a successful surgeon, and

[1] Later Sir John Sheppard, Provost of King's College, Cambridge.
[2] G. Lowes Dickinson.
[3] See *Sowing*, pp. 177-180.
[4] See *Sowing*, pp. 174-175.

Saxon[1], who was now a civil servant in the Treasury. I went to see the Russian dancers, Shaw's *Fanny's First Play*, *Traviata*, and Adeline Genee dance at the Coliseum. I went to the Corona Club dinner where I met many Ceylon civil servants, including J. P. Lewis[2]. The next night I went to the Society dinner where I sat between Lytton and Maynard Keynes, and met once more Moore[3] and Desmond Mac-Carthy[4]. All this in a fortnight. Then on Monday, July 3rd, only three weeks after I had arrived in England, I went and dined with Vanessa and Clive Bell in Gordon Square. I was alone with them at dinner, but afterwards Virginia, Duncan Grant, and Walter Lamb came in. This was, I suppose, so far as I was concerned, the beginning of what came to be called Bloomsbury.

'What came to be called Bloomsbury' by the outside world never existed in the form given to it by the outside world. For 'Bloomsbury' was and is currently used as a term —usually of abuse—applied to a largely imaginary group of persons with largely imaginary objects and characteristics. I was a member of this group and I was also one of a small number of persons who did in fact eventually form a kind of group of friends living in or around that district of London legitimately called Bloomsbury. The term Bloomsbury can legitimately be applied to this group and will be so applied in these pages. Bloomsbury, in this sense, did not exist in 1911 when I returned from Ceylon; it came into existence in the three years 1912 to 1914. We did ourselves use the term of ourselves before it was used by the outside world, for in the 1920's and 1930's, when our own younger generation were growing up and marrying and some of our generation were

---

[1] Saxon Sydney-Turner; see *Sowing*, pp. 103-108 and 113-119.
[2] See *Growing*, pp. 41-44.
[3] See *Sowing*, pp. 131-149 and 154-157.
[4] See *Sowing*, pp. 142-143, 173-174, and 197-199.

already dying, we used to talk of 'Old Bloomsbury', meaning the original members of our group of friends who between 1911 and 1914 came to live in or around Bloomsbury.

Old Bloomsbury consisted of the following people: The three Stephens: Vanessa, married to Clive Bell, Virginia, who married Leonard Woolf, and Adrian, who married Karin Costello; Lytton Strachey; Clive Bell; Leonard Woolf; Maynard Keynes; Duncan Grant; E. M. Forster (who will be referred to in this book as Morgan Forster or Morgan); Saxon Sydney-Turner; Roger Fry. Desmond MacCarthy and his wife Molly, though they actually lived in Chelsea, were always regarded by us as members of Old Bloomsbury. In the 1920's and 1930's, when Old Bloomsbury narrowed and widened into a newer Bloomsbury, it lost through death Lytton and Roger and added to its numbers Julian, Quentin, and Angelica Bell, and David (Bunny) Garnett, who married Angelica.[1]

That Monday night of July 3, 1911, when I dined with Vanessa and Clive in Gordon Square, as I said, Bloomsbury had not yet actually come into existence. The reasons were geographical. At that moment only Vanessa and Clive and Saxon lived in Bloomsbury. Virginia and Adrian lived in Fitzroy Square and Duncan in rooms nearby. Roger lived in a house outside Guildford; Lytton in Cambridge and Hampstead; Morgan Forster in Weybridge; Maynard Keynes, as a Fellow of King's College, in Cambridge. I was a visitor from Ceylon. Ten years later, when Old Bloomsbury had come into existence, Vanessa, Clive, Duncan,

---

[1] There is proof of this chronological classification. We had what we called a Memoir Club, i.e. we met from time to time and we each in turn read a chapter, as it were, of autobiography. The original thirteen members of the Memoir Club were the thirteen members of Old Bloomsbury given above. Twenty years later the four younger persons were members.

Maynard, Adrian, and Lytton all lived in Gordon Square; Virginia and I were in Tavistock Square; Morgan in Brunswick Square; Saxon in Great Ormond Street; Roger in Bernard Street. Thus we all lived geographically in Bloomsbury within a few minutes walk of one another.

I am not, in this book, writing a history of Bloomsbury in any of its forms or manifestations, real or imaginary, and I shall have, after these first pages, very little to say about it. I am trying to write my autobiography, a true account of my life in relation to the times and the society in which I have lived, to the work I have done, and to people, whether intimates, acquaintances, or public persons. The twelve included by me in the previous paragraph as members of Old Bloomsbury had a great influence upon my life. The account of what happened to me during the ten or twelve years after my return from Ceylon will necessarily show how we came to congregate in those nostalgic London squares and the real nature of our congregation. Here there are one or two facts about us which I want to insist upon before going on with my narrative. We were and always remained primarily and fundamentally a group of friends. Our roots and the roots of our friendship were in the University of Cambridge. Of the 13 persons mentioned above three are women and ten men; of the ten men nine had been at Cambridge, and all of us, except Roger, had been more or less contemporaries at Trinity and King's and were intimate friends before I went to Ceylon.

There is another point. In the first volume of my autobiography, in dealing with my years at Cambridge, I said that it was 'necessary here to say something about the Society —The Apostles—because of the immense importance it had for us, its influence upon our minds, our friendships, our lives.'[1] Of the ten men of Old Bloomsbury only Clive,

[1] See *Sowing*, particularly pp. 129-130 and 150-151.

Adrian and Duncan were not Apostles. Of the other seven of us, Desmond, Morgan, Lytton, Saxon, Maynard, and I, all overlapped more or less at Cambridge and had already grown into a peculiar intimacy there as active members of the Society. I tried in *Sowing* to give some idea of the character of G. E. Moore and of his tremendous intellectual (and also emotional) influence upon us and upon the Society of those days. The main things which Moore instilled deep into our minds and characters were his peculiar passion for truth, for clarity and common sense, and a passionate belief in certain values. I have said that Moore's influence upon us was lifelong. How profound it was is shown by what Maynard Keynes wrote in his book *Two Memoirs*. What Moore and his *Principia Ethica* gave to us as young men and what we 60 years ago embraced with the violence and optimism of youth Maynard calls a religion and he is affectionately critical of its and our adolescent one-sidedness and absurdities. But as a final summing up he writes

It seems to me looking back that this religion of ours was a very good one to grow up under. It remains nearer the truth than any other that I know, with less irrelevant extraneous matter and nothing to be ashamed of; though it is a comfort today to be able to discard with a good conscience the calculus and the mensuration and the duty to know *exactly* what one means and feels. It was a purer, sweeter air by far than Freud cum Marx. It is still my religion under the surface.

That is the point: under the surface all six of us, Desmond, Lytton, Saxon, Morgan, Maynard, and I, had been permanently inoculated with Moore and Moorism; and even Roger, who was seven years older than Moore and highly critical of his philosophy, continually proved by his criticism of Moorism that he was 'under the surface' a Moorist.

Through us and through *Principia Ethica* the four others, Vanessa and Virginia, Clive and Duncan, were deeply affected by the astringent influence of Moore and the purification of that divinely cathartic question which echoed through the Cambridge Courts of my youth as it had 2300 years before echoed through the streets of Socratic Athens: 'What do you mean by that?' Artistically the purification can, I think, be traced in the clarity, light, absence of humbug in Virginia's literary style and perhaps in Vanessa's painting. They have the quality noted by Maynard in Moorism, the getting rid of 'irrelevant extraneous matter'.

There have often been groups of people, writers and artists, who were not only friends, but were consciously united by a common doctrine and object, or purpose artistic or social. The utilitarians, the Lake poets, the French impressionists, the English Pre-Raphaelites were groups of this kind. Our group was quite different. Its basis was friendship, which in some cases developed into love and marriage. The colour of our minds and thought had been given to us by the climate of Cambridge and Moore's philosophy, much as the climate of England gives one colour to the face of an Englishman while the climate of India gives a quite different colour to the face of a Tamil. But we had no common theory, system, or principles which we wanted to convert the world to; we were not proselytizers, missionaries, crusaders, or even propagandists. It is true that Maynard produced the system or theory of Keynsian economics which has had a great effect upon the theory and practice of economics, finance, and politics; and that Roger, Vanessa, Duncan, and Clive played important parts, as painters or critics, in what came to be known as the Post-Impressionist Movement. But Maynard's crusade for Keynsian economics against the orthodoxy of the Banks and academic economists, and Roger's crusade for post-impressionism and 'significant form' against the orthodoxy of academic 'representational' painters and aestheticians were just as purely individual as Virginia's writing of *The Waves* —they had nothing to do with any group. For there was no more a communal connection between Roger's 'Critical and Speculative Essays on Art', Maynard's *The General Theory of Employment, Interest and Money*, and Virginia's *Orlando* than there was between Bentham's *Theory of Legislation*, Hazlitt's *Principal Picture Galleries in England*, and Byron's *Don Juan*.

I can now return to Monday night, July 3, 1911. In Cambridge during my week-end there, as I have said, I had had the reassuring pleasure of finding men and things, truths and values, to whom or to which I had given the love or loyalty of youth, unchanged and unchanging. In Gordon Square I re-entered a society which had completely changed since I left it seven years before, but in which I found myself immediately and completely at home. Nothing is more silly than the principle, which too often fatally influences practice, that you ought to be consistent in your feelings and your likes and dislikes. Where taste is concerned there is no law of contradiction. It is absurd to think, as many people do, that the love of cats or claret is a reason or excuse for not loving dogs or burgundy. So I get as much pleasure from the comfort of finding that nothing has changed as from the excitement of finding that everything is new.

There had certainly been a profound revolution in Gordon Square. I had dined in 46 Gordon Square with Thoby and his two sisters, the Misses Stephens, in 1904 only a few days before I left England for Ceylon. Now seven years later in the same rooms meeting again for the first time Vanessa, Virginia, Clive, Duncan, and Walter Lamb I found that almost the only things which had not changed were the furniture and the extraordinary beauty of the two Miss

Stephens. Vanessa was, I think, usually more beautiful than Virginia. The form of her features was more perfect, her eyes bigger and better, her complexion more glowing. If Rupert was a goddess's Adonis, Vanessa in her thirties had something of the physical splendour which Adonis must have seen when the goddess suddenly stood before him. To many people she appeared frightening and formidable, for she was blended of three goddesses with slightly more of Athene and Artemis in her and her face than of Aphrodite. I myself never found her formidable, partly because she had the most beautiful speaking voice that I have ever heard, and partly because of her tranquillity and quietude. (The tranquillity was to some extent superficial; it did not extend deep down in her mind, for there in the depths there was also an extreme sensitivity, a nervous tension which had some resemblance to the mental instability of Virginia.) There was something monumental, monolithic, granitic in most of the Stephens in the two generations which descended from the Sir James Stephen who ruled the Colonial Office in the middle of the 19th century. His son, Sir James Fitzjames Stephen, the judge, was an outsize monolithic Stephen; Leslie, his brother, and two sisters whom I knew personally—Miss Stephen the Quaker and Miss Stephen, Principal of Newnham—all had the quality, but less exaggeratedly. There was a magnificent and monumental simplicity in Thoby[1] which earned him his nickname The Goth. Vanessa had the same quality expressed in feminine terms. Like him she had a monolithic character and monolithic common sense and, as with him and her uncle, the judge, there was often something adamantine in the content and language of her judgments. It was the strange combination of great beauty and feminine charm with a kind of lapidification of character and her caustic humour which made her such a fascinating person.

[1] See *Sowing*, pp. 123-128.

Virginia was a very different kind of person beneath the strong family resemblances in the two sisters. She was, as I said, normally less beautiful than Vanessa. When she was well, unworried, happy, amused, and excited, her face lit up with an intense almost ethereal beauty. She was also extremely beautiful when, unexcited and unworried, she sat reading or thinking. But the expression, even the shape of her face changed with extraordinary rapidity as the winds of mental strain, illness, or worry passed over its surface. It was still beautiful, but her anxiety and pain made the beauty itself painful.

Virginia is the only person whom I have known intimately who had the quality which one had to call genius. One has to call it genius because the mental process seems to be fundamentally different from those of ordinary or normal people and indeed from the normal mental processes of these abnormal persons. Virginia had a great enjoyment of ordinary things, of eating, walking, desultory talking, shopping, playing bowls, reading. She liked and got on well with all kinds of everyday people, as soon as they got to know her well and she them. (She had a curious shyness with strangers which often made them uncomfortably shy.) In this day to day, everyday life and intercourse with other people she talked and thought and acted, to a great extent, no doubt, as other ordinary people, though it is a curious fact that there was about her something, some intangible aura, which made her very often seem strange to the 'ordinary' person.

During our life together there was one fantastic recurring example of this fact which again and again I noted with astonishment. If you walk in the streets of London or any other large European city, you will see every now and then persons, particularly women, who in the eye of God must appear indescribably ridiculous. There will be fat or lean, middle aged or elderly, women dressed up in some exaggera-

The author and Virginia, 1912

tion of the exaggerated contemporary fashion which could in fact only—and that doubtfully—be carried off by some rare and lovely young thing. They are ludicrous and laughable caricatures of female charm. Virginia, on the other hand, by any standard of taste was a very beautiful woman and many people would have applied to her the rather dubious description 'distinguished looking'; she had, too, I think, a flair for beautiful, if individual, dresses. Yet to the crowd in the street there was something in her appearance which struck them as strange and laughable. I am one of those people who merge in a crowd anywhere. Even in a foreign town, though I am not dressed exactly like the native inhabitants, no one notices and I pass—in appearance—for a Spaniard in Barcelona or a Swede in Stockholm. But in Barcelona and in Stockholm nine out of ten people would stare or stop and stare at Virginia. And not only in foreign towns; they would stop and stare and nudge one another— 'look at her'—even in England, in Picadilly or Lewes High Street, where almost anyone is allowed to pass unnoticed. They did not merely stop and stare and nudge one another; there was something in Virginia which they found ridiculous. Some monstrous female caricature, who was accepted as ordinary by the crowd, would go into fits of laughter at the sight of Virginia. I always found it difficult to understand exactly what the cause of this laughter was. It was only partly that her dress was never quite the same as other people's. It was partly, I think, because there was something strange and disquieting, and therefore to many people ridiculous, in her appearance, in the way she walked—she seemed so often to be 'thinking of something else', to be moving with a slightly shuffling movement along the streets in the shadow of a dream. The hags and harridans and bright young things could not restrain their laughter or their giggles.

This laughter of the street distressed her; she had an almost morbid horror of being looked at and still more of being photographed—which is the reason why there are very few photographs of her in which she looks her natural self, the real everyday self which one saw in her face in ordinary life from hour to hour. A curious example of this nervous misery which she suffered from being looked at occurred when Stephen Tomlin (Tommy, as he was always called) sculpted the bust of her now in the National Portrait Gallery. With the greatest reluctance she was eventually induced by him to sit for him. The object of each sitting was naturally to look at her, which Tommy did with prolonged intensity. It was a kind of Chinese torture to her. He was a slow worker and worked away for an hour or so quite unconscious of what was going on in the mind of his tortured sitter. The sittings ended only just in time; if they had gone on much longer, they would have made Virginia seriously ill. A shadow of her misery has, I think, been caught by Tommy and frozen into the clay of the portrait.

I was saying that in her day to day, everyday life she thought and talked and acted, to a great extent, as other people do, though there was always this element or aura in her which was strange and disquieting to ordinary people so that in self-defence, in order to reassure themselves, they giggled or roared with laughter. I think this element was closely connected with the streak in her which I call genius. For in conversation she might, at any moment, leave the ground, as I used to call it. She was an unusually amusing talker in the usual way of talk and talkers, her mind being very quick and intelligent, witty and humorous, appropriately serious or frivolous as the occasion or subject demanded. But at any moment, in a general conversation with five or six people or when we were alone together, she might suddenly 'leave the ground' and give some fantastic, entrancing, amusing, dreamlike, almost lyrical description of an event, a place, or a person. It always made me think of the breaking and gushing out of the springs in autumn after the first rains. The ordinary mental processes stopped, and in their place the waters of creativeness and imagination welled up and, almost undirected, carried her and her listeners into another world. Unlike most good or brilliant talkers, she was never boring, for these displays—and displays is a bad word to describe them for they were so spontaneous—were always short.

When she soared away into one of these fantasias, one felt it to be a kind of inspiration. The thoughts and images fountained up spontaneously, not directed and consciously controlled as they were ordinarily by her in conversation and are always by most people. In the description in her diary of how she wrote the last pages of *The Waves* I recognize the same mental process:

Saturday, February 7th
Here in the few minutes that remain, I must record, heaven be praised, the end of *The Waves*. I wrote the words O Death fifteen minutes ago, having reeled across the last ten pages with some moments of such intensity and intoxication that I seemed only to stumble after my own voice, or almost,after some sort of speaker (as when I was mad) I was almost afraid, remembering the voices that used to fly ahead.[1]

'Stumble after my own voice' and 'the voices that fly ahead' —here surely is an exact description of the inspiration of genius and madness, showing how terrifyingly thin is the fabric of thought often separating the one from the other, a fact recognized at least 2000 years ago and often recognized since. 'Nullum magnum ingenium sine mixtura dementiae

[1] *A Writer's Diary*, p. 165.

fuit'—there has never been great genius without a mixture of madness in it—says Seneca, which Dryden echoed in the hackneyed tag:

> *Great wits are sure to madness near allied,*
> *And thin partitions do their bounds divide*

This breaking away of the mind from the ordinary modes of thought which I have described in Virginia is, I think, a kind of inspiration or genius. It produces more often than other modes of thought what Sir Thomas Browne called 'a glimpse of incomprehensibles and thought of things which thoughts do but tenderly touch'. There is evidence that the greatest of great geniuses experience it. Beethoven, every now and again, used to have what his faithful disciple called 'a raptus', a kind of volcanic creative outburst. In one sense however, there is nothing mysterious about this. The raptus or inspiration is clearly only a rare and wonderful form of a well-known everyday mental process. Graham Wallas in *The Art of Thought* rightly insisted upon the importance of bouts of idleness and of not thinking for creative thought. Nearly everyone must have had the experience of grinding away unsuccessfully at some intellectual or even emotional problem and then suddenly, when one has given it up in desperation and is thinking of something entirely different, the solution comes with a flash—'like an inspiration'—into the mind. Or you may even go to bed with an unsolved problem and wake next morning to find you have solved it in your sleep. The most famous example of this phenomenon is the triumphant 'Eureka!' of Archimedes when he leapt from his bath, having seen in a sudden flash the scientific principle which had so long eluded him in his study. The writer's 'inspiration' and Beethoven's raptus are of the same nature. One proof of this is that the inspiration is only the end process of a prolonged period of persistent conscious thought, often of trial and error. In Beethoven's case this is proved by his Notebooks. It was also true of Virginia. I have never known any writer who thought, ruminated so continually and so consciously over what she was writing, turning her problems over in her mind persistently while sitting in a chair in front of the winter fire or going for her daily walk along the bank of the Sussex Ouse. She was able to reel across the last ten pages of *The Waves* stumbling after her own voice and the voices that flew ahead only because of the hours of intense, conscious thought she had given to the book for weeks and months before the words were actually put upon paper—just as Archimedes would never have been able to shout his 'I have found it!', if he had not already consciously and laboriously worked for hours upon the problem.

After this second digression—though it is a highly relevant digression—I can return once more to the evening of Monday, July 3, 1911. There were two things which immediately made me feel that I had entered a society wonderfully different from that which I had left in Gordon Square in 1904, not to speak of the Kiplingesque society in which I had lived from 1904 to 1911 in Ceylon. The first was an immediate sense of intimacy which was both emotional and intellectual. It carried back, and carried me back, to the Cambridge of my youth. What was so exhilarating in Cambridge and particularly in the Society in those years from 1900 to 1904 was the sense of profound intimacy with a number of people whom one liked and who were passionately interested in the same things and pursued the same ends—and who were always ready to laugh at themselves and at the universe, even the serious things in the universe that they took very seriously. But that was a state of things which applied only to Cambridge and the Society, to a small number of people who were Apostles. It did not in

1904 apply to Gordon Square and above all it excluded all women. What was so new and so exhilarating to me in the Gordon Square of July, 1911 was the sense of intimacy and complete freedom of thought and speech, much wider than in the Cambridge of seven years ago, and above all including women.

People who were born too late to experience in boyhood and adolescence the intellectual and moral pressure of Victorianism have no idea of the feeling of fog and fetters which weighed one down. In the first volume of my auto-biography, *Sowing*, I described the excitement with which we found ourselves, as young men at Cambridge, taking part 'in the springtime of a conscious revolt against the social, political, religious, moral, intellectual, and artistic institu-tions, beliefs, and standards of our fathers and grandfathers.[1]' Some reviewers lectured me severely for exaggerating or inventing this revolt and the part which my generation played in it. One can only congratulate the lecturers on their good fortune in never having suffered the burden of Vic-torianism and in having benefited so much from our revolt against it—clearly that revolt which Shaw and his generation began and my generation helped to extend was so effective that our successors are not even aware how and why, while we were born in chains, they are comparatively free.

In 1904 we had reached complete freedom of thought and speech among a few intimate friends, but the circle of friends was entirely male and extremely narrow and it is extraordinary to look back from today and remember how formal society was in those days. When I went to Ceylon— indeed even when I returned—I still called Lytton Strachey Strachey and Maynard Keynes Keynes, and to them I was still Woolf. When I stayed for a week with the Stracheys in the country in 1904 or dined in Gordon Square with the

[1] See *Sowing*, pp. 151-154 and 160-167.

Stephens, it would have been inconceivable that I should have called Lytton's or Thoby's sisters by their Christian names. The social significance of using Christian instead of surnames and of kissing instead of shaking hands is curious. Their effect is greater, I think, than those who have never lived in a more formal society imagine. They produce a sense—often unconscious—of intimacy and freedom and so break down barriers to thought and feeling. It was this feeling of greater intimacy and freedom, of the sweeping away of formalities and barriers, which I found so new and so exhilarating in 1911. To have discussed some subjects or to have called a (sexual) spade a spade in the presence of Miss Strachey or Miss Stephen would seven years before have been unimaginable; here for the first time I found a much more intimate (and wider) circle in which complete freedom of thought and speech was now extended to Vanessa and Virginia, Pippa and Marjorie.

In the last six months of 1911 I lived a life of pleasure, just unmitigated, pure, often acute pleasure, such as I had never had before and have never had again. To have a full six months of unalloyed pleasure and even happiness is a very rare thing and a salutary thing, temporarily smoothing the lines and wrinkles which time and life grave upon the face, the mind, and the soul. There was first the weather. I do not remember any year as sunny as 1911. The sun was always blazing in a cloudless sky. In Ceylon I had lived for years in a very hot district and had never suffered from the heat, but at Stockholm in the first week of August it was so hot that, for the first and only time in my life, it was almost too much for me. It seemed absurd to have to come from the equator to latitude 60° north in order to feel too hot.

The climate and the weather, the sun and the rain, and the wind on the heath, have an immense effect upon our happiness, as Jasper Petulengro so rightly and so poetically

35

explained to George Borrow. So too has the climate of opinion. In the decade before the 1914 war there was a political and social movement in the world, and particularly in Europe and Britain, which seemed at the time wonderfully hopeful and exciting. It seemed as though human beings might really be on the brink of becoming civilized. It was partly the feeling of relief and release as we broke out of the fog of Victorianism. The forces of reaction and barbarism were still there, but they were in retreat. They had suffered a tremendous defeat in the Dreyfus case. In the Zabern incident and the Denshawi incident a new note began to be heard in what may be called world opinion. It seemed at last to be generally agreed that for a German officer to beat a German cobbler was 'an outrage against law and order and decency and civilization'. When at Denshawi a British court passed savage sentences upon Egyptian villagers for killing a British officer who insisted upon killing the villagers' pigeons, a cry went up, not against the villagers, but against the insolence of the officers and the vindictiveness and savagery of the judges. For the first time in the history of the world the rights of Jews, cobblers, and coloured men not to be beaten, hanged, or judicially murdered by officers, Junkers, or white men were publicly admitted; it looked for a moment as if militarism, imperialism, and antisemitism were on the run.

We were, of course, mistaken in thinking that the world really might become civilized, but the fact that it didn't does not prove that our optimism was foolish or credulous. It is so easy and foolish to be historically wise after the event. It was, I still believe, touch and go whether the movement towards liberty and equality—political and social—and towards civilization, which was strong in the first decade of the 20th century, would become so strong as to carry everything before it. Its enemies saw the risk and the result was

36

the war of 1914; they postponed the danger of our becoming civilized for at least a hundred years. But the future could not alter the fact that it was exciting to be alive in London in 1911 and that there was reason for exhilaration. Profound changes were taking place in every direction, not merely politically and socially. The revolution of the motor car and the aeroplane had begun; Freud and Rutherford and Einstein were at work beginning to revolutionize our knowledge of our own minds and of the universe. Equally exciting things were happening in the arts. On the stage the shattering impact of Ibsen was still belatedly powerful and we felt that Ibsen had a worthy successor in Shaw as a revolutionary. In literature one seemed to feel the ominous lull before the storm which was to produce in a few years *A la Recherche du Temps Perdu, Ulysses, Prufrock* and *The Waste Land, Jacob's Room* and *Mrs. Dalloway*. In painting we were in the middle of the profound revolution of Cézanne, Matisse, and Picasso which miraculously followed so closely upon the no less profound revolution of Renoir, Monet, Degas, and Manet. And to crown all, night after night we flocked to Covent Garden, entranced by a new art, a revelation to us benighted British, the Russian Ballet in the greatest days of Diaghilev and Nijinsky.

For six months or more I lived in a kaleidoscopic dream and it is only by giving some details that I can give any idea of what life was like to the Ceylon civil servant on leave in Europe before the 1914 war. Two days after my dinner in Gordon Square Harry Gray took me, disguised as a surgeon, to West Ham Hospital to see him perform a terrific operation on an elderly man. I lived in those days on the principle that I wanted to know everything and experience everything and I therefore jumped at the chance when Harry offered to let me see a formidable operation. The spectacle was surprising and rather disconcerting. The operation was to take a growth out of the man's inside; it lasted an unconscionable time and what astonished me was that, after the first use of the knife, it was hardly used again, for Harry after a long and tremendous struggle and the use of great force, working away with his bare hands in the man's inside, at last triumphantly, as it seemed to me, drew out the growth. The heat and smells of the operating theatre and the sympathetic tension of those straining hands in the man's belly all but made me disgrace myself and Harry by fainting. I only just managed to remain conscious and on my feet.

Two days later I went and stayed for four days with Leopold at Frome. Leopold, who, when I knew him at Cambridge, was Leopold Colin Henry Douglas Campbell, was now the Rev. Leopold Colin Henry Douglas Campbell-Douglas, married and vicar of Frome in Somerset. The change from Gordon Square and the Russian dancers to the Somerset vicarage was fascinating. Leopold, it is true, was not by any means an ordinary English country parson. He was in the direct succession to the Barony of Blythswood and eventually, owing to the deaths of uncles, father, and brothers, did become Lord Blythswood. He was indelibly marked with the hereditary stigmata of Eton, the Scots Guards, Manchester Square, wealth and aristocracy. He really did call hunting and fishing 'huntin and fishin'. By some Freudian twist of the unconscious he had become a clergyman of the Church of England instead of Colonel of the Scots Guards, a post which had been occupied by his uncle, father, and brother and which they themselves seemed to regard as a kind of family heirloom. Up to a point Leopold took his religion pretty seriously and was about as High, I suppose, as an Anglican parson can be this side Rome and popery. It was probably true, as I wrote in *Sowing*, that 'the Church was to him exactly what the Scots Guards were to his father, his uncle, and his brother'.

It was fascinating to watch him now shepherding his sheep in the somnolent, typically agricultural, profoundly English parish instead of (and as if) paternally commanding his 'men' in the platoon, the company, or the regiment. He loved the High Church paraphernalia and properties, the incense, banners, images, genuflexions, chasubles, just as his relations had loved the standards, the uniforms, the pomp and circumstance of the daily drill on the Guards parade ground of the barracks in Birdcage Walk. In 1911 Somerset was still rural and Frome a typical market town with fewer than 10,000 inhabitants. These Somerset parishes were unlikely to be astonished by the idiosyncracies or antics of any incumbent presented to a living by a Lord of the Manor or still more remote owner of an advowson, since for 500 years or more they had experienced the strange, motley succession of rectors or vicars who had appeared in and disappeared from their village churches. There were things about the Rev. Leopold Campbell-Douglas which ecclesiastically some of his parishioners did not approve, but beneath the sometimes irritating and foolish surface he had a singularly simple, honest, and charming character which endeared him to most people. Owing to the incorrigible snobbery of all classes in rural England the fact that his father was Lord Blythswood and that he would almost certainly succeed one day to the title probably endeared him to even more people in Frome and more securely than the charm of his character.

Fifty years ago life in Somerset still moved exceedingly slow and the well oiled wheels of Leopold's life moved slowly in the rhythm of the life around him. It seemed almost incredibly archaic and remote and to have nothing to do with realities, the reality of life in Jaffna or Hambantota, the reality of the Dreyfus case or Zabern, the reality of the Russian dancers. I went to church with Leopold and heard him preach an absurd sermon which I do not think the rest

39

of the congregation thought absurd; I went with him to visit some of his parishioners which seemed to me even more absurd; we sat through the long sunny summer afternoons in the garden heavy with leaves and flowers; we ate heavy meals of juicy joints, Somerset cream and butter, home-made bread, peas and beans and raspberries; we drove slowly to Bath which with its peeling buildings still slept peacefully in the 18th century. Except that the car was ousting the parson's gig and the railway had ousted the stage coach, the life which I dipped into for four days in the Frome rectory in 1911 was centuries old. I don't think the essence or rhythm of it had changed much from the days of the Rev. Laurence Sterne, Vicar of Sutton-in-the-Forest in Yorkshire, or the Rev. Gilbert White in Selborne, Hampshire. I am glad to have lived in it briefly, just as I am glad to have lived briefly in the antediluvian life of the Ceylon jungle village. Both of them have finally passed away, becoming as extinct as the pterodactyl and the mammoth, destroyed by the motor car and the motor omnibus and the aeroplane and high explosives and bombs—man's passion for speed and destruction. Being a modern man, I too have a passion for speed, always moving faster and faster from place to place. But I am old enough and sensible enough to remember the pleasure of travelling slow and living slow and to recognize the folly and emptiness of speed.

On July 11th the kaleidoscope flickered violently again, for I went straight from Leopold and Frome and stayed with Lytton and Moore at Beckey House, Manaton, on Dartmoor. Beckey belongs also to an almost extinct past, for I doubt whether anything quite like it is now obtainable in England. It was a largish house in a remote, narrow, rocky Dartmoor valley. Behind it was a waterfall, the Beckey Falls, and through the valley and the trees past the house rushed the Beckey stream. A working class man and his wife and children lived in the house and they let lodgings, a large sitting-room and a few bedrooms. It was incredibly remote and rather primitive, but the people were very nice. The week I spent with Moore and Lytton was intellectually pretty astringent; to pass straight from the conversation of Leopold's parishioners to that of the authors of *Principia Ethica* and *Eminent Victorians* was as though one were stepping straight out of the society of the Vicar of Wakefield into that of Voltaire and Diderot. Astringency exactly describes the flavour of life with Moore and Lytton. Moore was never easy to talk to, though I found him less difficult in 1911 than he had been in 1904. It was extremely difficult to live up to his extraordinary simplicity and integrity, which were combined with great intellectual power. Talking to him one lived under the shadow of the eternal, though silent, question: 'What exactly do you mean by that?' It is a menacing question, particularly when you know that muddle and not knowing 'exactly what you mean by *that*' will cause to Moore almost physical pain which he will show involuntarily in his eyes.

In the morning Lytton used to sit in one part of the garden, with a panama hat on his head, groaning from time to time over his literary constipation as he wrote *Landmarks in French Literature* for the Home University Library; in another part of the garden sat Moore, a panama hat on his head, his forehead wet with perspiration, sighing from time to time over his literary constipation as he wrote *Ethics* for the Home University Library. Lytton used to complain that he was mentally constipated because nothing at all came into his mind, which remained as blank as the paper on his knees. Moore on the contrary said that his mental constipation came from the fact that as soon as he had written down a sentence, he saw either that it was just false or that it required a sentence to qualify it which would require another sentence to qualify the qualification. This, as we pointed out to him, would go on ad infinitum, and the 60,000 words which he had bound himself to write on ethics for the Home University Library would, after he had written a first sentence which was not 'just false', consist of an infinite series of qualifications to it only cut short by the fact that the publishers would not print more than 60,000 words.

In the afternoons we went for long walks over Dartmoor. Moore had a passion for bathing, and, whenever we came upon one of those long, deep, black pools which you find in the rocks among the Dartmoor tors, he would strip off his clothes and jump in. Nothing would induce Lytton to get into water in the open air, and so I felt I must follow Moore's example. It nearly killed me. I do not think that I have ever felt any water colder than in those Dartmoor rock pools; after the delicious evening plunge into the warm waves of the Indian Ocean at Hambantota, this was real torture. In the evenings Moore sang Adelaide, Schubert songs, or the Dichterliebe, or he played Beethoven sonatas. It was good to see again the sweat pour down his face and hear his passion in the music as he played the Waldstein or the Hammerklavier sonata.

A week after I got back from Dartmoor, I set off with my brother Edgar for Göteborg in Sweden. One of my aunts, my mother's sister, had married a Dane and lived in Copenhagen. When we were children, we used sometimes in the holidays to go and stay with her in Denmark. She had a large family and Charlotte, one of her daughters, had married a Swede who lived in Göteborg; he was a lawyer and Member of Parliament. Edgar and I went and stayed with Charlotte and her family at the fishing village of Fiskeback-shil in Bohuslan, on the coast north of Göteborg. From there we went by steamer through fiords and canals and reached Rattvik on Lake Siljan and thence to Stockholm. Finally we went to Denmark and stayed in a large country house with Aunt Flora not far from Copenhagen.

Even after 50 years I can recall those three weeks in Scandinavia with extraordinary vividness. It was just three years before the Serbian student Princip fired the shot in Sarajevo which killed the Archduke Francis Ferdinand of Austria and destroyed the civilization of Europe. Civilization is a way of life and the war of 1914 destroyed a new, and civilized or semi-civilized, way of life which had established itself or was establishing itself all over Europe. I doubt whether anyone born after 1900 has any idea of what life was like before 1914 in England, France, or Sweden. We live today, and have lived ever since the shot was fired at Serajevo, with a background of battle, murder, and sudden death. When the B.B.C. voice announces: 'This is the Home Service with the programme of news and current affairs', we know that the news is always bad; it will be 99 per cent. political and will tell us of some new acts of organized communal barbarism and violence in Russia or Hungary, Spain or Portugal, South Africa or Algeria. The motives and motifs in these events are fear and hatred, and we feel, as we listen to the announcer's voice—such a well-bred voice of doom—that the doom is threatening, not only our country and its allies, but ourselves, helpless individuals, in our personal lives with every kind of disaster and horror. Human beings are, we know, like Habbakuk, 'capable of anything'; they will accustom themselves to live their lives clinging to the side of a volcano which, they are aware, may at any moment overwhelm them with hot ashes and burning lava—and so we too in the last 50 years have schooled ourselves to live more or less contentedly under the menace of news and current affairs.

But it was really not like that before 1914. Thanks to the doctrines of nationalism and patriotism, of fascists, nazis, and communists, happiness is now politically a dirty word. I

43

think the main difference in the world before 1914 from the world after 1914 was in the sense of security and the growing belief that it was a supremely good thing for people to be communally and individually happy. Coming to Europe after seven years in the purely Asiatic civilization and barbarism of Ceylon, I was peculiarly sensitive to the civilized and barbarous variations in European countries. Life in Scandinavia, and particularly in Sweden, had a quality, an atmosphere and flavour, of its own, markedly different from that of Britain or France, Italy or Germany. Bohuslan has a lovely northern rocky coastline. In Fiskebackshil we lived in a house outside the village on a narrow estuary. The sea was studded with tiny islands of bare rock often only a few inches above the water. We used to row out to them and spend all day swimming in the sea or lying on the little islands talking, reading, eating, and sleeping. The sky and sea were bright blue; the sun beat down upon us in this marvellous eternal summer; the Swedes—advanced in everything—bathed, men, women, and children, naked and unashamed, so that scattered round one one saw tall, fair-haired, naked men and women on the little islands or plunging into the sea. In the evening we rowed back to the mainland and walked out to the headland overlooking the estuary and called altogether in a long-drawn, lilting unison across the water: 'Re-gi-na! Re-gi-na!' Then, from the tiny rocky bay across the estuary, came the ferry boat rowed by Regina, an elderly woman, statuesque, with a face of great beauty, touched slightly by sadness and nobility. And as Regina rowed us across the water, and the soft, lilting Swedish merged or mingled with the gentle lapping of the water against the prow, there descended upon us from the cloudless, darkening sky that delicious melancholy which steals over one when one is completely happy and at the end of a summer day twilight steals across one's happiness.

The Swedes were in those days, and still are, more civilized than most Europeans. Their civilization was their own. It was a little too self-conscious, too antiseptic and sterilized and municipalized for my taste, but it was refreshingly alive and vigorous. The Scandinavians have a passion for knowledge and for asking questions, and we were always having to try to satisfy this thirst for information in our cousins and their children and friends, in naked strangers whom we met on the rocks of Bohusland or in fully clothed strangers whom we met in trains, steamers, trams, and buses. 'Do you belong to the Church of England?' 'Do you believe in God?' 'What is the constitution of the Stock Exchange?' 'Can you divorce your wife in England if she is insane?' This conscientious, relentless, somewhat humourless pursuit of knowledge occasionally filled me with despair—Virginia used to say that in similar circumstances a look would sometimes cross my face which made her fear that I would stand up and howl like a child of three, suddenly aware that the bottom has dropped out of its world. Up to the age of 50, I did, I think, often feel like that, but one of the consolations of age is that, if one does not exactly learn to suffer bores gladly, one learns at least to disregard them with equanimity. These Swedish searchers for truth were, too, so sympathetic, so civilized, that it was impossible not to like them even when for the twentieth time one explained that one was not a member of the Church of England and was unfortunately ignorant of how the London Stock Exchange was governed.

Edgar and I saw a good deal of the life of Scandinavia in the short time that we were there. On Lake Siljan, in Gefvle, and Stockholm we saw it as tourists from the outside; in Göteborg, Fiskebackshil, and in Denmark we saw it from the inside, from the inside of an enormous Danish family. It was a bourgeois life and civilization, 19th-century bourgeois civilization developing to its apogee. Society in Britain,

France, and Italy has never been of a purely middle class type; it has always been tainted or tempered by an aristocracy, a peasantry, or a working class. If you wanted to see a bourgeois society in its purest and most advanced form, you had to go to Amsterdam and The Hague; but Scandinavia in 1911 was not far behind Holland. In my aunt's large country house at Gentofte, in the comfortable houses and flats of her innumerable relations in Copenhagen, in the house, swarming with children, which one of my cousins owned at a seaside place on The Sound, we sat down, usually ten to twenty or even thirty people, to vast meals; we swam and sailed and rowed; we talked interminably. Here, as in Sweden, I felt a sense of civilized stability and security, a wide and widening prosperity and communal happiness, humane, progressive, and, though partly philistine, also intellectually and artistically alive and eager.

It was a patriarchal or matriarchal society such as exists no longer, I suppose, anywhere in Europe. When my brother Herbert and I once went and stayed with my aunt and uncle one summer in their country house near Copenhagen, we came in for the wedding of their daughter Mary. The wedding ceremony was performed in the house in the presence of about 150 guests. After the ceremony there was a wedding breakfast for about 120 people, all relations. It was a colossal feast and lasted from 12 to 3.30 or 4. There were innumerable speeches, young women got up and recited poems, children in white dresses and pink sashes rose from their seats and sang what I imagined to be Danish epithalamiums. At 4 the bride and bridegroom drove away in a shower of confetti, white satin slippers, laughter, tears, and cheers. Then the guests began to drift away, although about 30 of them remained to dinner. The scale of family reunions was nearly always gigantic. The patriarch of patriarchs lived in Copenhagen, an incredibly ancient man in his nineties.

We were taken ceremonially to have lunch with him and I felt that I was expected to realize that I was going to have lunch with a kind of tribal totem or a cross between Methuselah and Melchizedek or even Jehovah. There were some 30 relations at lunch and Methuselah gave us, as Englishmen, an enormous sirloin of beef with marmalade.

Edgar and I returned to England in the middle of August and the next five months were the most exciting months of my life. During them 'Bloomsbury' really came into existence and I fell in love with Virginia. I felt the foundations of my personal life becoming more and more unstable, crisis after crisis confronting me, so that I had at short notice to make decisions whether I should or should not turn my life upside down. There is nothing more exhilarating than having to make that kind of decision, with the (no doubt false) feeling that you are the captain of your soul, the master of your fate. The shadow in the background of my life was Ceylon. Here in London and Cambridge during the next few months I was plunged into a life which was in every way the exact opposite of what I had left in Hambantota and what I should go back to at the end of my leave. Even before I decided to ask Virginia to marry me, I knew that I should sooner or later have to decide whether I would go back to the Ceylon Civil Service or throw the whole thing up.

A few days after I returned from Denmark I began to write *The Village in the Jungle*. The jungle and the people who lived in the Sinhalese jungle villages fascinated, almost obsessed, me in Ceylon. They continued to obsess me in London, in Putney or Bloomsbury, and in Cambridge. *The Village in the Jungle* was a novel in which I tried somehow or other vicariously to live their lives. It was also, in some curious way, the symbol of the anti-imperialism which had been growing upon me more and more in my last years in Ceylon. The Sinhalese way of life, in those entrancing

Kandyan hills or the rice fields and coconut plantations of the low country, and above all those strange jungle villages, was what engrossed me in Ceylon; the prospect of the sophisticated, Europeanized life of Colombo, the control of the wheels of the intricate machinery of central administration, with the dreary pomp and circumstance of imperial government, filled me with misgiving and disgust. And I knew that if I went back to Ceylon it was almost certain that I would be returning, not to the village in the jungle, but to the seats of power in Colombo. The more I wrote *The Village in the Jungle*, the more distasteful became the prospect of success in Colombo.

Virginia and Adrian Stephen at this time were living in a large house in Fitzroy Square and had an 'evening' once a week. Virginia also leased a red-brick villa house in Firle, near Lewes, and she asked me to come there for a long week-end in September. It was still the unending summer of that marvellous year, and it seemed as if the clouds would never again darken the sky as we sat reading in Firle Park or walked over the downs. This was the first time that I had seen the South Downs as it were from the inside and felt the beauty of the gentle white curves of the fields between the great green curves of their hollows; I have lived close to them ever since and have learnt that, in all seasons and circumstances, their physical loveliness and serenity can make one's happiness exquisite and assuage one's misery. After that I began to see a great deal of Virginia and the circle around her in Fitzroy Square, and around Vanessa and Clive Bell in Gordon Square. The Russian Ballet became for a time a curious centre for both fashionable and intellectual London. It was the great days of Diaghilev with Nijinsky at the height of his powers in the classical ballets. I have never seen anything more perfect, nor more exciting, on any stage than Scheherezade, Carnaval, Lac des Cygnes, and the other famous classics. There develops in nearly all arts, and indeed in games like cricket, at various periods after an archaic, vague, or inchoate beginning, a classical style which combines great power and freedom and beauty with a kind of self-imposed austerity and restraint. In the hands of a great master, like Sophocles, Thucydides, Virgil, Swift, La Fontaine, La Bruyere,[1] this combination of originality and freedom with formal purity and restraint is tremendously moving and exciting, and it was this element of classicism in the ballets of 1911 which made them so entrancing. One's pleasure was increased because night after night one could go to Covent Garden and find all round one one's friends, the people whom one liked best in the world, moved and excited as one was oneself. In all my long life in London this is the only instance in which I can remember the intellectuals going night after night to a theatre, opera, concert, or other performance as, I suppose, they have and do in other countries and cities, for instance Bayreuth or Paris.

Bayreuth recalls another motif of the autumn of 1911. Among the frequenters of the Russian Ballet there was, strangely enough, a vogue for Wagner—strangely, because one can hardly imagine two products of the human mind and soul more essentially hostile. Virginia and Adrian with Saxon Sydney-Turner used to go, almost ritualistically, to the great Wagner festival at Bayreuth, as Hugh Walpole and many others did later. It was, I think, Saxon who in our circle was the initiator or leader of the Wagner cult; the operas appealed to him, partly because, as I explained in *Sowing*,[2] he collected them as if they were postage stamps, and partly because the intricate interweaving of the 'themes'

---

[1] I saw the same classical qualities in the batting of W. G. Grace and A. C. Maclaren and in the bowling of J. T. Hearne, Richardson, and Rhodes.

[2] See page 104.

gave scope to his extraordinary ingenuity in solving riddles; spotting the Wotan or Siegfried theme interweaving with the fire music theme gave him the same kind of pleasure as that from fitting the right piece into a picture puzzle or solving a crossword puzzle. In 1911 I knew nothing about Wagner, but I saw that it was time for me to set about him seriously. I therefore took a box in Covent Garden for the *Ring* in October, and Virginia came to *Das Rheingold*, *Siegfried*, and *Götterdämmerung*, with Adrian and Rupert Brooke to *Die Walküre*. It was a formidable experience: the operas started in the afternoon and ended after 11, and we used to go back after them to supper in Fitzroy Square. I am glad that I sat through those four operas of the *Ring*, though I have never had the courage or desire to do it again. I see that in its way the *Ring* is a masterpiece, but I dislike it and dislike Wagner and his art. There are passages in *Das Rheingold*, *Walküre*, and *Götterdämmerung* of considerable beauty and it is occasionally moving and exciting, but I find it intolerably monotonous and boring. The Germans in the 19th century developed a tradition, a philosophy of life and art, barbarous, grandiose, phoney. Wagner was both cause and effect of this repulsive process which ended in the apogee and apotheosis of human bestiality and degradation, Hitler and the Nazis. There are, as I said, moments of beauty and excitement in the *Ring*; there is still more, perhaps, to be said for the early Wagner, as in *Lohengrin*, and for the *Meistersinger*. But I did not enjoy the *Ring* in my box, with Virginia by my side, in 1911, and *Tristan* and *Parsifal* when I came to hear them repelled me and far outdid the *Ring* in tediousness and monotony.

In October Virginia and Adrian had to find a new house as the lease of their house in Fitzroy Square came to an end. They took a large four-storied house in Brunswick Square, which they proposed to run on—for those days—original lines. Adrian occupied the second floor and Virginia the third. Maynard Keynes and Duncan Grant shared the ground floor, and I was offered the fourth floor, or rather a bedroom and sitting room there. They had a wonderful old family cook inherited from the 19th century, Sophie[1], and a

[1] The following letter from Sophie to Virginia, written in 1936, shows in an interesting way the curious psychology of these devoted female servants to the families for whom they worked—sometimes without exorbitant recognition—in the 19th century:

My dear Miss Genia,

You are much too good to me. I dont deserve such kindness. I am sure I dont.

Thank you very much your very generious cheque arrived this morning. It was sent from Dalingridge to 33 Chester Square ware Lady Margaret has a house until the end of August. then on to me.

Thank you also for your nice letter and all the bits of news. I do enjoy hearing all about Miss Nessa and her charming children there is nobody just like you all are to me. I shall look forward to seeing you all again one day. I keep all your letters and read them over and over I also have some snaps that Sir George sent me. he had taken them of you all when he went to Charlston with Mr Brony and her Ladyship. They are all Treasures of mine. I took them one day to show Mr & Mrs Gerald. I am including one that Miss Stella took of me at St Ives also one Mr Gerald took. At least it might have been a copy of them thay was found with some others after Sir George died he always thought he had taken them. One day your beloved Mother found me in the kitchen shelling peas. and said thats whot I like to see you doing wait until I fetch Miss Stella to take a snap of you. then come Mr Gerald oh said I like to see you stirring with a big spoon. So hear they are Lady Margaret gave them to me after Sir George died Will you Please dear Miss Genia return them. . . . Thanks again for all your kindness to me. May I send my love to Mr Woolf and to you. I am quite well but feel old I am going to be 76 next May. its 50 years last Friday that I fust cooked your Christmas dinner. May I send my Love to Miss Nessa and remain yours obediently   Sophia

Sir George was George Duckworth, half-brother of Vanessa and Virginia; Lady Margaret was his wife; Mr. and Mrs. Gerald were

parlourmaid of the same vintage. Breakfast was provided for all the occupants and every morning one notified in writing on a tablet in the hall whether one would be in for lunch and dinner. All meals were put on trays in the hall and one carried one's tray up to one's room and, having eaten, left it again in the hall. We shared all the expenses of the house and establishment. On December 4 I went into residence and from that moment began to see Virginia continually. We often lunched or dined together, we went together to Gordon Square to see Vanessa or have a meal there, we walked in the country, we went to the theatre or to the Russian Ballet.

By the end of 1911 I knew that I was in love with Virginia and that I should have to make up my mind rapidly what I was to do about it. Should I ask her to marry me? What was I to do about Ceylon? In a few months time my leave would end and I should have to return to Colombo. If she married me, I should, of course, resign, but what should I do if she refused me? As I explained at the end of my book, *Growing*, if she did not marry me, I did not want to go back to Ceylon and succeed in the Civil Service and end as a Governor. I had a vague notion that I might return and immerse myself for ever in the administration of a remote, backward district like Hambantota, but at the back of my mind I must have known that this was a mere fantasy. For a few weeks in a kind of perpetual social motion I contrived to put off the moment of making a decision. I went to Cambridge and stayed in Trinity as Hardy's guest, and the following week I was there again as Moore's guest for the Commem. feast. I stayed with Bob Trevelyan in his bitterly cold house on the North Downs near Dorking. In the new

Gerald Duckworth and his wife; Miss Stella was George and Gerald Duckworth's sister. Miss Nessa was Vanessa Bell. Sophie's life, as the letter shows, had become entirely absorbed in the life of the Stephen family.

year—on January 8, 1912—I went down to Frome in Somerset to stay for a week with Leopold.

The change from the incessant whirl of London to the quiet somnolence of a Somerset rectory was like passing straight from a tornado into a calm, or from a saturnalia into a monastery. At last I had time to think. It took me 48 hours to come to a decision and on Wednesday I wired to Virginia asking whether I could see her next day. Next day I went up to London and asked her to marry me. She said she did not know and must have time—indefinite time—to see more of me before she could make up her mind. This put me in a quandary with regard to my leave and I thought, so far as my decision was concerned, I had better postpone taking any irrevocable step until it was forced on me. So I wrote to the Secretary of State for the Colonies, as I recounted in the last chapter of *Growing*, and asked him to extend my leave. When he refused, I resigned from the Ceylon Civil Service. In *Growing* I gave verbatim the correspondence which I had with the Colonial Office about my leave and resignation, and I was a little surprised and amused by the reactions of some reviewers to this. One reviewer could not understand why I included these rather dull letters verbatim. I did so because I thought—and still think—them interesting as a period piece. They show, I think, the economy and restraint on both sides which 50 years ago was considered right and proper in official relations and communications. As an official, I was in those days a stickler for what was officially right and proper. The result seems to me slightly interesting and amusing. Another reviewer criticized me severely on the ground that the Colonial Office behaved so well to me and I gave no recognition of this. But one of the reasons why I gave the letters in full was just that: to show how decently the Secretary of State treated his subordinate, giving me every opportunity to withdraw my resignation. I saw no reason to say this, just as I saw no reason to say that the Secretary of State's treatment of me may have been in part due to the fact that he knew that I had been a highly competent civil servant.

My resignation from the Ceylon Civil Service came into effect on May 20, 1912. Until that date I drew my salary of £22 a month, on which I found it possible to live comfortably in London before the war. Those were the days of economic paradise for the bourgeoisie, and my total bill for the most comfortable lodging and first-class cooking at Brunswick Square was between £11 and £12 a month. But I had to face the fact that after May 20 I should be without a job and means of subsistence. It is true that I had saved a sum of about £600. This was mainly the result of my winning £690 in a sweepstake in 1908. That £690 has given rise to one of those completely false legends the origin of which is inexplicable. I have often been told and I have seen it stated more than once in print that Virginia and I started the Hogarth Press on the money which I had won in the sweepstake. The statement is ludicrously untrue. We started the Hogarth Press in 1917 on a capital of £41. 15s. 3d. This sum was made up of £38. 8s. 3d., which we spent on a small printing machine and type, and £3. 7s. 0d., which was the total cost of production of the first book which we printed and published. We made a profit of £6. 7s. 0d. in the first year on the first publication and that 'went back into the business', so that at the end of 1917 the total capital which we had put into the Hogarth Press was £35. After that the business financed itself out of profits and we never had to 'find capital' for it.

However this is a digression and I must return to the economic problem which faced me at the beginning of 1912. The problem faced me, but in fact I did not face the problem. I simply ignored it or rather postponed any serious con-

LONDON AND MARRIAGE, 1911 AND 1912

sideration of it. I could keep going in my present way of life on my £600 for about two years. After that I should have to find some means of earning a living. I had a vague idea of trying to earn a living by writing, but I decided that for the present I should make no attempt to find a job—I would go on writing *The Village in the Jungle*.

During the first six months of 1912 I lived an extremely social life. I went up to Cambridge more than once for week-ends, and even read a paper to the Society. I stayed with Roger Fry in Guildford, with Bob Trevelyan near Dorking. I got to know the Morrells—Philip, the Liberal M.P., and Lady Ottoline, his wife—and went to the kind of salon Ottoline presided over in Bedford Square, and later for week-ends in Garsington Manor near Oxford. I saw a good deal of Henry Lamb, the artist, who painted my portrait. I used to take him out riding on Wimbledon Common. We hired horses in Putney, lazy, somnolent old hacks, as that kind of horse practically always is, but Henry was a congenitally incompetent rider. The ancient hacks, of course, realized this as soon as he was on their backs, and often when we got to the middle of the Common his horse would take charge of him and canter back down Putney Hill to its stable near Putney Bridge. I found that it was no good my trying to stop this, for as soon as I pursued Henry's horse to turn it back, its canter would change to a gallop, and, though Henry could just stick on at a trot or canter, he was liable to fall off if his horse broke into a gallop. Sometimes Philip Morrell, Adrian Stephen, and Ka Cox joined Henry and me on these rides over Wimbledon Common or in Richmond Park.

All this time I was seeing a great deal of Virginia, and an event took place which in future years greatly affected our lives for it brought us permanently into Sussex. When I was staying with her in her Firle villa, we walked over the downs one day from Firle to the Ouse valley, and in one of those lovely folds or hollows in the down we came upon an extra-ordinarily romantic-looking house. It was upon the Lewes-Seaford Road, but a great field, full of sheep, lay between it and the road. It faced due west, and from its windows and terrace in front of the house you looked across the great field and the Ouse valley to the line of downs on the west of the river. Behind it was a steep down, on the south and north were lines of elm trees running down on each side of the field to the road. There were barns behind the house, but there were no other buildings anywhere visible from it, indeed the only building anywhere near it was the shepherd's cottage. Its name was Asham House, sometimes written Asheham or Ascham. The house was empty, though it was, I think, occasionally occupied by a worker on the farm—Itford Farm. Its history was curious. The large Itford Farm was bought about 1820 by a Lewes solicitor. It was worked by a bailiff who lived in the very ancient farm-house at Itford over a quarter of a mile from Asham. The solicitor built himself Asham House in the hollow of the down and used it as a summer residence. An L-shaped house, it had two large sitting-rooms on the ground floor, four bedrooms on the second, and a vast attic. Its front was flat, plain, serene, yellow washed, with large french windows opening on to a small terrace. Just below the terrace was a small piece of grass and from it the great field swept straight away, joining with the Ouse valley to meet the downs which lay two miles away as the crow flies across the river.

We made enquiries and found that Asham and the whole farm belonged to the solicitor's granddaughter who lived in Rugby. From her Virginia got a five-year lease of Asham, and she gave up her Firle villa. On February 9 there was a house warming, a week-end party consisting of Virginia, Vanessa, Clive, Adrian, Roger Fry, Duncan Grant, and

Asham House

myself. It was the first of many such week-ends. Asham was a strange house. The country people on the farm were convinced that it was haunted, that there was treasure buried in the cellar, and no one would stay the night in it. It is true that at night one often heard extraordinary noises both in the cellars and in the attic. It sounded as if two people were walking from room to room, opening and shutting doors, sighing, whispering. It was, no doubt, the wind sighing in the chimneys, and, when there was no wind, probably rats in the cellar or the attic. I have never known a house which had such a strong character, personality of its own—romantic, gentle, melancholy, lovely. It was Asham and its ghostly footsteps and whisperings which gave Virginia the idea for *A Haunted House*, and I can immediately see, hear, and smell the house when I read the opening words:

> Whatever hour you woke there was a door shutting. From room to room they went, hand in hand, lifting here, opening there, making sure—a ghostly couple.

There was a small, dishevelled walled garden on one side of the house. The great elms towered up above it on the south. The grass of the garden and field seemed almost to come up to the sitting rooms and into the windows facing west. One often had a feeling as if one were living under water in the depths of the sea behind the thick, rough glass of the room's long windows—a sea of green trees, green grass, green air. One day when Virginia was ill in London, after we were married, I had to go down by myself to Asham to get something or make some arrangements. I arrived late in the evening of an early summer day and spent the night there, sleeping outside on a mattress. In the night there was not a sound—I might have been miles from any other human being. Suddenly in the early morning there burst out a tremendous chorus as if every thrush and blackbird in

England had started to sing round the house and every wood pigeon in Sussex had started 'bubbling with content'—in Virginia's *Haunted House* 'from the deepest wells of silence the wood pigeon drew its bubble of sound'. When this ecstatic hosanna or alleluia woke me, I really felt, lying there on the ground, for a moment that I was submerged by the uncut grass towering above my head, the rose leaves above the grass, and the elms above the rose leaves. I wonder if it is age and its dullness of hearing, the spraying of crops, or insecticides which make it seem that there are now no such great convocations of birds in my garden, no such passionate bursts of song, no such 'fantastic summer's heat' as one knew 40 years ago.

It was a lovely house and the rooms within it were lovely. There was a slight sadness always over it and in it—an almost comforting sadness. Behind it was one of the most perfect hollows running right back into the down, the hill rising perpendicular behind and on each side of it. In the late summer and autumn the hollow was full of mushrooms. It was so remote and undisturbed that once a vixen had her cubs in an earth half way up the down behind the house and one could go out and watch the fox cubs playing about on the grass, with the mother lying full length outside her earth keeping an eye on them. There was only one objection to Asham House, but it was, as we eventually found, a serious one. With the down behind it on the east and the elms high above it on the south, for a great part of the year it was in shadow the better part of the day. The sun shone upon it so little that it felt damp spring, autumn, and winter, even though in fact the floors, walls, and ceilings were quite dry. The consequence was that, if one stayed in it for more than a week or two, one began to feel slightly depressed or even vaguely unwell.

All through the spring and summer of 1912, usually

twice a month, I went with Virginia for the week-end to Asham. As a rule, Adrian, Vanessa, and Roger Fry came too, sometimes Lytton or Marjorie Strachey. The shepherd's wife, Mrs. Funnell, from the cottage across the road came up and 'did' for us, making the beds, cleaning the house, and washing up. She was a great character and a great talker. After washing up, she used to come into the sitting room and stand talking for a long time. She was pure Sussex and used ancient words which have now, after 50 years, completely dropped out of the Sussex villagers' vocabulary. They were words like 'dishabille' and 'terrify'. After a storm she would tell us that all the flowers in her garden were 'dishabille'. When we first went to Rodmell, I had a man who did my garden and talked the same language. Dedman would say to me: 'Them birds do so terrify the peas, I must put a net over them.'

Mrs. Funnell was a woman of iron will, but, in so far as her hard life allowed it, of good will. She became fond of Virginia and, to a much lesser degree, of me. She brought up a family of sons and daughters, in spotless cleanliness and considerable fear of their mother, on the starvation wage of her husband. Within the limits of her profound ignorance of the world outside a four-mile radius from her cottage— there were no buses in those days and it was only rarely that she could leave her cottage and go the four miles to Lewes or Newhaven—she had sagacity, understanding, curiosity, intelligence. I think she had scarcely ever read a book, but one day one of our visitors left a copy of Ethel M. Dell's *The Way of an Eagle* in the kitchen and Mrs. Funnell became completely engrossed in it—it was my first experience of the mysterious, devastating power of the great born best seller, which acts like a force of nature, an earthquake or hurricane, upon the mind and heart of unsophisticated millions.

I only once saw Mrs. Funnell in any way upset or put out.

One evening about an hour after she had done the washing up and talking and had gone back to her cottage, there was a knock on the sitting room door and there stood Mrs. Funnell again, obviously 'in a state', a dark, fierce, but worried look upon her broad, lined, handsome face. Without beating about the bush, she told us that her unmarried daughter was at that moment giving birth to a child and that it was quite impossible to get a doctor. So bare was the home of a Sussex shepherd 50 years ago that she had not the necessary towels, basins, cans, and she had come to borrow them from us. The child was safely delivered, the father being, it was said, the bailiff, but Mrs. Funnell never mentioned the subject again.

In the 50 years since we had Asham House, the physical basis of life in the English countryside has been revolutionized. Conditions in Sussex in 1912 were pretty primitive, and our daily life was probably nearer that of Chaucer's than of the modern man with water from the main, electricity, gas, cars, motor buses, telephone, wireless. When we went down to Asham for a week-end we sometimes got a fly, which the dictionary tells us correctly was 'a one-horse hackney carriage', from Lewes; but more often than not, wet or dry, we walked the four miles along the river bank and across the fields with knapsacks on our backs. All the water we used in the house we had to pump from the well. Sanitation consisted of an earth closet. We cooked on an oil stove or a primus; at night we used candles and oil lamps. Even in 1919, when we bought Monks House and moved across the river to a house in the middle of a village, conditions were just the same—no buses, no water, no gas or electricity and the only 'sanitary convenience', as it was called, an earth closet discretely, but ineffectively, hidden in a grove of cherry laurels in the middle of the garden.

In 1917 when we had to renew our lease of Asham in the

middle of the war, Mr. Hoper, the Rugby solicitor, told us
that they found the farm too big and that after the war they
would divide it into two. They would then require Asham
House for a bailiff to live in, and so could give us only a
yearly tenancy while the war lasted. In 1918, when the war
at last ended, they gave us a year's notice, which meant that
we should have to leave Asham in September, 1919. Then
began a desperate attempt to find a house to take the place of
Asham. We could find nothing to suit us and our purse, and
in despair in the middle of the year we bought for £300 a
very strange little house up on the hill in the middle of Lewes
near the castle. It was called The Round House and it was
indeed completely round, for it had been converted into a
house from the old mill.

No sooner had we bought The Round House than in the
village of Rodmell two miles away from Asham across the
river old Jacob Verrall died; and Monks House, in which he
had lived for many years, was to be sold by auction on July 1,
1919. As soon as we saw Monks House, we decided that we
must, if we possibly could, buy it. It was said to date from
the 15th or 16th century, a weatherboarded house with eight
or nine oak-beamed rooms. But the rooms were mostly small
as four of them had in fact been formed by thin partitions
from what originally were biggish rooms, and we removed
the partitions and restored the house to what it originally
must have been. It had about an acre of garden which ad-
joined the churchyard, and it was said to have got its name
because it belonged in the 15th century to the monks of
Lewes Priory who used it for their 'retreats'. I hope this
story is true, but I never believe such legends about houses
unless there is documentary evidence for them, for if you
know an English village for 50 years, you see strange things
happen. For instance, I have seen two cottages converted
into a gentleman's residence to be sold twenty years later

61

as a 15th century Sussex farmhouse. Our monks, I am afraid, are probably equally mythological.

Chronologically I have got too far ahead, for Monks House and all this belong to life after I married and after the 1914 war, and should therefore come in a later volume. And in my experience what cuts the deepest channels in our lives are the different houses in which we live—deeper even than 'marriage and death and division', so that perhaps the chapters of one's autobiography should be determined by the different periods in which one has lived in different houses, and the man who had lived the whole of his life in one house would have no life to write about. On the other hand the purchase of and move across the river to Monks House follow logically on our seven years interlude with Asham House and Mrs. Funnell, and I shall therefore ignore chronology for a moment and finish the story of our acquisition of Monks House.

We had often noticed the house and garden before 1919, for walking up or down the lane between Rodmell church and the village street you could look over the wall into the orchard and garden and catch a glimpse of the back of the house. The orchard was lovely and the garden was the kind I like, much subdivided into a kind of patchwork quilt of trees, shrubs, flowers, vegetables, fruit, roses and crocus tending to merge into cabbages and currant bushes. In the middle of the 19th century it had belonged to the miller whose windmill stood on Mill Hill, the down above the village, and the great millstones were brought to Monks House, when the mill was pulled down, and still pave the garden. Jacob Verrall, the last owner, was a great character. The first extant reference to him is in the Rodmell Vestry Minute Book of 1882. He was then the Surveyor of Highways, the Assessor and Collector of Taxes, and an Overseer of the Poor. As Surveyor he was paid a sum of £10 per

annum. In the first minutes recorded in this book, for the
Vestry Meeting on March 25, 1882, the Overseers were
requested to provide a new Vestry Minute Book as 'the old
one cannot be found'; it is clear therefore that Jacob Verrall
held all these parish posts even before 1882. He continued
to hold them and to attend every Vestry Meeting until 1910,
and even in 1918 just before his death at the age of 74 he
attended the Parish Meeting, which had taken the place of
the old Vestry Meeting.

Old Verrall, as he was always called when I first knew
Rodmell, lies now in his narrow cell beneath rugged elms
and the yew-trees' shade in Rodmell churchyard. He was, I
think, a typical rude forefather of the hamlet such as Gray
described in his famous Elegy in 1751; these kind of men
and the society to which they belonged still existed 250 years
after Gray wrote when I first knew Rodmell. They have died
out with the earth closets in the laurel shrubberies. I am glad
that I knew them and for a short time lived in the village
among them, just as I am glad to have lived for a time in the
primeval and rapidly disappearing life of the Ceylon jungle
village. There was a great deal to be said against both, and
yet one can say without any sentimentality that there was an
element of earthy strength and individuality which gave not
only some aesthetic satisfaction to the outsider, but some
compensation to the victims.

Verrall's wife Lydia was a descendant of the miller and I
think it was she who brought him Monks House. She died
seven years before him and of course, like him, lies under the
elms and the yews in the churchyard. After she died, he
lived by himself, cultivating his garden, grafting (not entirely successfully) his fruit trees, and collecting riddles for
which he had a passion. Every Monday morning Mrs.
Dedman came in from the neighbouring cottage and cooked
him a large joint which he ate hot the first day and cold for

the remainder of the week. The rest of his diet consisted of the vegetables from his garden, which he always ate raw, and the produce of his fruit trees. In the last years of his life he spent most of his time lying in bed in the tiniest room in the house which overlooked the garden and an immense gaunt cherry tree which grew out of a flower border into which the cabbages had to some extent penetrated. In the cherry season Verrall lay on his bed with one end of a long cord attached to his big toe while the other end of the cord was attached to a large bell hanging from the topmost bough of the cherry tree. Whenever he saw any birds approaching the tree, he jerked his foot so that the bell rang and scared the birds away.

Most of my information about Verrall came from the Rodmell rector who belonged entirely to that same ancient English village way of life which in Sussex has completely disappeared. The first time I ever saw Mr. Hawkesford, I mistook him for a farm hand. He came suddenly round a corner into the footpath along which I was walking, a tall grizzled man of about 60 with an untidy beard in dirty old clothes carrying a ladder on his shoulder. He looked at me with the rapid, sideways, cautious glance with which the countryman in those days habitually greeted a stranger. Later on I got to know him fairly well for he liked to come and sit with me in the garden and talk about flowers and vegetables, the village history, and the curious characters of men and women who now lay buried in the churchyard. I never heard him say a word about religion or his work as a clergyman. Sometimes on Sunday I have seen him come out of the church during the service and stand in the churchyard smoking a cigarette, while the congregation sang the hymn or the psalm. His wife, poor woman, suffered intensely, but not silently, from the boredom of village life. People today have no conception of the long-drawn-out torture of boredom and empty lives in villages which in those days devoured the minds and souls of large numbers of middle class women whose only interests and pleasures could be found in the bourgeois society of a London suburb. There were no 'gentry' in the neighbourhood with whom Mrs. Hawkesford could consort. She hated Rodmell, for she had nothing to look forward to—so she one day told us—but the hot bath on Thursday night when Mary, the devoted maid, carried up the brass cans full of hot water to the hipbath in front of the fire in her bedroom. Mrs. Hawkesford had once stayed for a few days with a friend or relation in a house in West Kensington which overlooked Queen's Club, where in those days the Oxford and Cambridge football matches and high class tennis tournaments were held. She more than once told us about this and how she had never enjoyed herself more than sitting at the window and watching these exciting events; her ambition in life, never to be attained, was to live in a house backing on Queen's Club.

When the rector died, Mrs. Hawkesford went and lived in Brighton. And there she lived for years until indeed she became an old bedridden woman who had lost even her memory. Her maid, Mary, went with her and looked after her—served her, as they used to say, devotedly—until they were parted by death. The lives of modern, civilized human beings can be incredibly strange—and sad. For the greater part of a long life Mrs. Hawkesford lived in a nice large house, in a charming village, in beautiful country, comfortably off and with no apparent troubles, but miserable, bored, discontented, longing for a house in West Kensington. And to this peevish—though probably quite nice— woman and to her family Mary devoted absolutely the whole of *her* life. Not only her life but her universe seemed to be the Hawkesford family, her youth, her middle age, all the best years of her life, passing, until she too became old, in looking after the children, carrying up brass cans of hot water, cooking meals, looking after Mrs. Hawkesford (in her second childhood), first in Rodmell rectory and then in the end in a Brighton flat. In 1919 there were hundreds of Marys all over England. Next to the war memorial in White-hall there should be another to the millions of daughters who gave their lives to looking after selfish parents and millions of Marys who gave their lives to looking after Mrs. Hawkesfords.

In Southease, the next village to Rodmell, was another rector, the Rev. Mr. Thomas. He had succeeded his father, and, when Mr. Thomas junior died, the parish of Southease had had only two rectors in nearly 100 years. The number of his parishioners, men, women, and children, was well under 50 and the total size of Southease parish was 850 acres. Outside his services the rector had simply nothing to do. He was unmarried and lived in a pleasant rectory with a fair sized garden, looked after by his two antediluvian un-married sisters. One of the sisters kept bees and sold honey, and to go into the rectory to buy honey from her was like walking into the 16th century and talking to someone who was unaware of the 20th century or of a world outside the Southease rectory. The rector himself spent most of his time sitting in his study, which looked across the water-meadows to the railway line from Lewes to Newhaven and Seaford, and counting the number of trucks in the goods trains which he could see passing along the line. The great war of 1914-1918 was a landmark in the life of the rector of Southease, not because it launched a thousand ships and killed ten million men and destroyed European civilization, but because it caused the longest goods trains which Mr. Thomas had ever seen to pass along the railway line to Newhaven. This was because Newhaven became one of the Channel ports through which our army in France was supplied, and all day long for four years the rector watched from his study longer and longer goods trains pass backwards and forwards along the line and counted the number of trucks. Whenever I happened to meet him in Southease village he used to tell me of a train which he had seen with a record number of trucks. The only other interest in life which the rector seemed to have was the weather. He had the appearance and gave one the feeling of an unusually happy and contented man.

The country life of a Sussex village 50 years ago and the people who lived it have, as I said, now completely disappeared. They were probably nearer to Chaucer's England than to the England of 1963. In many ways it was a terribly hard life and an uncivilized society, both physically and spiritually. It was full of unhappy Mrs. Hawkesfords, village women worn out by childbearing and domestic slavery, men of considerable brutality. It took ten to fifteen years before the villagers regarded one as other than a stranger—and all strangers were regarded with distrust and some hostility. But when they got to know you and allowed you to get to know them, you found that beneath the surface, side by side with the grimness and brutality, life was complex, with deep down sometimes happiness and sensitiveness to beauty. No writer has so clearly felt and re-created this than the countryman Hardy in his novels.

I never felt it in real life more intensely than when I got to know the carter on the Rodmell farm. In the early summer morning one heard him bring the horses up from the brooks and, after working them all day, he brought them slowly down to the fields in the evening. There is no doubt that he had a passion for his horses and that to have anything to do with them gave him intense pleasure. On Sunday afternoon, whenever it was fine, dressed in his Sunday clothes he walked through the churchyard and down the field to the watermeadows. There, leaning over a gate, he would stand for an hour or more in contemplation and there for a time I would sometimes join him. It is a lovely, profoundly peaceful place, with the great stretch of watermeadows lying in the circle of the downs. Our conversation was desultory, broken by long silences, and I have no doubt that he went there, as I did, instinctively to allow the beauty to seep soothingly into the soul. One day he came to me and asked me to make his will for him. He had several sons and one daughter and he wanted me to write out on a sheet of paper a statement, which he would sign in the presence of his children and of me, saying that he left everything to his daughter. I told him that this would not be a legal will and that he ought to go to a solicitor and sign a proper legal will. He refused to do this and said that if I would do what he asked, his sons would carry it out after his death. So I did do what he asked. I wrote out the statement and took it round to his cottage one Sunday morning. He, his sons, and his daughter were all there in their best clothes. I read aloud the document and he signed it and they all thanked me and we shook hands. When he died, everything went to the daughter without difficulty.

I must return to the spring and early summer of 1912. I had tried in February to get an extension of my leave, but, as recorded in *Growing*, the Ceylon Government were not prepared to grant it unless I stated 'the exact nature of the private affairs' on account of which I was applying for an extension. This on my part I was not prepared to do, and in April I had to make a decision either to go back to Ceylon and give up the possibility of marrying Virginia or to resign from the Ceylon Civil Service and start afresh in London in the hope that Virginia might decide to marry me. On April 25 I sent in my resignation and it was accepted by the Secretary of State on May 7. Life went on for me much as it had in the preceding months. I continued to write *The*

68

Village in the Jungle, and in rather a desultory way, when staying for a week-end in May in Cambridge, I went to the Appointments Board to see whether there was any likelihood of my getting a job from which I could earn a living.

Then on May 29 I had lunch with Virginia in her room and we sat talking afterwards, when suddenly Virginia told me that she loved me and would marry me. It was a wonderful summer afternoon and we felt that we must get away from London for a time. We took the train to Maidenhead and I hired a boat and rowed up the river to Marlow and then we came back and dined at the riverside restaurant in Maidenhead. We both felt that in those 10 hours from after lunch to midnight when we got back to Brunswick Square we had seemed to drift through a beautiful, vivid dream. First, after the intense emotion of Virginia's saying that she would marry me, the gentle rhythm of the row up the river. There is always to me something of the noiseless drift of dreaming in the gliding of the boat through the water of the river. Then the complete unreality of the brash restaurant and the blatant riverside crowd. As a rule it is disquieting to find oneself insulated and isolated in a crowd, in the herd, but not of it. But there are rare moments when this seems appropriate and comforting. In the restaurant and coming back in a crowded train, I think we both felt a strange happiness of being for a moment alone together in an empty universe.

Such moments are indeed only moments; they pass in a flash, and before one knows it one is again in and of the herd. Virginia and I were married on Saturday, August 10, at St. Pancras Register Office in a room which, in those days, looked down into a cemetery. In the ceremony before a Registrar one makes no promise 'to love and to cherish, till death us do part, according to God's holy ordinance', but in the St. Pancras Office, facing the window and looking through it at the tombstones behind the Registrar's head, one was, I suppose appropriately, reminded of the words 'till death us do part'. Apart from the tombstones, our wedding ceremony was provided with an element of comic relief (quite unintended) characteristic of the Stephens. In the middle of the proceedings Vanessa interrupted the Registrar, saying: 'Excuse me interrupting; I have just remembered: we registered my son—he is two years old—in the name of Clement, and we now want to change his name to Quentin— can you tell me what I have to do?' There was a moment of astonished silence in the room as we all looked round sympathetically and saw the serious, slightly puzzled look on Vanessa's face. There was a pause while the Registrar stared at her with his mouth open. Then he said severely: 'One thing at a time, please, Madam.'

In the seven weeks between our visit to Maidenhead and our visit to the St. Pancras Register Office we lived rather a hectic life. In those days we went continually to theatres, concerts, operas. We had a vast number of friends and acquaintances and so lived a very social life. I was taken off to be exhibited to many of Virginia's relations whom hitherto I had not met. The most interesting was Lady Ritchie, Aunt Anny as she was always called. Aunt Anny had been born in 1837 and was therefore 75 when I dined in the Ritchies' house in St. George's Square, slightly oppressed and de-pressed by the solid Victorian gloom of their dining-room. She was Thackeray's eldest daughter and the sister of Virginia's father's first wife. At the age of 40 she married her cousin Richmond Thackeray Ritchie, who was 17 years younger than she. He was an extremely able, formidable man and, sitting at the head of his table, he seemed to me rather saturnine; he was Under Secretary of State in the India Office.

Aunt Anny was a rare instance of the child of a man of

genius inheriting some of that genius. You can see it in her books, even in her now unread novels, but particularly in her autobiographical books. Her genius, like most things about her and in her, was a shade out of control. This erratic streak in her made her miss trains, confuse dates, and get the chapters of most of her novels so muddled that the last chapter was printed as the first (and nobody noticed it). This flightiness was absurd and, as Virginia records in her essay 'The Enchanted Organ', amused the great Charles Darwin, who said apologetically: 'I can't for the life of me help laughing.' But it—and still more she—was not entirely absurd. It was part of her great charm and of her flashes of genius and imagination. Virginia noted that 'she said things that no human being could possibly mean; yet she meant them'.

That evening in 1912 she sat at one end of the dining table, with Richmond at the other, looking very frail, living not entirely in the same world as we were living in, and suddenly from time to time saying one of these things which no human being could possibly mean, but which she meant. From time to time too Richmond from the opposite end of the table heard one of these strange pronouncements which obviously irritated him like a little thorn which had been for so many years domestically and matrimonially embedded in his mind, and he put her somewhat sharply in her place. The curious thing was that when I thought about what she had in fact said, the absurdity remained, but through the absurdity I seemed to see something imaginative, something which only Aunt Anny had seen and which we could not quite get at, and Richmond's irritation irritated me. I think I must have shown her something of what I felt about her and about what she was saying, for in a letter which she wrote to Virginia some time later she said: 'I always feel glad when I think of your dear husband who belongs to the order of those to whom my heart goes out.' The first sentence of this letter is worth quoting, because it is a good example of her style and of some of her peculiarities which I have described above: 'My dearest Virginia, I meant to have a pretty card for you also, but only Nessa's butterflies flew off and yours posted itself as cards do, and there is only the outside wrapping to send with my love and blessing.'[1]

We went down and had luncheon at Wellington College with the headmaster, Virginia's cousin Will Vaughan. He was married to Madge, a daughter of John Addington Symonds. There were also present Symonds's widow and his biographer, Horatio Brown. The atmosphere of this luncheon party was curious; it was compounded of two opposite, antipathetic, and entirely unmixable elements. Will was the public school headmaster in excelsis, a product of Rugby and New College, breezy, his feet planted with no nonsense on the solid earth of the English public school, a liberal of course, but accepted as invincibly safe by the most conservative of conservatives. He was charming to me, treating me at once as a favourite prefect. Madge too was charming and Virginia was fond of her. But she, her mother, and Horatio Brown oozed the precious, incense laden, Italianate culture of Walter Pater and the eighties and nineties. I don't suppose anyone now reads Symonds, but he

[1] The following letter which she wrote to me is also characteristic; I had asked her to support the Adult Suffrage movement: 'O my dear Leonard What will you think of me. It seems to me ten thousand pities to give equal votes to unequal men I should like to give 100 to one man and ¼ of a vote to another I would give you a great many to you and to Virginia too and my love to her. I have a friend to tea at the Sesame at 4 o'c next Thursday and I have asked a charming Mrs. Kendall who writes plays Could you come there or *here* the following Thursday. We have had dear poor Blanche Cornish here for a month tell Virginia She has lost that dear Gerald who used to know Virginia and Nessa so well Yrs with affectionate sympathy and what is the word?—dissidence?—Anne Ritchie'

George Duckworth, Stella Duckworth, and J. W. Hills

had a reputation in the last decade of the 19th century which still existed, in a rather decrepit state, in 1912. Symonds was a littérateur, lock, stock, and barrel. He lived in Venice and wrote a large number of books on Italian literature and history. Horatio, who seemed to me a kind of caricature pussycat littérateur, also lived in Venice. His relation to Symonds was that of the lesser to the greater fleas; besides the biography, he wrote books about Venice and literature and history, with titles like *Life on the Lagoons* and *Venetian Studies*.

Madge worshipped her father as so many daughters have since the time of Electra, in a way which was not fully understood until the second eating of the apple on the tree of knowledge by Sigmund Freud. She had the same kind of literary gift as her father and, when young, had followed in his footsteps with a book, *Days Spent on a Doge's Farm*. She was rather intense, and the atmosphere of the Doge's farm and Venetian lagoons would not mix with that of Wellington and Will, who treated her across the luncheon table much as Richmond had treated Aunt Anny across the dining table. I find few things more distressing than the note of matrimonial exasperation in one's host or hostess when they speak to each other.

Another visit we made was to Virginia's half-brother, Sir George Duckworth. Eton, Trinity College, Cambridge, married to Lady Margaret Herbert, very handsome, immensely kind and charming, and—it has to be admitted—a snob. He lived in a large house in largish grounds near East Grinstead, and he kept some Highland cattle in a field. We went down for lunch and there was one other visitor, Reginald Farrer. I was much amused to meet him again in such very different circumstances. For the last time I had seen him was when he appeared as an English Buddhist in Kandy, and, at the request of the Diyawadana Nilame, the

73

Manager of the Temple, I opened the shrine and showed Farrer the famous relic, the Buddha's tooth.[1] He gave no sign of recognizing me so I did not recall to him our meeting. I could see nothing of the Buddhist in him as I watched him in Dalingridge Place, rather a drawing-room pussycat, talking to the Lady Margaret.

I was glad when the tour of introductions ended. The children of Sir Leslie Stephen had, at the turn of the century, when their father died, broken away from the society into which they were born. That society consisted of the upper levels of the professional middle class and county families, interpenetrated to a certain extent by the aristocracy. But, although Vanessa, Virginia, and Adrian had broken away from it and from Kensington and Mayfair to live in Bloomsbury what seemed to their relations and old family friends a Bohemian life, there was no complete rupture; they still from time to time saw socially their Stephen and Duckworth relations and the old family friends. It was a social class and way of life into which hitherto I had only dipped from time to time as an outsider, when, for instance, I stayed as a young man with the Stracheys.[2] I was an outsider to this class, because, although I and my father before me belonged to the professional middle class, we had only recently struggled up into it from the stratum of Jewish shopkeepers. We had no roots in it. The psychology of the different strata of English society is extremely important in its effects upon the individual (or was 50 years ago). The Stephens and the Stracheys, the Ritchies, Thackerays, and Duckworths had an intricate tangle of ancient roots and tendrils stretching far and wide through the upper middle classes, the county

[1] See *Growing*, p. 143.
[2] See *Sowing*, pp. 186-191. I dipped into another, but different, section of the same social class when I used to lunch with Leopold Campbell in Manchester Square (*Sowing*, pp. 177-180).

families, and the aristocracy. Socially they assumed things unconsciously which I could never assume either unconsciously or consciously. They lived in a peculiar atmosphere of influence, manners, respectability, and it was so natural to them that they were unaware of it as mammals are unaware of the air and fish of the water in which they live. Now that I was going to marry Virginia and went round to see her relations, I began to see this stratum of society from the inside. I said in *Sowing* that I know that I am ambivalent to aristocratic societies, disliking and despising them and at the same time envying them their insolent urbanity. In a milder form there was the same ambivalence in my attitude to the society which I found in Dalingridge Place and St. George's Square. I disliked its respectability and assumptions while envying and fearing its assurance and manners. I should, perhaps, add that the class stratum or strata which I have been writing about in this paragraph are now practically extinct; they were almost destroyed by the 1914 war and were finally wiped away in the 1939 war.

During the time that I lived in the same house as Virginia in Brunswick Square, and particularly in the months before we married, I became for the first time aware of the menace of nervous or mental breakdown under which she always lived. I had had no experience at all of nervous or mental illness and it was some time before I realized the nature and meaning of it in Virginia. It played a large part in her life and our lives and it was the cause of her death. If in the following pages I am to give an accurate and understandable account of our life from 1912 to 1941, when she committed suicide, it is necessary at this point that I should explain the nature of her illness. The doctors called it neurasthenia and she had suffered from it all her life. In the 30 years of our married life, we consulted a considerable number of nerve and mental specialists in and around Harley Street. I do not

think that any of them knew the cause or—except superficially—the nature of the disease which they called neurasthenia. It was a name, a label, like neuralgia or rheumatism,
which covered a multitude of sins, symptoms, and miseries.
They knew the symptoms, or some of them, and they could
prognosticate, within limits, what would alleviate and what
would exacerbate the symptoms. Superficially the nature of
the disease was clear and simple. If Virginia lived a quiet,
vegetative life, eating well, going to bed early, and not tiring
herself mentally or physically, she remained perfectly well.
But if she tired herself in any way, if she was subjected to any
severe physical, mental, or emotional strain, symptoms at
once appeared which in the ordinary person are negligible
and transient, but with her were serious danger signals. The
first symptoms were a peculiar 'headache' low down at the
back of the head, insomnia, and a tendency for the thoughts
to race. If she went to bed and lay doing nothing in a
darkened room, drinking large quantities of milk and eating
well, the symptoms would slowly disappear and in a week or
ten days she would be well again.

But if she did not take these drastic steps at once, if she
ignored the symptoms and went on working and walking
and going to parties and sitting up late, then suddenly the
headache, the sleeplessness, the racing thoughts would
become intense and it might be several weeks before she
could begin again to live a normal life. But four times in her
life the symptoms would not go and she passed across the
border which divides what we call insanity from sanity. She
had a minor breakdown in her childhood; she had a major
breakdown after her mother's death in 1895, another in
1914, and a fourth in 1940. In all these cases of breakdown
there were two distinct stages which are technically called
manic-depressive. In the manic stage she was extremely
excited; the mind raced; she talked volubly and, at the height

of the attack, incoherently; she had delusions and heard voices, for instance she told me that in her second attack she heard the birds in the garden outside her window talking Greek; she was violent with the nurses. In her third attack, which began in 1914, this stage lasted for several months and ended by her falling into a coma for two days. During the depressive stage all her thoughts and emotions were the exact opposite of what they had been in the manic stage. She was in the depths of melancholia and despair; she scarcely spoke; refused to eat; refused to believe that she was ill and insisted that her condition was due to her own guilt; at the height of this stage she tried to commit suicide, in the 1895 attack by jumping out of a window, in 1915 by taking an overdose of veronal; in 1941 she drowned herself in the river Ouse.

This is, of course, a very summary account of extremely complicated mental reactions of a most sensitive and sophisticated mind. One or two things should be noted. The initial symptoms of fatigue, which were, as I have said, in Virginia's case danger signals, were exactly the same, except in one or two particulars, as almost everyone experiences if they overtire themselves. Most people have had the experience of going to bed 'dead tired' and finding that, although they were half asleep before going to bed, they cannot sleep because their mind is 'racing'. With an ordinary person the fatigue and symptoms disappear as soon as he has had a night's rest. Virginia differed from the ordinary person only because the symptoms of fatigue appeared much more easily, were much more severe, and required, not a night's rest, but a week's rest to get rid of them. They differed, therefore, from the ordinary person's symptoms in degree rather than in kind. And this is true also in most respects of the symptoms in the later stages of an attack, even when she had passed from sanity to insanity; they differed mainly from the initial

77

symptoms by becoming much more violent and severe. Even the delusions, the volubility, and the incoherence were exaggerations of the 'racing' thoughts.

All this is true, and because it is true, one might be inclined to say that 'insanity' of the kind which was a perpetual menace and terrifying curse in Virginia's life is solely a matter of degree, the degree of duration or violence of mental states which habitually, in certain circumstances, occur in everyone. In that case everyone is slightly and incipiently insane, and Virginia differed from ordinary 'sane' persons only because, when she had a 'breakdown', there was a great increase in the degree of intensity and duration of symptoms which occurred in her when she was 'sane' and occur in all other people, 'sane' or 'insane'. I do not think this view is correct. For nearly 30 years I had to study Virginia's mind with the greatest intensity, for it was only by recognizing the first, most tenuous mental symptoms of fatigue that we could take in time the steps to prevent a serious breakdown. I am sure that, when she had a breakdown, there was a moment when she passed from what can be rightly called sanity to insanity. On one side of this line was a kind of mental balance, a psychological coherence between intellect and emotion, an awareness and acceptance of the outside world and a rational reaction to it; on the other side were violent emotional instability and oscillation, a sudden change in a large number of intellectual assumptions upon which, often unconsciously, the mental outlook and actions of everyone are based, a refusal to admit or accept facts in the outside world.

The human mind is so complex and so self-contradictory that one can never safely make any statement about it without qualification. In the previous paragraph I have seemed to maintain that there is generally and was in Virginia a definite line between sanity and insanity—that normally she was sane, but four times in her life passed over the line which divides the sane from the insane. This is partly true and partly untrue. When Virginia was quite well, she would discuss her illness; she would recognize that she had been mad, that she had had delusions, heard voices which did not exist, lived for weeks or months in a nightmare world of frenzy, despair, violence. When she was like that, she was obviously well and sane. But even then she was not well and sane in the way in which the vast majority of human beings are well and sane. If, when she was well, any situation or argument arose which was closely connected with her breakdowns or the causes of them, there would sometimes rise to the surface of her mind traces or echoes of the nightmares and delusions of her madness, so that it seemed as if deep down in her mind she was never completely sane.

For instance, one of the most troublesome symptoms of her breakdowns was a refusal to eat. In the worst period of the depressive stage, for weeks almost at every meal one had to sit, often for an hour or more, trying to induce her to eat a few mouthfuls. What made one despair was that by not eating and weakening herself she was doing precisely the thing calculated to prolong the breakdown, for it was only by building up her bodily strength and by resting that she could regain mental equilibrium. Deep down this refusal to eat was connected with some strange feeling of guilt: she would maintain that she was not ill, that her mental condition was due to her own fault—laziness, inanition, gluttony. This was her attitude to food when she was in the depths of the depressive stage of her insanity. But something of this attitude remained with her always, even when she appeared to have completely recovered. It was always extremely difficult to induce her to eat enough food to keep her well. Every doctor whom we consulted told her that to eat well and drink two or three glasses of milk every day was essential if she was to remain well and keep off the initial symptoms which were the danger signals of an approaching breakdown. Everything which I observed between 1912 and 1941 confirmed their diagnosis. But I do not think that she ever accepted it. Left to herself, she ate extraordinarily little and it was with the greatest difficulty that she could be induced to drink a glass of milk regularly every day. It was a perpetual, and only partially successful, struggle; our quarrels and arguments were rare and almost always about eating or resting. And if the argument became heated, even when she was apparently quite well, in a mild, vague form the delusions seemed to rise again to the surface of her mind. Her hostility to the doctors and nurses which was very marked during the breakdowns would reappear. She would argue as if she had never been ill—that the whole treatment had been wrong, that she ate too much and lived a life too lethargic and quiet. Below the surface of her mind and of her argument there was, I felt, some strange, irrational sense of guilt.

Some pages back I referred to the ancient belief that genius is near allied to madness. I am quite sure that Virginia's genius was closely connected with what manifested itself as mental instability and insanity. The creative imagination in her novels, her ability to 'leave the ground' in conversation, and the voluble delusions of the breakdowns all came from the same place in her mind—she 'stumbled after her own voice' and followed 'the voices that fly ahead'. And that in itself was the crux of her life, the tragedy of genius. It was mental or physical strain and fatigue which endangered her mental stability; if she lived a quiet, vegetative life, she was well and sane. But to tell her, as doctors always did and I often had to tell her, that she must live a quiet, vegetative life, was absurd, terribly ironical. If she tired herself by walking too long and too far, if she sat up later than 11 two or three nights running, if she went to too many parties, the physical strain would very soon bring on the dangerous symptoms, the danger signals. As soon as they appeared, one could reasonably tell her that she must really stop and go to bed and do nothing for a few days, and, by continual vigilance and (to her) tiresome interludes of inanition, we were successful in dealing with this kind of strain. But the mental strain of her imagination or genius, of her own mind, was equally or rather more dangerous, and though you can tell a person like Virginia not to go for a walk or to a party, you cannot tell her not to think, work, or write. I have never known any writer work with such concentration and assiduity as she did. When she was writing a novel, she did the writing in the morning from 10 to 1, but she was thinking about it almost all day long. And she put the whole of herself into the writing and the thinking. Even with a review, she would write and rewrite it and rewrite it again from end to end five or six times, and she once opened a cupboard and found in it (and burnt) a whole mountain of MSS.; it was *The Voyage Out* which she had rewritten (I think) five times from beginning to end. Thus the connection between her madness and her writing was close and complicated, and it is significant that, whenever she finished a book, she was in a state of mental exhaustion and for weeks in danger of a breakdown. In 1936 she only just escaped a breakdown when finishing *The Years*; in 1941 she wrote the last words of *Between the Acts* on February 26, and 23 days later on March 21 she committed suicide.

When we married, I had no clear knowledge or understanding of all this, but I had become extremely uneasy about Virginia's health. It was obvious that exertion and strains which had no effect at all upon me were disastrous to her. She was at the time writing *The Voyage Out* and in March 1912 she read some of it to me. I thought it extraordinarily good, but noticed even then what a strain it was upon her.

Then came the emotional strain of our engagement and she got a severe headache and insomnia and had to go for a time to a nursing home in Twickenham and rest there. Her doctor was Sir George Savage, a mental specialist at the head of his profession. He was also a friend of her family and had known her ever since her birth. I went to see him quite early on in 1912 and he discussed Virginia's health with me as a doctor and as an old friend. He was very friendly to me, but impressed me much more as a man of the world than as a doctor. In the next few months, I became more and more uneasy about one thing. We both wanted to have children, but the more I saw the dangerous effect of any strain or stress upon her, the more I began to doubt whether she would be able to stand the strain and stress of childbearing. I went and consulted Sir George Savage; he brushed my doubts aside. But now my doubts about Sir George Savage were added to my doubts about Virginia's health. There seemed to be more of the man of the world ('Do her a world of good, my dear fellow; do her a world of good!') in his opinion than of the mental specialist. So I went off and consulted two other well known doctors, Maurice Craig and T. B. Hyslop, and also the lady who ran the mental nursing home where Virginia had several times stayed. They confirmed my fears and were strongly against her having children. We followed their advice.

We were married, as I said some pages back, on Saturday, August 10, 1912. Then we went off for a long meandering honeymoon. In those days I had the *wanderlust* almost perpetually upon me. I suppose it was partly due to Ceylon: during my last three years there in the Hambantota District I was continually on the move, never more than two weeks at a time sedentary in my bungalow, continually travelling on circuit, sleeping anywhere in tents or in the bare circuit bungalows. I had got into the habit of thinking that one could go anywhere anyhow at any time, and rather on that principle we wandered about, first in Provence and then into and all over Spain. It was very pleasant, but of course we occasionally got into difficulties staying in posadas off the beaten track and hiring mulecarts in out-of-the-way villages. I did not realize at the time that this kind of travelling was probably much too tiring for Virginia. Eventually we got to Valencia, and there by chance I found a Hungarian ship on the point of sailing to Marseille and willing to take us as the only passengers. Not being able to make ourselves under-stood in English, French, Sinhalese, or Tamil, and not understanding Hungarian, we did not realize that we should have dined at 6.30 p.m. and that after 7.30 it was contrary to the laws of the Medes and Persians, and of the Hungarians and Austrians, to give any food to a passenger. We went to bed hungry; the Mediterranean was extremely rough; the boat bucked and rolled, creaked and groaned. In the middle of the night I woke up and realized that I was not alone in my bunk; three large cats had joined me. At 7.30 in the morning I staggered up on to the deck and found the Third Officer who spoke English. I explained to him that I was very hungry and why. He took me up on to the bridge and had breakfast sent to me there; the first course was an enormous gherkin swimming in oil and vinegar. One of the bravest things I have ever done, I think, was to eat this, followed by two fried eggs and bacon, coffee and rolls, with the boat, the sea, and the coast of France going up and down all round me. From Marseille we took the train to Venice, where for a week or two we rested in a pension on the Grand Canal, experiencing for the first time its strange beauties and the wind which, whistling through its canals, can sometimes seem the coldest wind in Europe. And at the end of November we returned to London.

Part Two

THE YEARS 1913 AND 1914

IN December 1912, when we got back from our honeymoon, we went to live in Cliffords Inn in Fleet Street. It was still then the old Cliffords Inn, rather beautiful, our rooms incredibly ancient, also incredibly draughty and dirty, for 50 years ago in the City of London all day and all night long there fell a slow gentle rain of smuts, so that, if you sat writing by an open window, a thin veil of smuts covered the paper before you had finished a page. The City is—or rather was—one of the pleasantest of all London districts to live in. From Monday to Saturday morning there was something peculiarly exhilarating about it. It was not residential, and yet, with Fleet Street and the Temple and Fetter Lane and Gough Square at one's door, one felt that it had been lived in for hundreds of years by Chaucer, Shakespeare, Pepys, Johnson, Boswell. And though Fleet Street was one of the noisiest streets in London, in Cliffords Inn one heard only the incessant muted hum or rumble of the traffic. On Saturday morning and all through Sunday the whole place changed completely; it became a deserted city. There was practically no traffic and only an occasional solitary policeman or pedestrian. On Sunday you could walk—and we often did—for miles eastward through empty streets. No Londoner who has never lived east of Chancery Lane really knows what the essence of London is. I have lived in Kensington, Bloomsbury, Westminster, and the City—I would give the palm to the City.

I went back to Cliffords Inn in November 1941 after

Virginia's death. I had been bombed out of Mecklenburgh Square and I took a flat in Cliffords Inn. They had pulled down the old building and put up in its place a great block of modern flats. I found it intolerable. I had a little box consisting of a sitting room and bedroom and all round me, above and below, to the right and to the left, were dozens of other people, each and all in his or her precisely similar little box—many of them journalists whom I knew, Francis Williams and Ritchie Calder and Hubert Philips. I felt as if I was being weighed down and suffocated by the sound and smell and weight of human animals all round me; it was a kind of andro-claustrophobia. I could not stand it for more than a few months. In April 1942 I got two rooms in my bombed house in Mecklenburgh Square patched up and moved in there. The first night of my return as I was letting myself in with my latchkey, a voice behind me said: 'What are you doing there?' I turned round and found that it was a policeman. When I said that I was going to sleep in my house, he told me that I would be the only person sleeping in the square as all the houses were uninhabitable. It was certainly an odd life, though I think he exaggerated when he said that all the other residents had had to move out. My two rooms had, of course, no glass in the windows, which were boarded up so that one had to have the electric light on day and night. The ceilings were down and the sparrows got in through holes in the roof and scrambled about all day long on the rafters above one's head. The water pipes had been so shaken by the bombings that every now and then there was no water in them or in the middle of the night one would suddenly burst and I would wake up to hear water cascading down the stairs. But I preferred it to Cliffords Inn.

As I have jumped forward in time to 1942, I may as well say something more about the house in Mecklenburgh Square during the great bombing. We had moved into it

from Tavistock Square in 1939 on the very day of the outbreak of war. When in March 1924 we left Richmond and
took 52 Tavistock Square, we had as sub-tenants on the
ground floor and first floor a firm of solicitors; old Mr.
Pritchard was the senior and young Mr. George Pritchard
was the junior partner. They were extraordinarily nice
people and, when we moved to Mecklenburgh Square, they
came with us, again as sub-tenants occupying the ground
floor and first floor. The house was not actually hit by a
bomb, but bombs fell all round it and the house next door
was completely destroyed by an incendiary bomb. All the
ceilings of my house were blown down and all the windows
blown out by bombs and a landmine; the front door and
many of the other doors were blown off their hinges. The
roof was so much damaged that, as I said, the sparrows came
in and fluttered about the skeleton of the house. But all
through the war Mr. George Pritchard, now senior partner,
imperturbably refused to budge. He sat at his desk day after
day in a leather coat and hat—to protect himself from the
cold and the dust and dirt which the sparrows, scrabbling on
the rafters above his head, rained down upon him—and continued his 'business as usual'. It was comforting and reassuring to see him sitting there surrounded by the deed boxes
and the papers.

But I must get back to 1912. Life in Cliffords Inn was
extraordinarily pleasant. The old buildings, the rooms, the
court were almost exactly the same as a Cambridge College
and it was as though I had returned to live in the Great Court
of Trinity. We felt wonderfully free. We had, of course, no
servants; only a daily char came in and made the beds, swept
up the smuts, and washed up the dishes. Every night we
crossed Fleet Street and dined at the Cock Tavern. The
Cock still remembered Tennyson; it had in its furniture and
its food an air and flavour of considerable antiquity. It was

a real old city eating house. One sat in wooden partitions and at night it was almost always pretty empty, only journalists from the dailies and lawyers from the Temple dropping in until quite late. Henry was a vintage head waiter, belonging to an era and tradition which, even in 1912, one felt was passing. Large, white faced, redheaded, he was incredibly solemn, slow, unruffled. It was a great day when at last he recognized one as a 'regular'. He would greet one with the ghost of the shadow of a smile, and, as one sat down, he would whisper confidentially: 'I can recommend the devilled bone tonight, Sir,' or: 'I am afraid I can't recommend the steak and kidney pudding tonight, Sir; it's not *quite* as good as usual.'

We both worked hard when we settled in to Cliffords Inn. Virginia was rewriting the last chapters of *The Voyage Out* for the tenth or, it may have been, the twentieth time. She finished it in February and I read it in early March and took it on March 9 to Gerald Duckworth, her half-brother, who owned the publishing firm of Duckworth & Co., in Henrietta Street. Edward Garnett wrote an extremely appreciative reader's report on it and Gerald agreed to publish it. The terms of the agreement are interesting: the publishers agreed to pay the author

> on the published price of twelve out of thirteen copies sold the following royalties: 15% on the first 5,000 copies sold, 20% on all sales above 5,000.

There was to be no advance payment on account of royalties. The book was not actually published until 1915. It was held up for the two years because of Virginia's breakdown. They printed 2,000 copies, and 14 years later, when in 1929 the Hogarth Press acquired the rights from Duckworth, there were still a few copies unsold. In the ten years before the Hogarth Press took the book over, 1919-1929, Duckworth sold 479 copies for which Virginia received in royalties £26. 2s. 10d. The fate of *The Voyage Out* in its first 15 years after publication shows what a long time it takes for a writer like Virginia to get any sale for her books or to make any money out of them. *The Voyage Out* had an extraordinarily good press; the reviewers were nearly all complimentary and she was recognized from the first as an important novelist. By 1929 she had published *To The Lighthouse* and *Orlando* and had established herself as a highly successful writer. 4,000 copies of *To The Lighthouse* were sold in the first year of publication and *Orlando* sold 4,000 copies in its first month. But it took 15 years to sell 2,000 copies of *The Voyage Out*, as I said, and the earnings of the author from it in those 15 years were less than £120. However as soon as an author really establishes himself, all his books sell. That is why when we in the Hogarth Press reprinted *The Voyage Out* in 1929, we sold 781 in the first year, though it had sold fewer than 500 copies in the previous ten years.

Meanwhile in 1913 Edward Arnold published my novel *The Village in the Jungle*. The book was not unsuccessful in its way. It had very good reviews. The first edition sold out at once and it was reprinted twice before the end of 1913 and again in 1925. Four editions of one's first book in 12 years sounds pretty good, but in fact the sound was a good deal better than the material reality. Arnold did not take a rosy view of the selling prospects of the book, and when the first edition sold out, he printed only a few hundred copies. Rather to his dismay, I think, he sold these immediately and had to reprint for the second time. By 1929 the book had sold 2,149 copies. My agreement with Arnold was less favourable for the author than Virginia's with Duckworth. I got 10% royalty on the first 1,000 sold and 15% thereafter, and, as the price of *The Village in the Jungle* was 5s. while *The Voyage Out* was 6s., by 1929, though my book had sold a few more copies than hers, I had earned £63. 3s. 0d. against her £110 to £120. As a publisher myself today, I am amused to find that in 1913 when I bought one of my own books (published price 5s.) from Arnold, he charged me 4s. and also 4d. for sending it to me in Brunswick Square. He was therefore charging the author 4s. 4d. for a book for which he would get from a London bookseller either 3s. 9d. or 3s. 4d.

I give these figures about the sales of the books which we wrote, partly because our earnings as writers had an important effect upon what we actually did in life, but also because they have a more general interest. Professional writers rarely reveal, even in autobiographies, accurately and in detail what exactly they earned by their books. I propose, off and on throughout this book, to give such figures in order to show the effect of our earnings upon our writing and our lives, and also because of the light which they shed upon the economics of the literary profession in the 20th century. Consider for a moment the fate of these two novels *The Voyage Out* and *The Village in the Jungle*. They are two very different books, but both have survived. In the year 1961, 46 years after the date of its first publication, 441 copies of *The Voyage Out* were sold in England at the published price of 10s. 6d. and the royalties paid amounted to £23. 3s. 1d.—compare this with the 479 copies sold and royalties £26. 2s. 10d. in the ten years 1919 to 1929. In the year 1961, 48 years after its first publication, *The Village in the Jungle* sold 610 copies at the published price of 7s. 6d. and the royalties paid amounted to £12. 3s. 6d.[1]—compare this with the 770 copies sold and royalties £28. 7s. 11d. paid in the ten years 1919 to 1929.

In the years immediately following our marriage these kind of figures became of great practical importance to us.

[1] The reason why the royalties on the 610 copies are so small is because most of them were sold at export prices to Ceylon.

Virginia had a certain amount of capital invested in stocks and shares, theoretically worth about £9,000; it gave her an income of rather less than £400. In 1917 our expenditure was £697, in 1918 £717, and in 1919 £845. It was obvious therefore that somehow or other we must between us earn between £400 and £500 a year. In fact our financial position was a good deal darker or more precarious than these figures suggest. In 1915, when Virginia's mental breakdown was at its worst, we had nurses—sometimes four—in the house for months and she was visited continually by Harley Street doctors. The doctors' and nurses' bills must have been more than £500 for the 12 months. Any hope that we could earn this by writing books soon faded. Virginia had taken more than four years to write *The Voyage Out*. It took her six years to write her second novel *Night and Day*, which was published by Duckworth in 1919. The agreement was much the same as for the first book. Duckworth printed 2,000 copies and the published price was 9s. They reprinted 1,000 copies in 1920 and began to sell them at a published price of 3s. 6d. in 1923. When the Hogarth Press acquired the rights from Duckworth in 1929, they had sold 1,768 of the 9s. impression and 566 of the 3s. 6d., so that they still had over 500 copies unsold. Virginia had earned in royalties £119. 3s. 11d. There was also an American edition published by Doran; 1,326 copies were sold in 1921 and Virginia received £27. 13s. 7d. in royalties. The total, therefore, which she received in the first ten years, 1919 to 1929, for this book was £146. 17s. 4d. The first book of hers to be published after *Night and Day* was *Monday or Tuesday*, a book of sketches and short stories in 1921. Up to the end of 1921 she had earned less than £100 on *The Voyage Out* and £108 on *Night and Day*. In the twelve years from 1909 (when she began to write *The Voyage Out*) to 1921, therefore, she had earned by writing books say £205 or £17. 1s. 8d. per annum.

My second novel *The Wise Virgins* was published in 1914 simultaneously with the outbreak of war. The war killed it dead and my total earnings from it were £20. By the end of 1921 *The Village in the Jungle* had brought me in £42, so that my income as a novelist had been £62 in 10 years, or £6. 4s. od. per annum. It looked therefore as if Virginia and I could not count on earning more than £23 between us per annum by writing novels, and we must obviously make somehow or other by other means, say, £477 a year if we were to be certain of making both ends meet.

The attitude to money and financial security in different people is very curious. I am not, I think, a worrier by nature, at any rate about material things. If I am to tell the truth, the whole truth, and nothing but the truth, I must admit that I am, I think, a psychological worrier at the back of my mind, in the depths of my soul, or in the pit of my stomach (probably all three). I have always felt psychologically insecure. I am afraid of making a fool of myself, of my first day at school, of going out to dinner, or of a week-end at Garsington with the Morrells. What shall I say to Mr. Jones, or to Lady Ottoline Morrell, or Aldous Huxley? My hand trembles at the thought of it, and so do my soul, heart, and stomach. Of course, I have learnt to conceal everything except the trembling hand: one of the consolations of growing old is that one learns to talk to Mr. Jones and Lady Ottoline Morrell—one has learnt that even the dreariest dinner party or longest week-end does come to an end, that even the weariest river winds somewhere safe to sea. I have had to be extremely careful about money for long periods in my life, but I have never worried about it, probably because I learnt by experience as a child and a youth to be insecure and comparatively poor and not to worry about it.

Virginia's experience had been very different and had had a very different effect upon her. Her family belonged to the

Victorian professional upper middle class which was finan-
cially as impregnably secure as (almost) the Bank of England.
In their current account in the Westminster or Barclays
Bank there was always a balance of hundreds of pounds, and
both the heavens and justice would have fallen before that
balance fell below zero. The consequence was that her father,
Sir Leslie Stephen, K.C.B., author of the *History of English
Thought in the 18th Century*, editor of *The Cornhill Magazine*
and *The Dictionary of National Biography*, owner of a large
house in Hyde Park Gate, another in Emperor's Gate, and
another in St. Ives, Cornwall, with capital invested in gilt-
edged securities bringing him in dividends sufficient to
maintain his whole family in comfort—the highest income
tax which he ever paid was 1s. 3d. in the £ and it varied
between 3d. and 8d. in the £ until a few years before his
death at the age of 72—this fortunate man, whose bank
balance was virtually impregnable, never stopped worrying
himself and his children about money. He lived in a perpetual
fear of bankruptcy, convinced every Monday morning that
he was being ruined by what were called by Victorian fathers
and their women folk the household books. When his wife
died in 1895, Vanessa, then aged 16, took over the running
of the house in Hyde Park Gate, helped by Sophie, that
perfect example of the devoted Victorian cook, whose letter
I have quoted on page 51. For the next nine years, until
Sir Leslie's death in 1904, every Monday morning Vanessa
brought to him the household books in order that he might
give her a cheque to cover the previous week's expenditure.
Then for ten minutes or more he sighed and groaned[1] over

[1] Leslie Stephen in old age was much given to groaning audibly,
like many distinguished Victorians, particularly if they were widowers.
(I think Tennyson groaned freely and so did Watts, the painter.) Mr.
Gibbs was an old friend of the Stephen family and at more or less
regular intervals used to come and dine with them at Hyde Park Gate.
He had been tutor for six or seven years to the Prince of Wales, later

The Stephen family on the brink of the workhouse

Leslie Stephen, Lady Albutt, Mrs. Stephen, Gerald Duckworth, Sir C. Albutt
Vanessa, Virginia, and Adrian

the enormous sums which they were spending on food, wages, light, coal—at this rate ruin stared them in the face and they would soon all be in the workhouse. 'Ruin staring us in the face' and 'the workhouse' were the economic nightmares which haunted so many wealthy Victorians. Yet Leslie Stephen was an extremely kind and affectionate man, and generous except on Monday mornings.

The cloud of impending bankruptcy and poverty, not to say positive starvation, which hung over her father and sister on Monday mornings had an effect upon the impressionable Virginia between the ages of 13 and 22. She never suffered from her father's obsession about ruin and bankruptcy; she was usually quite sensible about money, not worrying about it, and, when she had it, she enjoyed spending it. But every now and again she would get into a sudden panic about our finances, particularly in the first seven or eight years of our marriage when we had no regular or even probable means of earning the £400 or £500 which we needed to cover our expenditure. But the panic did not last and we took no immediate steps to find me a paid job. It was more or less understood that Virginia should go on writing novels and reviewing for *The Times Literary Supplement*; I decided to stop writing novels and to see what I could earn by journalism.

The first job which I took was a curious one. The second Post-Impressionist Exhibition, organized by Roger Fry, opened in the Grafton Galleries in the autumn of 1912. In Spain on our honeymoon I got an urgent message from Roger asking me whether I would act as secretary of the show on

---

Edward VII, and in spite or because of this was a bit of a bore—I think Mr. Pepper in *The Voyage Out* has some of his characteristics. On the nights when Mr. Gibbs came to dinner, towards 10 o'clock, Leslie Stephen would start groaning and saying at intervals quite audibly: 'O why doesn't he go; O why doesn't he go!'

our return. I agreed to do so until, I think, the end of the year. It was a strange and for me new experience. The first room was filled with Cézanne water-colours. The highlights in the second room were two enormous pictures of more than life-size figures by Matisse and three or four Picassos. There was also a Bonnard and a good picture by Marchand. Large numbers of people came to the exhibition, and nine out of ten of them either roared with laughter at the pictures or were enraged by them. The British middle class—and, as far as that goes, the aristocracy and working class—are incorrigibly philistine, and their taste is impeccably bad. Anything new in the arts, particularly if it is good, infuriates them and they condemn it as either immoral or ridiculous or both. As secretary I sat at my table in the large second room of the galleries prepared to deal with enquiries from possible purchasers or answer any questions about the pictures. I was kept busy all the time. The whole business gave me a lamentable view of human nature, its rank stupidity and uncharitableness. I used to think, as I sat there, how much nicer were the Tamil or Sinhalese villagers who crowded into the veranda of my Ceylon kachcheri than these smug, well dressed, ill-mannered, well-to-do Londoners. Hardly any of them made the slightest attempt to look at, let alone understand, the pictures, and the same inane questions or remarks were repeated to me all day long. And every now and then some well groomed, red faced gentlemen, oozing the undercut of the best beef and the most succulent of chops, carrying his top hat and grey suede gloves, would come up to my table and abuse the pictures and me with the greatest rudeness.

There were, of course, consolations. Dealing with possible purchasers was always amusing and sometimes exciting. Occasionally one had an interesting conversation with a stranger. Sometimes it was amusing to go round the rooms with Roger and a distinguished visitor. I have described in

Sowing Henry James's visit. Roger came to the gallery every day and spent quite a lot of time there. We used to go down into the bowels of the earth about 4 o'clock and have tea with Miss Wotherston, the secretary, who inhabited the vast basement, and we were often joined by Herbert Cook who owned Doughty House, Richmond, and a superb collection of pictures. I saw so much of Roger that at the end of my time at the Grafton Galleries I knew him much better than when I first went there. His character was more full of contradictions even than that of most human beings. He was one of the most charming and gentle of men; born a double dyed Quaker, he had in many respects revolted against the beliefs and morals of The Friends, and yet deep down in his mind and character he remained profoundly, and I think unconsciously, influenced by them. Like his six remarkable sisters, he had a Quaker's uncompromising sense of public duty and responsibility and, though he would have indignantly repudiated this, ultimately the Quaker's ethical austerity. And yet there were elements in his psychology which contradicted all these characteristics. I was more than once surprised by his ruthlessness and what to me seemed to be almost unscrupulousness in business. For instance, we discovered, shortly after I took on the secretaryship, that when Roger had been preparing the exhibition and asking people to exhibit, owing to a mistake of his, they had been offered much too favourable terms—the figure for the Exhibition's commission on sales was much too low. When the time came to pay artists their share of the purchase amounts of pictures sold, Roger insisted upon deducting a higher commission without any explanation or apology to the painters. Most of them meekly accepted what they were given, but Wyndham Lewis, at best of times a bilious and cantankerous man, protested violently. Roger was adamant in ignoring him and his demands; Lewis never forgave

Roger, and, as I was a kind of buffer between them, he also never forgave me.

There was another odd—and rather endearing—contradiction in Roger's psychology. He had been educated as a scientist both at Clifton and at Cambridge, and in many ways he had the scientific careful, sceptical mind and methods. This was notably the case in that province of knowledge where he was a great expert, the science of the Kunstforscher. I once saw an interesting display of this. One evening when he and Virginia and I were at Clive Bell's flat, a well-known politician, who was something of a buyer of pictures, came in after dinner accompanied by a large canvas. He wanted Roger's opinion as to whether the picture was or was not a Poussin. Roger examined it with the greatest care, but refused to commit himself. The picture was placed on the floor against the wall and we all began talking about something else. The conversation was general, but I noticed that, as it went on, all the time at intervals Roger's eyes wandered to the picture. After about an hour, Roger suddenly said that he had made up his mind, that it was not a Poussin. He then gave his reasons at great length; he may or may not have been right, but the performance was extraordinarily convincing; it was an opinion based on expert knowledge and scientific investigation. This was the scientific side of Roger's mind, but there was another side which was amazingly credulous. He was really capable of believing anything, particularly the most extravagant assertions of the great quacks. He believed in the famous black box and sent a drop of his blood to America so that it might be put into the black box and all his ailments—and he always had a good supply of ailments—might be diagnosed thereby. Another characteristic example of his capacity to believe the unbelievable was the following. One evening when we were all sitting round the fire, he suddenly said with intense and gloomy seriousness: 'I am convinced that the future is not with man, but with the birds.' When some of us laughed, he was a little upset and explained at considerable length that he had read in some obscure authority that a curious development in the intestines of birds as compared with that of the human inside would inevitably lead in the course of evolution and the struggle for existence to the extinction of man and the survival of birds.

The quality in Roger's mind which produced this rather ridiculous credulity also produced his unflagging curiosity and the fertility of his thought and imagination. His mind was packed with information on almost every subject, so that he was also the most erudite of men. As he was, like me, an indefatigable arguer, I found him a fascinating companion. Virginia and I went with him and his sister Margery for a month to Greece in 1932. They were wonderful travellers. Their knowledge was encyclopaedic. Roger always everywhere knew the most important thing which nobody else knew, e.g. the most perfect Byzantine building on the top of some formidable mountain far off the beaten track or a perfect moussaka only obtainable in one small dingy restaurant in an alley of Athens. He was 66 years old and not at all well. But his energy was terrific. We hired a large open car, driven by a chauffeur, and went to Delphi and all over the Peloponnese. The sun was very hot, but the winds (the chauffeur always called them draughts) that blew between the mountains were icy cold so that Virginia and I trembled and shivered under the blazing sun. The Frys, impervious to heat or cold, every now and again stopped the car, leapt out, and rapidly painted a picture. At the end of a strenuous 16-hour day, after dinner at 11 Roger would say to me: 'There's just time for a game of chess before we go to bed.'

One last picture of Roger in Greece. In 1932 the roads

there were nearly all appallingly bad. We drove to Delphi by the long road which circled Mt. Parnassus and was fairly good. Roger said that there was a marvellous monastery called Hosios Loucas and that there was a road to it direct from Delphi. The chauffeur said that the road was almost impassable and that it was terribly dangerous to attempt it. Roger was ruthless. The road, he said, is marked as a main road on the map and is obviously just as good as the road which we had driven over from Athens to Delphi. We stood in the Delphi street where outside every house the people were roasting the Paschal lamb on wooden skewers—it was Easter—and the chauffeur and Roger argued interminably. At last, just before it was time to go into the inn and have dinner, the Greek gave in; 'All right', he said, 'but we shall all be killed.' About half an hour after dinner, they brought us a message to say that the chauffeur was outside and wanted to speak to us. Next minute we were back again all four in the street among the roasting lambs. The chauffeur, with a long face, told us that they had just brought two dead American young men into Delphi; they had tried to drive their car on Roger's 'main road' from Hosios Loucas and had ended upside down at the bottom of a ravine. He definitely refused to follow their example. Reluctantly and with unconcealed scepticism Roger gave way. So next day we drove back the same way all round Mt. Parnassus to the crossroads where Oedipus met and killed his father. From near there the road was indeed so bad that we got out of the car and, with Roger riding on a mule, we walked up to the monastery. It should be added that the face of Greece has greatly changed in the last 30 years. When I visited it again in 1961, I found that the road which the chauffeur refused to drive on was now a first class main road. When I reached Hosios Loucas by it, I found an hotel there and half a dozen omnibuses.

Roger Fry in Greece

I must return to the Grafton Galleries, but only for a moment, for I handed my duties to Sydney Waterlow at the end of the year. My seven years as a civil servant in Ceylon had made me very much a political animal, and I have remained such ever since. Once one has been personally concerned with communal affairs and has felt personally responsible for them, one can never again escape a feeling of political responsibility. Consequently, as soon as I had resigned from the Ceylon civil service I began to look at the politics and economics of London and Britain—and very soon Europe—in the way in which I had looked at those of the Hambantota District and Ceylon. I had to study the details of the social system in which I was now going to live as carefully as I had studied that of the Tamils of Jaffna and the Sinhalese of Kandy or the Southern Province—to understand its merits and its defects. I had been so absorbed in the administrative problems of Ceylon and my district there that in England I was to a great extent politically both ignorant and uncommitted. In 1912 I was, I think, a liberal, but not a Liberal, and half way to socialism.

My first political experience made me complete my journey to the Left. Virginia had a cousin, Marny Vaughan, who, like many serious, middle class, maiden ladies of the Victorian era engaged in 'good works', and her particular good work was a Care Committee connected with the Charity Organisation Society. She induced me to join it. It was in Hoxton, in those days a typical London east end district, full of dreary depressed sordid streets, houses, and people. Our business was to help the poor, to dispense charity. I cannot remember exactly what kind of charity we proposed to dispense, whether it was hard cash or charity in kind. What happened was that, when the committee assembled, the secretary put before us a number of applications or recommendations for relief. Relief was given only if

99

we were satisfied that the case was deserving, and usually in order to satisfy ourselves about this one of us was sent off to interview the applicant in his or her home. I made, I think, two visits of this kind. There was no doubt about the poverty in the east end of London in 1912; I would rather have lived in a hut in a Ceylon village in the jungle than in the poverty stricken, sordid, dilapidated, god-forsaken hovels of Hoxton. And the moment that I stood in their grim rooms and began to speak to the dejected inhabitants, whose voices and faces revealed nothing but the depths of their hopelessness, I realized my hopelessness and helplessness there. In the Ceylon jungle village there was still a place or excuse for governmental paternalism. Life and the people there were still simple and primitive enough to make a simple and primitive relationship between ruler and ruled possible. Even so I had resigned from the Ceylon Civil Service largely because I personally did not like being a ruler of the ruled. Having refused to remain the benevolent ruler of Silindu and Hinnihami in Beddegama, I was not going to try to play the part of benevolent father to Mr. and Mrs. Smith in a Hoxton slum. Besides, one only had to spend a quarter of an hour sitting with Marny Vaughan on a Care Committee and another quarter of an hour with the victim, Mr. and Mrs. Smith in the Hoxton slum, to see that in Hoxton one was confronted by some vast, dangerous fault in the social structure, some destructive disease in the social organism, which could not be touched by paternalism or charity or good works. Nothing but a social revolution, a major operation, could deal with it. I resigned from the Care Committee and the C.O.S.

Hoxton turned me from a liberal into a socialist, and this led directly to my next political step. At Cambridge I had known Theodore and Crompton Llewelyn Davies (because they were Apostles) although they were a good deal older

than I was.[1] They belonged to a remarkable family. Their
father had four sons and one daughter, all of them extremely
intelligent, finely built, beautiful—they all had great personal
charm, immense energy. Though they were almost fanatical
in their integrity and high principles, they were, unlike so
many exceptionally serious and good people, amusing and
interesting, companionable and lovable. They were friends
of the Stephen family and Virginia often saw Margaret
Llewelyn Davies, the daughter. She was secretary of the
Women's Co-operative Guild. To the vast majority of my
readers the last sentence will convey little or nothing and it
would have conveyed even less in 1912. Yet Margaret was
one of the most eminent women I have known and created
something of great value—and at the time unique—in the
Guild. If she had been a man, her achievements would have
filled probably half a page in *Who's Who*; though she lived
to be over 70, you will not find the name of Margaret
Llewelyn Davies in any edition of it—the kind of fact which
made—and makes—feminism the belief or policy of all
sensible men.

I am writing an autobiography, not a political or social
treatise, and I shall enter into political questions and problems as little as possible; but I shall have to say something
about them when or where they affected my life. And
strangely enough, the Co-operative Movement, the Guild,
and Margaret did affect my life. The Co-operative Movement is a peculiar and enormous system of manufacture,
retail trade and banking, based upon the consumers organized in retail Co-operative Societies and controlling through
them retail trade, through the Co-operative Wholesale
Societies wholesale trade and manufactures, and through
Co-operative banks finance. It originated in 1844; it was a
working class movement and in 1912 the membership of

[1] See *Sowing*, pp. 143-144 and 198.

consumers' co-operative societies was overwhelmingly working class. The Women's Co-operative Guild or W.C.G. was
an organization of women members of Co-operative Societies.
When I first knew it, it had a membership of about 30,000
and its objects were 'to educate its members, advance co-
operative principles, and to obtain for women's interests the
recognition which within and without the movement is due
to them'. It sounds dreary and superficially it was dreary, for
on its surface were the drabness and cheerlessness which,
not without reason, infected the working classes and their
institutions at the beginning of the 20th century. In fact it
was a unique and even exciting regiment of women whose
energy and vitality were exhilarating. They were almost all
of them working class women who had had little or no
regular education, and they were organized, in the traditional
working class way, in 'Branches'—i.e. the women members
of a Co-operative Society, say the York Co-operative Society,
formed a York Branch of the W.C.G. which was federated
with all the other branches in the Guild which had its head
office in London. Each branch held its weekly, fortnightly,
or monthly meetings, and sent its delegate to the Annual
Congress of the Guild, held in London or Manchester or
some other big town.

The vitality and inspiration of the Guild—and also its
organization—were mainly due to Margaret. I think that
what had primarily moved and shocked her was the grimness,
hardship, narrowness of the lives to which most working
class wives and mothers were condemned. Then when she got
to know them individually and in the mass, she was deeply
moved and exhilarated to find in them great strength and
resilience of character, great potentialities, not merely as
human beings, but also as political animals. She was that
strange and usually inexplicable phenomenon 'a born leader'.
Of course one could explain it by her immense energy and

enthusiasm; by her laugh which was so characteristically Margaret, a deep contralto spontaneous laugh; by the feminine charm which was also so spontaneous and unconscious, and sometimes among her regiment of working women, her blue books, and Co-operative Stores so endearingly incongruous; and by her beauty, which remained even when she had grown fat and almost an old woman, the fresh English beauty of hair and eyes and skin marvellously united with a chiselled classical beauty of Greek features—nearly all the Llewelyn Davieses had this pure chiselled nobility of face, particularly in profile, which perhaps should be called Roman rather than Greek. But when one has catalogued all these charms and powers, one feels that there was something beyond them which made her glow in the co-operative drabness so that she was able to inspire thousands of uneducated women with her own passion, both for 'sweetness and light', and also for liberty, equality, and fraternity. This something can, I think, only be described as a kind of virginal purity of mind and motive which—I am afraid it sounds rather absurd, but is nonetheless true—made her a kind of Joan of Arc to her cohorts of Lancashire and Yorkshire housewives in her crusade against ignorance, poverty, and injustice.

When I first knew Margaret she was a middle-aged woman, but she still had the quicksilver eagerness of the young which remained with her until she was an old woman. I do not know why she never married—partly, I suppose, because, like thousands of other middle class Victorian virgins, she was devoted to and devoted her life to, her father,[1] partly because it would have been only a very

[1] Not but what her father, the Rev. John Llewelyn Davies, was himself a remarkable man and worthy of some filial devotion. Born in 1826 he was an admirable scholar and a Fellow of Trinity College, Cambridge. A friend of Charles Kingsley and F. D. Maurice, he was, like them, a Christian Socialist and shared their austere sense of social responsibility. He was for 20 years Vicar of the small and remote

superior young man whom the terribly serious, austere, dynamic young Margaret would not have scared away, and partly because it would probably have been only a super-superior, terribly serious, austere, and dynamic young man whom the young Margaret would have considered for one moment as a possible husband.

There is a peculiar contradiction in the Co-operative Movement and in everything connected with it. On the face of it it is one of the most depressingly drab and dreary creations of the human ant, and of the working class human ant in particular. Its embodiment seems to be the dingy Co-operative grocery store in some rain-sodden street in a hideous grimy northern industrial town. A great deal of the co-operative spirit which moves the vast co-operative machine is as drab and dreary as its material surface. And yet from its very beginnings in 1844, there has been working below this surface a passionate belief in a social ideal. The spirit and the contradiction—passion and imagination yoked to dreariness—can be traced back even to the strange man who invented the co-operative system and movement, Robert Owen, who was accurately described as 'one of those bores who are the salt of the earth'.

This dichotomy of dreariness and inspiration, of deadness

Westmorland village of Kirkby Lonsdale and there too, of course, for the best 20 years of her life Margaret lived. When I knew him first, he was nearly 90, and a few years later, when the time came for him to die, he was mentally and physically so strong that life refused to leave him. During the weeks of his struggle for death I used often to go up to Hampstead, where they lived, to see Margaret. A few hours before he died, she told me, though he was quite blind, he suddenly saw a cat and a large portrait of Mr. Gladstone. But, though almost everything else in him was already dead, his clearness of mind and its tenacity of truth were such that he knew that his visions were hallucinations. The mystery of why a blind dying clergyman should know that he is seeing a non-existent cat and non-existent portrait of Mr. Gladstone remains, unexplained either by the clergyman's God or even by Dr. Freud.

and life, extended, it must be admitted, to Margaret, for, like all fanatics, and the first prophet of co-operation, Owen, she could be a bore. But she not only saw the practical, material importance of consumers' co-operation and recognized the potentialities of the Movement and Guild as economic, political, and educational instruments for the working class; she saw, to some extent, that behind the unpromising multiplicity of Retail and Wholesale Societies there existed, thanks to Owen's stroke of imaginative genius, an immensely valuable method or principle of economics and social organization.[1] Impressed by her enthusiasm, I embarked on a thorough study of the movement, both its principles and its practice. This study completed my conversion to socialism, but I became and have remained a socialist of a rather peculiar sort. To regard socialism as an end in itself in the way in which many socialists and all communists do has always seemed to me ridiculous mumbojumboism. But I do not think that in the modern overpopulated world of large-scale industry and monopolies you can have a civilized society unless the community, in some form and by some method, exercises considerable control over the whole economic system. There are considerable disadvantages and dangers if that control is exercised by the state, and still more if it is exercised by the community organized as workers or producers. Owen seemed to me to have devised in the Co-operative Movement a system which, if extended and developed, would place large sections of the economy in the control of the community organized as consumers. The advantages of this form of socialism were that

[1] One of the first persons to see the significance of the Consumers' Co-operative Movement was Mrs. Sidney Webb ; her book published in 1891 and for long a classic, *The Co-operative Movement in Great Britain*, was a revelation both to co-operators and to people who had ignored and despised the movement.

it could eliminate profit and class conflict and make some democratic control of the economic system possible.

I wrote a book, published in 1919, *Co-operation and the Future of Industry*, describing the Movement and its methods and its potentialities for the socialist. I still agree with the greater part of what I wrote in that book 45 years ago, though my vision of a socialist society based on consumers' control now sounds utopian, because the events of history have turned in the opposite direction. The view that everything which has not happened was always utopian, however, seems to me false—it is one of the commonest forms of stupidity after the event. At any rate, started off by Margaret I soon became a believer in the theory and principles of co-operation and have remained one ever since. But I decided that I must also see for myself how the principles and the machinery worked.

I began by going up to Newcastle in June 1913 to attend the annual congress of the Women's Guild. I was enormously impressed by this unofficial parliament of 650 working class women. In the eyes of a middle class person they were lamentably ignorant and most of them were completely uneducated except in what is called the hard school of life. But they showed an extraordinary native, intuitive understanding of their own ignorance and therefore of their own problems and, what was more unexpected, of the problems of the working class. They showed a passionate desire for education and it was clear that the Guild meant everything to them as an instrument of self education. When I wrote the words 'passionate desire' in the last sentence, I paused in hesitation. I think it is true that there was in those working women what may rightly be called a passion of desire for education and for other social or political ends, and when I got to know them much better than I did in 1913 I was often aware of it. But it would have been quite possible for a careless observer to miss the passion altogether, for it was almost always well below the surface. One of the most inveterate and gross vulgar errors is that women are more emotional than men and more flighty. Ten minutes with the 650 women in the hall at Newcastle would have proved to anyone how untrue this old error is. They were much more un-emotional, stable, quiet, matter of fact than any similar male assembly. They were in fact a little too serious; I remember once at one of their congresses, when during a very serious debate on divorce there was a burst of laughter at something that one of the speakers said, a delegate rose and with a strong Yorkshire accent, shouted: 'Shame on you! Shame on you!'

There was, however, another characteristic both in individuals and in the congress generally which was remark-able; it was a kind of intensity of patience, learnt perhaps by those particular women over babies, saucepans and frying pans, and coppers. For instance, at Newcastle one of the questions discussed was the proposal that there should be a 'fusion of labour forces', i.e. some sort of union between the Co-operative Movement, the trade unions, and the Labour Party. Many Co-operators and many of the women in the Congress were strongly opposed to this. Then one of the delegates spoke in favour of the proposal and I described her intervention at the time as follows:

This Northern delegate, a typical working-class woman both in speech and appearance, spoke with passionate and yet restrained earnestness in favour of the resolution. She told with an eloquent simplicity, which made her speech a work of art, how, as a child, she had learnt from her father to believe that the one hope for the working classes was to forget their differences and to work together loyally for the same ideals and the same ends. Then she paused, and told the delegates that she did not wish her words to influence their votes: if they had come prepared to vote against the resolution they should do so; but then they should go home and think over what she had said, and, if it convinced them, they should return to Congress next year and vote in favour of the resolution. 'We can wait,' she said, 'we can wait. We women have waited years, thousands of years, even to be able to discuss things like this. We can wait.'

Later on I got to know many of these women well and the better I knew them the more they confirmed my first impressions. The Guild used to arrange week-end classes or short courses of lectures in London and big towns like Manchester and Leeds for their members, and I used to take classes or give lectures on subjects like taxation, international affairs, or the colonial empire. Superficially there was no resemblance, either in mind, body, experience, or environment, between the wife of a Lancashire textile worker or Durham miner and a Sinhalese villager. Yet I think that the days, weeks, months, years I had spent talking to those strange, alien men and women in Kandyan hills or among the rice fields and jungles of Hambantota helped me to understand and get in touch with Mrs. Barton and Mrs. Harris. It is not true that the poor and primitive are more 'real' than the rich and sophisticated, that there is more 'reality' in the Congo or a coalfield than in Cambridge or Cavendish Square; but those who live, physically unprotected and mentally almost naked, close to and desperately vulnerable to the catastrophes of nature or the economic system, acquire a crystalline simplicity, a straight disillusioned look in the eye which are to me humanly and aesthetically attractive. In Ceylon I learnt, I think, after a long time to sit under a kumbuk tree by a village tank and talk to a villager or even an old village woman so that they would talk to me, and somehow or other this helped me to be able to talk to the women Co-operators. At any rate I was not unnaturally pleased and flattered when one of them, after being lectured by me for an hour on taxation, came up to me and said: 'You are the only *gentleman* whom we can always understand when you talk to us.'

In March 1913 I went for a fortnight to the North of England and Scotland, visiting Liverpool, Manchester, Bolton, Leeds, Glasgow, Sheffield, and Leicester. I had introductions to the officials of the Co-operative Societies in each of these towns and of the English and Scottish Wholesale Societies, and I had arranged with them to be taken over the stores and factories. I 'inspected' them as I would have inspected them if they had been in my district in Ceylon and I cross-examined the officials minutely on the structure of the Movement, the organization of the societies, the way in which it worked and the way in which they worked it. It was my first experience of the industrialized towns of the North and of the strange race which inhabits them. The inhabitants differ as much from the southerner, the Londoner or the Sussex man, as the Tamil in the north of Ceylon differs from the Sinhalese in the south, or as the German who is born and bred in East Prussia differs from the Italian born and bred in Calabria. Large scale, highly developed, 20th-century industrial civilization, if it can be called civilization, fills me with despair. The melancholy which descended upon me in Manchester grew blacker in Bolton and still blacker in Glasgow. I cannot believe that what used to be called 'the good life' can be lived by millions of men and women spending all their days in monotonous manual labour in order to produce parts or particles of salable articles of which some are necessary, some useful, but most of them ugly or shoddy, while in order to achieve this end these unfortunate people have to live in surroundings of grey and grimy ugliness and discomfort. This judgment is not refuted by the fact that these men and women are generally very nice people and no less civilized than those who live in Bermondsey or Brighton. It is just an inexplicable miracle that human nature can remain as nice as it is in a Manchester slum or a Ceylon village.

My rapid, but pretty thorough, look at the Co-operative Movement impressed me, but it also depressed me. Many of the societies were very well managed, and so on the whole were the Wholesale Societies which, in addition to manufacturing a vast number of things, from boots and soap to flour and mustard, controlled a very large wholesale and banking business. The Movement was still growing rapidly both in numbers of co-operators and in the volume and variety of their trade. I met several secretaries or managers of societies who were intelligent and efficient men, proud of and devoted to their own societies and to co-operation. That this vast organization had been built up entirely by working class men and women was indeed something to be proud of —it was an amazing achievement. But from my point of view there was something wrong about the Movement as a whole, or rather something which filled me with doubt and suspicion. There was too often in the societies and their officials a narrow parochialism, a social and economic stuffiness, timidity, dreariness. 'The Co-op', product and emblem of the Movement, was more often than not a third-rate, badly arranged grocery shop in one of those terrible side-streets of such sordid respectability that they ought to have a sign, not of NO ENTRY, but ABANDON HOPE ALL THOSE WHO ENTER HERE. Most of those who were engaged in the practical work of the societies, and still more of the rank and file co-operators, seemed quite content with co-operation provided it went on making and selling soap and other things at a low price and in an ever expanding circle. The possibilities in consumers' co-operation for economic revolution and social evolution, which had been perceived, if dimly, by Robert Owen and did inspire some of the men in the societies and women in the Guild, meant nothing at all to the vast majority. The Englishman, indeed the Briton—though I think the Englishman more than the Scot—is taught in every class to dislike and distrust the intellect and the intellectual. He likes to know what to do and he is very good at seeing how to do it; he hates to think—he does not want to know—why he does it or should do it. He has no use for theories or principles, being socially and politically a plain, practical man, a human species which is responsible for a great deal of good, but also for some of the worst human disasters. Nearly all co-operators that I came across were plain, practical men, and so were the trade unionists and working class members of the Labour Party with whom later on I worked.

That the Co-ops should make their own soap and mustard and sell them to millions of members is, I think, a very good thing, but that is not what I was primarily interested in. What attracted me in co-operation was its potentialities as a socialistic alternative to the profit-making capitalist system and as a means of applying some of the principles of democracy to the economic system. The Movement also had an educational side, nearly all societies spending a certain amount of money on organizing educational classes or lectures. My two weeks tour of the northern societies had to some extent depressed me, but the enthusiasm of the Women's Guild and of some of the leading men in the North encouraged me, and for many years I did a good deal of work on the educational side of the Movement, trying to make the co-operators see the social potentialities of co-operation.

The most interesting experience I had trying to educate co-operators was during the 1914 war. I think it was the Co-operative Union which asked me to give a series of

lectures on international government to a number of Lancashire and Cheshire Co-operative Societies. I spent some time
going from society to society and giving a lecture in the
evening to audiences ranging in numbers from 30 or 40 to
100 or a little more. I was given what in labour organizations
is called hospitality, i.e. someone put me up for the night.
The hospitality was fascinating, for I had an extraordinary
variety of hosts. At the end of my lecture tour, I felt that I
had probably learnt a great deal more than I had taught—at
any rate, I came back with a knowledge of the class structure
of industrial society in the north of England which I had not
had when I started out from Euston to Manchester. In
Manchester I stayed with Mrs. Eckhard who was the
mother-in-law of Sydney Waterlow. I started therefore in the
middle classes, for the Eckhards belonged to the well-to-do
Manchester bourgeoisie. They lived in a large comfortable
ugly Didsbury 'villa residence'. Mrs. Eckhard was one of
those immensely energetic, dominating Jewish matriarchs
who amuse me and with whom I get on quite well provided
that our meetings are not too long and the moment does not
come when I have to show that even in the drawing-room,
the dining-room, and the bedroom I want liberty, equality,
and fraternity. What the horse power of her energy was may
be shown by this: one day at lunch I said to her that her
garden and house would be much improved if she cut down
a large tree near her front door. She jumped up, abandoned
our lunch, fetched an axe and saw, and we spent the rest of
the afternoon felling her tree and sawing it up. Hot, dishevelled, and dirty I only just caught the train to take me to my
evening lecture.

    In Bolton and some of the other towns I stayed with
working class families. They were extraordinarily nice to me.
After the lecture we went back to my host's house and had
an enormous high tea, usually fried fish with delicious rolls

and cakes. In a Cheshire town, Macclesfield I think, I stayed with the local editor, a man and a family quite unlike anything which I had ever come across in the south of England. They seemed socially to be hybrid between the middle and working classes and much more alive and intelligent than a bourgeois or working class family in Sussex. When we got back from the lecture, the whole family sat in a large room and we drank quantities of tea and ate splendid plates of fried fish, and the fried plaice and the fire and the warmth and humanity of our souls produced an immediate understanding and intimacy between us. We sat until quite late at night and we talked and argued seriously about politics and classes and the war and education and what the children would do or wanted to do and we told old tales and laughed while every now and again Mrs. Brown would say: 'Now really children you must go off to bed,' and the children would say: 'Now really, Mum, you have said that before.'

Finally at Oldham I stayed in a house such as I had never seen before and have never seen since; it belonged to a different world from that of Mr. Brown of Macclesfield. In it lived Dame Lees, who was Mayor of Oldham and a very wealthy widow of a textile manufacturer. Miss Lees, the daughter, met me at the station, took me to the meeting, and after the meeting back to the house where I was to stay the night. Werneth Park stood in the middle of Oldham and was indeed a park, but it was exactly like the bleakest of public parks, consisting entirely of slabs of grass intersected by asphalt paths and low railings about $1\frac{1}{2}$ feet high which in my childhood disfigured Kensington Gardens and practically all public parks in England. The house itself was very large, and every inch of every wall of every room, staircase, and landing (including the W.C.) was covered by heavily framed pictures. The pictures were all by R.A.'s or A.R.A.'s and must have cost Dame Lees thousands of pounds—when they were sold, if they ever were sold, they would, I suppose, have fetched a few hundreds. It is probable that in the heyday of the British Empire wealthy industrialists all over the north of England were papering their vast houses with pictures which they bought, like Dame Lees, for large sums at the annual exhibition of the Royal Academy in Burlington House. The effect of this miniature Royal Academy upon me was depressing and intimidating as Miss Lees led me into the Billiard Room apologizing for the absence of the Mayor, her mother, who was ill in bed with a cold. In the Billiard Room, however, were cakes, biscuits, lemonade, and Lord and Lady Emmott. Lord Emmott, in dinner jacket and black tie, was the Mayor's son-in-law and had been Liberal M.P. for Oldham. The only relic of our conversation which I remember was Lord Emmott saying to me in a muted voice as we went up to bed: 'I had better show you the geography of the house', a euphemism used in those days by the upper middle classes for the W.C. But all our conversation was in the same key of muted respectability.

I must now retrace the footsteps of my memory to 1913 and explain how the Co-operative Movement affected my life, professionally and economically. In June, 1913, the *Manchester Guardian* published an article which I wrote for them about the Newcastle Congress of the Women's Guild. The Webbs, sitting in the centre of their Fabian spider-web, always kept an eager eye watching for some promising young man who might be ensnared by them. They read and were impressed by my article, and the result was an invitation to lunch, and on July 12 I ate my first of many plates of mutton in Grosvenor Road. The Webbs thought as well of me as they had thought of my article and they got me to join the Fabian Society at once. This led, as I shall explain, to my doing work for the Fabians and for the *New Statesman*, but before I deal with that I should like to say something about those two strange human beings, Beatrice and Sidney Webb.

I came to know them, I think, as well personally as any-one of my age could get to know them. Hundreds of people have poked their fun at the Webbs and they were so absurd that you could not caricature them for they were always caricaturing themselves. But behind the fantastic façade there were two human beings for whom I eventually acquired real affection. I do not think that Sidney ever felt much affection for anyone except Beatrice, but he liked me and I liked him. Beatrice, who was highly strung and neurotic, came to have a certain amount of affection for Virginia and me, and I had a real affection for her. But however long one knew them, one never got accustomed to their absurdities, to the ludicrous way in which they caricatured the Webbs. What astonished one again and again was that they were so intelligent and in many ways so quick in their perceptions and yet seemed to be quite unconscious of their own absurdities. I cannot resist giving one or two examples of this.

It was another lunch in Grosvenor Road and this time Virginia was with me—also the long lean bearded Noel Buxton, a Buxton of the Buxtons and in the cockles of his heart and the convolutions of his brain a Liberal of the Liberals, but still on the day of the lunch a Labour M.P. and later a Labour peer, Lord Noel-Buxton. The conversation drifted, if conversation with the Webbs can ever accurately be said to have drifted, into the subject of education. Beatrice said that she thought it would be a good idea if Education Authorities provided for the small children in government schools sets of 'municipal bricks' inscribed with the names of various organizations; in playing continually with these the children would more or less unconsciously 'learn their civic duties'. Beatrice was quite serious, but Virginia, who described the meal in her diary, said that 'even Sidney had his mild joke at her'. She also says, perhaps rather unfairly, that 'Noel Buxton obsequiously offered his son for the experiment. Rich men nowadays can be seen divesting themselves of particles of gold with a view to the eye of the needle'.

I am going to relate another conversation with the Webbs because it is the best thing which I ever heard them say, but it is possible that I may have related it somewhere before. I am not sure that other people have not recorded similar remarks by the Webbs, and it is probable that they did sometimes say to other people what they said that day to Virginia and me. At any rate I can vouch for the accuracy of what follows. In September, 1918, we boldly, if not recklessly, asked Beatrice and Sidney to come to us for a week-end at Asham and we were rather astonished and a little dismayed when they accepted. They arrived on a Saturday, and also Joris Young.[1] On Sunday afternoon the Webbs, Virginia, and I went for a walk across the bridge over the river to Southease and the down above Telscombe. Even a walk with the Webbs tended to become regularized or institutionalized and organized, like the municipal bricks, and therefore on the way out I walked with Beatrice and Virginia with Sidney, and on the way back we changed partners. Sidney and I walked rather faster than the ladies and got a good way ahead of them; so we stopped on the top of a small hill just before we got to Asham and waited for them. When they came into view some distance away, Sidney said to me: 'I know what

[1] George Young, who, when his father died, later became Sir George Young, Bart. He was a brother of Geoffrey Young and Hilton Young (Lord Kennet). For many years I saw a good deal of him as he joined the Labour Party and, having been in the diplomatic service, considered himself and was considered an authority on foreign affairs. He was a nice, absurd, cantankerous man. Desmond MacCarthy said truly (but not in fact originally) that Hilton Young was a sphinx without a riddle. There was a faint shadowy sphinxiness about Joris's face; it was rather like a very blurred, out-of-focus photograph of a sphinx—but there was not even a shadow of a riddle.

she is saying to your wife; she is saying that marriage is the waste paper basket of the emotions.' In the evening when we were at last alone I asked Virginia whether on the road from Southease to Asham Beatrice Webb had told her that marriage was the waste paper basket of the emotions. She said she had. As soon as Sidney and I had started off ahead of them Beatrice had asked Virginia what she intended to do now that she was married. Virginia said that she wanted to go on writing novels. Beatrice seemed to approve and warned Virginia against allowing her work to be interfered with by emotional relations. 'Marriage, we always say,' she said, 'is the waste paper basket of the emotions.'[1] To which, just as they came to the level crossing, Virginia replied: 'But wouldn't an old servant do as well?' 'We were entangled', Virginia writes in her diary, 'at the gates of the level-crossing when she remarked: "Yes, I daresay an old family servant would do as well."' Virginia continues her account of her walk with Beatrice:

On the way up the hill she stated her position that one should wish well to all the world, but discriminate no one. According to her the differences are not great; the defects

[1] It is a curious fact that in Virginia's diary she records this conversation as follows: 'One should have only one great personal relationship in one's life, she said; or at most two—marriage and parenthood. Marriage was necessary as a waste pipe for emotion, as security in old age when personal attractiveness fails and as a help to work.' This shows how difficult it is to be certain of any accuracy in recorded conversations. I am absolutely certain that Sidney used the words 'waste paper basket of the emotions' in speaking to me, and I am almost certain that those were the words that Virginia agreed Beatrice used to her. But did Beatrice in fact say 'waste pipe' and not 'waste paper basket'? It is impossible now to know. Virginia was never an accurate recorder of what people said, and it is quite possible, if not probable, that when she came to write her diary, three days after the events, she dashed down (inaccurately) waste pipe. But it is, as I say impossible now to know.

invariable; one must cultivate impersonality above all things. In old age people become of little account, she said; one speculated chiefly upon the possibility, or the impossibility, of a future life. This grey view depressed me more and more; partly I suppose from the egotistical sense of my own nothingness in her field of vision. And then we wound up with a light political gossip and chatter of reminscences, in which Mr. and Mrs. Webb did their parts equally and so to bed; and to my horror, in came Mrs. W. early next morning to say Goodbye, and perched in all her long impersonality on the edge of my bed, looking past my stockings, drawers, and po. This has taken so long to write that we are now arrived at

Monday, September 23rd

and so many things have accumulated that I can hardly proceed to that masterly summing up of the Webbs which I intended. I had intended to dwell upon the half carping half humorously cynical view which steals into one's description of the Webbs. I had meant to point out the good qualities which come from such well kept brisk intellectual habits, how open minded they showed themselves; how completely and consistently *sensible*. . . . Their horizon is entirely clear, unless, in the case of Mrs. Webb, as the medium said, a cloud of dust surrounds them.

It should be added to complete a true picture of the Webbs, what I have rarely, if ever, seen properly recorded, that their mutual affection and devotion were unmistakably deep. When they stayed with us they brought with them all the paraphernalia for making tea, including kettle and spirit lamp. Very early in the morning, 6 o'clock I think it was, Sidney made tea in his room and carried it along to Beatrice, and he then read aloud to her until it was time to get up. And one vivid memory which I have of them is Sidney standing

on the terrace at Asham, his little figure and beard sil-
houetted against the lovely line of downs and a flaming
September sunset, explaining to us that they were in their
sixties and therefore their expectation of life was now some
four or five years, and 'I wish,' he said, 'I could compound
with'—here he characteristically used the correct technical
insurance term—'the Almighty so that she and I would die
at exactly the same moment'—Sidney always referred to
Beatrice as 'she'.

One other reminiscence of the Webbs. One summer we
went and stayed with them for a week-end at a house which
they had taken for a month near Three Bridges. Bernard
Shaw and Mrs. Shaw were the only other week-end guests.
Beatrice had a characteristic habit of classifying all her
friends or acquaintances in a kind of psychological and
occupational card index. Thus Virginia was 'the novelist', I
was 'the ex-colonial-civil-servant'—and anything connected
with novels which arose in conversation would be referred
to Virginia, anything connected with Asia or Africa to me.
Beatrice always treated Shaw as the generalized or universal
artist and his department was therefore not only the arts
generally but anything connected with the embellishment,
non-utility side of life. A curious example of this habit of hers
took place at lunch one day. There was on the table a vase
in which were some flowers. The flowers were sweet peas or
pinks—I have forgotten exactly what they were, but they
were so common or garden that everyone in Europe except
the Webbs would have known their name. Beatrice did not
know their name, and as the question came within Shaw's
sphere of knowledge according to the psychological-
occupational card index, it was solemnly referred to him.

Perhaps as I have dealt with the Webbs here, not with
chronological exactitude, I had better go on and deal with
Shaw, whom I first met at the Webbs and who for many

years was inseparably connected with them. One of the strangest things about him was that he was personally the kindest, most friendly, most charming of men, yet personally he was almost the most impersonal person I have ever known. He was always extremely nice to Virginia and me. If one met him anywhere, he would come up and greet one with what seemed to be warmth and pleasure and he would start straight away with a fountain of words scintillating with wit and humour. You might easily flatter yourself that you were the one person in Europe to whom at that moment the famous George Bernard Shaw wanted to talk, but if you happened to look into that slightly fishy, ice-blue eye of his, you got a shock. It was not looking at you; you were nowhere in its orbit; it was looking through you or over you into a distant world or universe inhabited almost entirely by G.B.S., his thoughts and feelings, fancies and phantasies. Writing this, I remember three more or less casual meetings with him which seem to me wonderfully characteristic. The first was at Golders Green; Virginia and I went to the cremation of H. G. Wells's wife. When we came out, Maynard and Lydia Keynes came up to speak to us. Lydia was in tears. Then Shaw came up and put his hand on Lydia's shoulder and made a kind of oration to her telling her not to cry, that death was not an event to shed tears upon. It was a kindly, even a beautiful and eloquent speech, and yet, though he knew Lydia well and certainly liked her, one felt that it was hardly addressed to this highly individual and warm-hearted woman, who had danced as Lydia Lopokova in Diaghilev's Russian Ballet and out of it into marriage with John Maynard Keynes, but rather to 'someone in tears', who indeed might have been any woman in tears.[1]

[1] The same scene is described—rather differently—by Mrs. Bernard Shaw in a letter to T. E. Lawrence (in *Mrs. G.B.S.* by Janet Dunbar, p. 289):

The second was in a Committee Room in the House of Commons. It was, I think, a Fabian Committee of which Webb was chairman and I was secretary. Shaw was sitting next to me; on committees he was just like the Shaw not on a committee; he loved to talk paradoxically and amusingly and at considerable length. If Webb was the chairman, G.B.S. was never allowed to get going; he was kept to the point or to silence, and it was usually to silence. On this afternoon, he had been allowed scarcely two sentences, and when the proceedings came to an end, he must have been bursting with words and ideas. He turned to the man sitting on his left, who was an M.P. and one of the dullest and stupidest men I have ever known, and began an extraordinarily brilliant and amusing monologue. I had to discuss some matter of business with Sidney Webb, who was sitting on my right, and, when I had finished, I found that Shaw's splendid display was still going on. Indeed the fireworks went on for another 5 or 10 minutes; it was superb, but I don't think that the M.P. understood, let alone appreciated, a single one of Shaw's squibs, crackers, or rockets. But it made no difference to G.B.S.; it made no difference to him whether he talked to the dummy M.P. or the cleverest man in Europe—the ice-

---

The moment the coffin was shoved through the door into the furnace, and H.G. and the boys went round, G.B.S. trotted through another door into the garden and I took quite a little time to get quiet. Then we went into the yard to look for the car and found the rest of the congregation—mostly in tears (it was as bad as that). First thing I knew Lopokova flung herself into my arms sobbing and shaking. A tiny thing she is: she felt like a bit of thistledown that had been out in a rainstorm. Then Sydney Olivier, with red eyes, held out a shaking hand: and Virginia herself, looking very stately and calm, and remote, relieved me of Lopokova ... G.B.S., of course, began to 'behave badly' at once, making jokes to everyone, and finally—putting H.G. into his car—he actually got a sort of grin out of *him*.

(I have to thank Miss Dunbar for allowing me to quote this.)

blue eye went through or over the M.P., fixed upon the universe of G.B.S.

The third occasion was in Kensington Gardens. One fine Sunday afternoon Virginia and I went for a walk in the Park and we had just crossed from Hyde Park into Kensington Gardens and were making for the Flower Walk when we met Shaw coming from the opposite direction. He stopped and immediately began to tell us about his voyage round the world in a 'luxury' liner from which he had just got back. For the next quarter of an hour or twenty minutes he stood in front of us in the characteristic G.B.S. attitude, very erect with folded arms, his beard wagging as he talked, and gave us a brilliant unflagging monologue, describing the ship, the passengers, his audiences, what he said to them, his triumphs. When the fountain of words at last died down and we parted, I found that we were the centre of a wide circle of 15 or 20 people; they had recognized Shaw and had stopped to listen to his oration as though it were a public entertainment. And it struck me then that that was just exactly what it was. Although we were fond of him and he, I think, in his curious way really liked both of us, the sparkling display to which we had just listened might just as well have been addressed to the 20 strangers gaping at him as to us.

Though Shaw had, quite rightly, a very high opinion of Shaw, he was entirely without the pretentiousness and personal prickliness which nearly always make the great or still more The Very Important Person such an intolerable nuisance. Like the Webbs, he seemed never to resent or to be offended by anything which a younger person said or did to him. No one but Sidney and Beatrice Webb would have shown no resentment when in the heyday of the Fabian Society G. D. H. Cole treated them with the ruthless arrogance of brilliant and foolish youth. When about the same time I wrote *International Government* for the Fabian

Society, I found that Shaw had written a preface for it, I insisted that the book should be published in England without Shaw's preface on the ground that, as a young man and writer, I wanted my book to be judged on its merits and defects; it should stand solely on its own legs, and not on those of a great man's preface. I agreed to the preface later appearing in an American and a French edition. Most great men would, I think, have felt some slight resentment or hurt at this treatment of what was a kind and generous act on his part. Many years later I found that the opposite was true of Shaw, for Sir Frederic Osborn showed me a letter written to him in 1917 by Shaw explaining why he would not write a preface to some book and adding:

> I think you will see, on consideration, that Woolf, the author of the Fabian Research Department's book on Supernational Organisation, to which I, as chairman of the Department, had to supply a preface, was quite right in insisting that the English edition should appear in the first instance without my preface.

In the war years, when Virginia and I, recently married, were each just beginning our literary careers, Shaw with H. G. Wells and Arnold Bennett were at the height of their powers and stood together at the zenith of the literary heavens. Of course there was Hardy—and, of course, Conrad and Galsworthy. But Hardy stood by himself, an Olympian surviving from a previous age. Galsworthy seemed to us and to all of our generation a second rate novelist and stuffy, respectable, reactionary. Conrad had been welcomed by all of us in our youth as a writer of great prose—though always, a little uneasily—but he too was 'respectable' and had no contact with or message for our generation. Shaw, Wells, and Bennett were stars which formed a very different kind of constellation. We criticized them, and, being of a younger generation, naturally and healthily reacted against them in some directions—as, for instance, Virginia did against Bennett in *Mr. Bennett and Mrs. Brown*. But we understood them and respected them and to some extent they understood us; at any rate, as European civilization began to break up under the attacks of the barbarians, we found ourselves always on the same side of the barricades with Shaw, Wells, and Bennett.

It is the fate of even stars to fade or die. The red giants dwindle to white dwarfs or to dead black suns. The light of the three giants of 1917 has dimmed, particularly of Wells and Bennett. No doubt this is natural, right and proper, in the logic of time. But looking back over the last 45 years I still see them as a remarkable trinity—not negligible men or writers. It was fascinating to see the three of them together with the sparks flying. I got to know Wells, as I shall explain later, during the war, and early on in our careers, when I was Literary Editor of the *Nation*, we were asked to dinner by Mrs. Wells. We arrived at Whitehall Court punctually and found only H. G. and his wife, son, and secretary there. But soon the door opened and the maid announced Mr. and Mrs. Bernard Shaw, and a few minutes later it opened again and she announced Mr. and Mrs. Arnold Bennett. We had hardly met Bennett before, and I felt rather overwhelmed by the galaxy. Bennett did not put me at my ease. I had reviewed his novel, *Lord Raingo*, rather critically in the *Nation*. When we sat down to dinner, Bennett was on Mrs. Wells's left and I was on her right with Mrs. Shaw on my right; Virginia was at the other end of the table between Shaw and H.G. As soon as we had sat down Bennett fixed me with his eye, leant across, and said 'W-w-woolf d-d-does not l-l-like my novels.' I tried to expostulate that this was not the case, but several times during the dinner the minute gun was fired at me across the table: 'W-w-woolf d-d-does not l-l-like my novels.' The three great men were all personally rather formidable;

what interested me, as the evening went on, was to see how dominating Shaw was. At intervals, through our conversation, one heard the fountain of his words going up at the other end of the table, and towards the end we were all dominated by Shaw. Arnold with his slow stutter had no chance of getting a word in and soon resigned himself to firing the minute gun at me. H.G. did not give way without a struggle, but he was no match for Shaw and the Shavian pyrotechnical monologue.

I have said that Shaw was extraordinarily charming and that I think he did, in his own way, like Virginia and me. The following letter which he wrote to Virginia seems to prove this. She had written to him with regard to some point when she was working on her life of Roger Fry:

My dear Virginia,   10th May, 1940.

I do not remember the occasion described by Roger; and I could hardly have dismissed art so summarily from consideration as a social factor as if I had just looked into it as a foreign subject for five minutes or so. As a matter of fact I am an artist to my finger tips, and always contend that I am a highly educated person because I had continual contacts with literature and art, including music, in my childhood, and found school and its Latin and Greek grind nothing but a brutalizing imprisonment which interfered disastrously with my real education. Now that I am nearly 84 I am more convinced than ever that an aesthetic education is the best now available, and that the neglect of the aesthetic factor in science has deprived it of its claim to be scientific.

Probably what Roger heard me say was that nothing fundamental can be done by art until the economical problem is solved. I am fond of saying that 12 hours hunger will reduce any saint, artist, or philosopher to the level of a highwayman.

I think my first private meeting with Roger was also my first meeting with Elgar. We three lunched with Madame Vandervelde, then wedded to the late Belgian Socialist Minister. Elgar, who had enjoyed my musical criticisms when he was a student and remembered all my silly jokes, talked music so voluminously that Roger had nothing to do but eat his lunch in silence. At last we stopped to breathe and eat something ourselves; and Roger, feeling that our hostess expected him to contribute something, began in his beautiful voice (his and Forbes Robertson's were the only voices one could listen to for their own sakes) 'After all, there is only one art: all the arts are the same.' I heard no more; for my attention was taken by a growl from the other side of the table. It was Elgar, with his fangs bared and all his hackles bristling, in an appalling rage. 'Music,' he spluttered, 'is written on the skies for you to note down. And you compare that to a DAMNED imitation.'

There was nothing for Roger to do but either to seize the decanter and split Elgar's head with it, or else take it like an angel with perfect dignity. Which latter he did.

I have a picture by Roger which I will give you if you care to have it: a landscape.

I wish we could see more of you and Leonard; but we two are now so frightfully old that we no longer dare to offer our company as a treat to friends who are still in the prime of life.

There is a play of mine called Heartbreak House which I always connect with you because I conceived it in that house somewhere in Sussex where I first met you and, of course, fell in love with you. I suppose every man did.

always yours, consequently

G. Bernard Shaw

I must once more retrace my steps to the point at which I left my career a few pages back and the influence of the Webbs upon it. After my first lunch with them in Grosvenor Road they at once took me in hand and made me come up to a Fabian Society Conference for two days in Keswick. This too was the moment at which the *New Statesman* was being brought to birth and every week the Webbs had a *New Statesman* lunch on, I think, Monday. They invited me to one of the earliest, if not the first, of these. There for the first time I met Clifford Sharp, the editor; Jack (later Sir John) Squire, the Literary Editor; Robert Lynd, one of those impeccable journalists who every week for 30 or 40 years turn out an impeccable essay (called in the technical jargon of journalism a 'middle') like an impeccable sausage, about anything or everything or nothing; John Roberts, the manager.

The name of Robert Lynd reminds me of an absurd incident which I cannot refrain from relating out of its order and I will therefore interrupt my account of luncheon with the Webbs by an account of a dinner with Rose Macaulay. Rose, whom we both liked very much, some time, I suppose, in the late twenties asked Virginia and me to dine with her. We thought it was just an ordinary dinner and that we should be alone with her or at most with one or two other guests. When the day came we printed all the afternoon, Virginia setting and I machining, and we got very late. We dashed off without changing, dishevelled and probably with traces of printer's ink still on our persons. To our horror we found a formal dinner party of ten or twelve people (in a restaurant just across the road from Rose's flat), all literary gents and ladies and all immaculate in evening dress. Though we loved Rose, it was the kind of party that both of us loathed, for the literary gent, who may be quite nice when he is in small numbers and in literary mufti, is a bore when he

is in a formal herd and evening dress. Being the last to come
and obviously having kept them all waiting, conscious of our
dirt and dishevelment, we both lost our nerve. I sat by Mrs.
Lynd and Virginia on the other side of the table was between
Robert Lynd and Conal O'Riordan, a prolific novelist who
described himself with grim truth in *Who's Who* as a Man
of Letters. I began badly; my hand trembled so that I could
not eat my soup, and my spoon startled everyone by clatter-
ing threateningly upon my plate and splashing the soup
perilously near to Sylvia Lynd upon the table cloth. I could
think of nothing to say while the conversation began to hum
and boom all round the table. Suddenly however it came to
a stop in one of those complete silences which fall upon even
a literary dinner party. And then in the deathly silence
Virginia's beautiful clear voice was heard to say on the other
side of the table: 'What do you mean by The Holy Ghost?'
To which O'Riordan replied angrily: 'I did not say "Holy
Ghost", I said "the whole coast".' I felt that Virginia had dis-
graced herself and that the whole table felt it too, but everyone tried to hide it by turning and talking animatedly to their
neighbours. I turned to Mrs. Lynd, and noticing, as I
thought, that she had dropped her white napkin on the floor,
leaned down and picked it up to give to her. Unfortunately I
found that it was not her napkin, but her white petticoat
which (wrongly) showed below her skirt. She took it badly
and we slunk away as soon as we could after dinner.

To return to Grosvenor Road, it was the first of many
New Statesman lunches which I have sat through in my life.
At this one I was obviously asked by the Webbs for a purpose. They never, as far as I saw, ever interfered at all with
Sharp and the editorial side of the paper. But they wanted to
introduce me to the editor and his staff in order to give them
a chance of employing me and me a chance of being
employed by them. In this they were successful. Squire sent

me books to review and in a year or two I was reviewing for him practically all the books published on the war, foreign affairs, and international questions. He used to send me enormous parcels of these kinds of books and leave it to me to decide whether to review them or not.

The editor, Clifford Sharp, was the exact opposite, in almost every characteristic, of his literary editor, Jack Squire. Jack was the best type of gay, casual, good tempered, generous Bohemian, a literary gent of the kind which has been indigenous round about Fleet Street since the 18th century. Sharp was a curiously chilly and saturnine man with a face or complexion which always looked to me as if it had recently been given a good rub with emery paper. He was unlovable—not a nice man. But, as time went on, I got to feel something towards him which might perhaps be called affection. It was the affection which one sometimes acquires for an old, mangy, surly, slightly dangerous dog. One is rather proud of being one of the few people whom he will—with a growl—allow to pat him gingerly on the head. He was by training an engineer, and he seemed to me to bring to human relations and politics, and so to journalism, the attitude of the engineer, of a sanitary inspector or super-plumber. When he stood in his room—I hardly ever saw him sit down—listening to what one had to say, there was about him an atmosphere of intellectual Jeyes' Fluid, moral carbolic soap, spiritual detergents—to such an extent that I sometimes had the illusion that he himself smelt strongly of soap and his room of disinfectants. Temperamentally and fundamentally he was a conservative of the Disraelian, Rule Britannia, 1878 vintage; but he was also, as the Webbs used to point out with quiet enjoyment, a collectivist. Indeed, collectivism and drainage—material or spiritual—were, I think, the only things Sharp believed in with any flicker of enthusiasm. He liked to think of himself as the hard-boiled

BEGINNING AGAIN

tough, without sentimentality, without illusions, without
emotions—the realist and no damned nonsense; and his face,
particularly the eyes and nose, which made him look like a
hooded falcon, helped him to sustain this character. In fact
he had the sentimentality of those who make a fuss about
being anti-sentimental.

After my first *New Statesman* lunch Sharp told me that he
would like to consider articles by me and that I was to come
and suggest subjects to him. As a beginner in journalism, I
found his methods rather disheartening, until I came to
know him better. He was one of those editors who believe in
keeping his contributors up to the mark by a liberal use of
cold water (perhaps another instance of his sanitation complex). I used to go to the office in Gt. Queen Street and suggest
an article to him. He would stand in front of the fireplace,
his head thrust forward, fix me with a cold eye, and listen
in complete silence. He then poured down my back several
metaphorical buckets of cold water, and when he had convinced me that the subject suggested was silly and the way I
proposed to treat it imbecile and that I had wasted a good
deal of his valuable time, he would say: 'Well, Woolf, you
may as well go off and see what you can do. I don't say it
won't make an article.' I slunk off with my tail between my
legs and gloomily wrote what seemed to me a depressed and
depressing article. I then took it to Sharp dejectedly expect-
ing him to reject it. He always did take it, and I do not think
that it is the euphoria of memory and senility that makes me
believe that occasionally he gave it and me a word of grim
and tepid praise.

I have known a good many well-known editors: the
famous Scott of the *Manchester Guardian*, Wickham Steed of
The Times, Massingham of the *Daily Chronicle* and *Nation*,
Sir Gerald Barry of the *News Chronicle* and *Week-end Review*,
Sir Bruce Richmond of *The Times Literary Supplement*,

130

Kingsley Martin of the *New Statesman*. As professional journalists go, Sharp was not a bad editor, though he was not in the very front rank. He performed the first duty of an editor, he impressed upon his paper an indelible character, a journalistic aroma which ultimately was the personal aroma of Sharp. It pervaded every corner of the paper, every article whether signed or unsigned. The way in which a real or 'good' editor pervades his paper is very remarkable; when you write for him his unseen presence broods over your pen or typewriter and unconsciously your thoughts and your words are infected by him. You become a ventriloquist's puppet. For a short time I used to write unsigned articles occasionally for Sharp in the *New Statesman* and for Massingham in the *Nation*. You could not find two men more different in temperament, style, and editorial methods, and, though, when writing for them, I was never conscious of being influenced by them, I know that my articles in the *Statesman* were in the image of Clifford Sharp and in the *Nation* in the image of H. W. Massingham. The image of Sharp was rather bleak and acrid, and to read—or write for —the *New Statesman* always seemed to me rather like sitting in a cold draughty room in which the fire was smoking a little. You might not like it; but at least the paper had a character of its own; it knew what it thought and said it in its own peculiar way—an important and by no means common journalistic merit.

Sharp ruined himself by drinking—a by no means uncommon journalistic failing. It is curious that, though I fairly often used to go and see him at the office latish in the day, when, according to all accounts, he was usually in an obviously drunken state, I had no idea that he drank until the final disaster. Journalism is a highly dangerous profession. Among its many occupational diseases is not only drink, but a kind of fatty degeneration of the mind. Only a few very strong minded men escape the latter disease, the nemesis of successful journalism. I have practised journalism, not unsuccessfully, for 50 years and have been an editor on three different papers. In 1924 I became Literary Editor of the *Nation*, practically a full time job, though I made conditions that I would only go the office for 2½ days a week. Its effect upon me and my mind was, I am sure, bad, and I resigned after six years, because I felt that it was destroying what mind I had. I made up what mind it had left me never again to take a full time journalistic job.

There are two great mental dangers in journalism. The first is most virulent among editors. It creates a kaleidoscopic, chaotic, perpetual motion rhythm of the mind. As soon as you have produced one number of your paper, you have to begin thinking of and planning the next. Your mind gets into the habit of opening and shutting at regular intervals of 24 hours or seven days like the shells of a mussel or the shutter of a camera, and everything in your mind—and indeed in your life—gets to be determined and conditioned by this interval. What you wrote for or published in last week's or yesterday's issue was written or published for a moment of time, last week or yesterday; it is now dead and forgotten and now all that concerns you is what you are publishing or writing for this week or for today. Your mind thus develops a curiously feverish habit of regular and ephemeral opening and shutting. You become a shell fish or a camera, but, unlike them, you soon delude yourself into thinking that the opening and shutting of your mind and the contents of the mollusc or camera are of immense importance. Nearly all good editors—like the owners of some of them, the great newspaper owners—become megalomaniacs and suffer from the hallucination that they control and exercise great power. The hallucination of power corrupts as efficiently as power.

The second occupational disease of journalism is connected closely with the first, but it affects all journalists, not merely editors. What you write for a paper you write for a moment of time, the moment being a morning or an evening, a week, a month, or three months. Whatever the length of the moment, what you produce is written under the shadow of ephemerality; you write it not in the mould of eternity, but for consumption with the kipper or eggs and bacon at the breakfast table or to distract someone from falling asleep in a railway carriage. There is, however, writing which is quite different from this, 'serious' literature or the art of literature. Literature may be a novel or a history, an essay or a poem; it is written not with the eggs and bacon, but sub specie aeternitatis. It is incompatible with journalese. Of course, occasionally and accidentally a work of serious literature has got into a newspaper and nearly all modern serious writers write for the papers. But generally habitual or professional journalism destroys any ability to write literature. In the vast majority of journalists this does not matter, for they are journalists and not potentially artists. But every now and again a serious writer is destroyed or maimed by journalism.

This is, I think, a point which has become more and more important with the enormous growth of popular journalism and of the incomes of popular journalists during my lifetime. The temptation in journalism is terrific for the young man or woman who has to earn a living and yet wants to be and perhaps might be a serious writer. 'I will earn my living in Fleet Street,' they think, 'and write my masterpiece in the evenings and at week-ends.' But newspaper offices are paved with unwritten masterpieces. If you want to write a masterpiece in the evening, the last thing you should do during the day is to write journalism or indeed to have anything to do with writing. When I was Literary Editor of the *Nation*, young men and women from Oxford and Cambridge were continually coming to me for advice; they wanted to write masterpieces, usually novels, and their idea was to earn their living by journalism or in a publishing office; they wanted me to tell them how to start. My advice was: 'Don't. If you want to write a masterpiece in the evening, you have an infinitely better chance of doing so by being a cook or a gardener during the day than if you write second rate stuff or mess about with books and writing all day.' I do not think that any of them took my advice or that any of them has written a masterpiece.

There is another snare and delusion in journalism for the young writer. When you write for an editor and a paper, particularly when you write what is unsigned, but even if your name appears, in a curious way you escape responsibility. This often has a very bad, if not fatal, effect upon a would-be serious writer. I am thinking of a person like Desmond MacCarthy. I was given a good dressing down by *The Times Literary Supplement* reviewer of my book *Sowing* because I wrote in it that when we were young men at Cambridge we thought of Desmond as 'someone upon whom the good fairies appeared to have lavished every possible gift both of body and of mind', that he seemed to be 'in the making a writer, a novelist of the highest quality', and that 'as a writer he never achieved anything at all of what he promised'. The reviewer, who admittedly only met Desmond, middle-aged or elderly, entertaining aristocratic or non-aristocratic dinner tables with his entrancing conversation, says that this is complete nonsense, Desmond 'surely could never have been a novelist even of passable quality, for he lacked that power of organization demanded by the novel, and indeed by even the shortest of short stories. This was manifest in his appearance, which, in the most engaging way, suggested a dishevelled bird just fallen out of the nest'. And not only did his middle-aged appearance show that he could never have written even a passable short story, 'his special gift for conversation' might also have revealed it to us in 1903.

The reviewer is mistaken and he arrives at his wrong conclusion by making a number of mistakes, large and small, on the way. First, he like many other people is really assuming that because a thing happened it and nothing else had to happen. Because Desmond never did write a novel, he never could have written a novel. This simplifies life, history, and people, and, if it were true, it would be unnecessary to write or review biographies or autobiographies. But there is no reason to believe it to be true and his own arguments are so bad that they tell against him. Take for instance his view that because Desmond looked like a dishevelled bird it proved that he could not write a passable novel. It is true that Desmond did look like a dishevelled bird when he was middle-aged, and he knew it himself—hence his character- istic pen name Affable Hawk. But when I first saw Desmond —he was 26 and just returned from a Grand Tour of Europe—there was nothing of the dishevelled fledgling fallen from the nest about him; he looked like a superb young eagle who with one sweep of his great wing could soar to any height he chose. He not only looked it; the good fairies had lavished upon him every possible gift and particularly those gifts which every would-be writer and novelist would pray for. Why did he never fulfil his promises? Why did the splendid eagle degenerate into an affable hawk, a dishevelled fledg- ling? The answer is infinitely more complicated than the reviewer's superficial explanation.

It is infinitely more complicated because the human being is psychologically so infuriatingly complex that you can never explain his thoughts, actions, or character by trotting out a single superficial cause. One of the difficulties is that in the human mind the same element is at the same time both a cause and an effect. Thus in the case of Desmond it is probably true to say that 'his special gift of conversation' was a cause of his not writing novels, but it is also true that (1) it was an *excuse* for his not writing novels, and (2) his not writing novels was a cause of his special gift for conversation. One summer Desmond came to stay for a few days with us in the country at Asham House. He was slightly depressed when he arrived and soon told us the reason. His friend A. F. Wedgwood, the novelist, had recently died leaving a post-humous novel and Desmond had promised the widow to write an introduction and memoir of the author for the book. He had continually put off doing this; the book had been printed, was ready for binding, and was completely held up for Desmond's introduction; the publisher was desperate and desperately bombarding Desmond with reply paid tele-grams. Desmond had sworn that he would write the thing over the week-end and post it to the publisher on Monday morning. He asked me to promise that next morning I would lock him up in a room by himself and not let him out until he had finished the introduction. And he told me then that he really suffered from a disease: the moment he knew that he ought to do something, no matter what that some-thing was, he felt absolutely unable to do it and would do anything else in order to prevent himself from doing it. It did not matter what 'it' might be; it might be something which he actually wanted to do, but if it was also something which he knew he *ought* to do, he would find himself doing something which he did not want to do in order to prevent himself doing something which he ought to do and wanted to do.

Here for instance was a fairly common situation in Desmond's life: he is engaged to dine at 7.30 with someone whom he likes very much in Chelsea; he looks forward to the

The author and Virginia
at Asham House, 1914

G. E. Moore
at Asham House, 1914

evening; at 7 he is sitting in a room at the other end of London talking to two or three people whom he does not very much like and who are in fact boring him; at 7.5 he begins to feel that he ought to get up and leave for Chelsea; at 7.30 he is still sitting with the people whom he does not much like and is uncomfortably keeping them from their dinner; at 8 they insist that he must stay and dine with them; at 8.5 he rings up his Chelsea friends, apologizes, and says that he will be with them in 20 minutes.

I should add that that evening at Asham Desmond recovered his spirits and was in fine form. After we had gone to bed, we heard him for a short time walking up and down the corridor groaning: 'O God! God!' Next morning he was quite cheerful when I locked him in the sitting room. An hour later he thumped on the door and shouted: 'You must let me out, Leonard, you must let me out.' He had run out of cigarettes and I weakly let him out so that he could walk over to Rodmell, a mile away, and buy some at the village shop. I cannot remember whether when he left us on Monday or Tuesday morning, he had finished the introduction. I rather think he had not.

Now one of the several reasons why Desmond never fulfilled his youthful aquiline promise and never wrote that brilliant novel which in 1903 lay embryonically in his mind was that he thought that he *ought* to write a novel and that the novel *ought* to be absolutely first class. Desmond was in many ways Moore's favourite apostle and Desmond loved and followed Moore with the purity and intensity of the disciple devoted to the guru or sage. He, as an impressionable young man, like all of us in the Cambridge of those days, took *Principia Ethica* as a bible of conduct. In *Sowing*, pp. 131-135, I tried to describe and define this influence of Moore and his book upon us. The book told us what we *ought* to do and what we ought not to do, and, when one thought of those words, it was impossible not to see and hear Moore himself, the impassioned shake of his head on the emphasized words as he said: 'I think one *ought* to do that,' or 'I think one ought *not* to do that.' So when Desmond sat down to write, an invisible Moore, with the 'oughts' and 'ought nots', stood behind his chair. But both as a man and a writer his gifts were of a lyrical kind; they had to be given a free hand; his imagination would not work and so he could not write on a tight, intellectual rein.

The best, said the Greeks, is the enemy of the good. The vision of the best, the ghostly echoes of *Principia Ethica*, the catechism which always begins with the terrifying words: 'What exactly do you *mean* by *that*?,' inhibited Desmond. When he wrote 'seriously', he began to labour, and the more he tinkered with what he wrote the more laboured and laborious it became. This brings me back to the point from which I started, the effect of journalism upon Desmond and writers like him. Journalism provided him with the easy way out of his difficult and complicated situation as regards writing a novel. He thought that he ought to write a novel—something serious—and as the habit grew upon him of not being able to do what he thought he ought to do, the habit of always doing something else in order to avoid doing what he ought to do, writing the weekly article for the *New Statesman* or *Sunday Times* became his refuge and shelter from his duty to be a great writer. (Of course, there was the further stage that, when the moment came at which he *ought* to begin writing the article, he had to find something else to prevent his doing so, and it was only a devoted and efficient secretary who managed somehow or other to get Affable Hawk's article, usually a few minutes after the very last moment, to an infuriated printer.)

But writing an article as a refuge for Desmond against doing what he thought he ought to do, i.e. writing a novel, was only part of the story. In literature he had tremendously high standards, and, if he had ever been inclined to lower them, the memories of Cambridge, Moore, and *Principia Ethica* would have warned him off. To write a book, say a novel, as a serious artist, requires a good many qualities, by no means common, besides the ability to write. However sensitive you may be to praise or blame, you have to be at some point ruthless and impervious—and ruthless to yourself. The moment comes when the writer must say to himself: 'I don't care what they say about it and me; I shall publish and be damned to them.' And he has to accept responsibility, the responsibility for what he has written; he must strip himself artistically naked before the public and take the icy plunge. People like Desmond, once they begin to doubt whether what they are writing is really any good—and such doubts occasionally torture practically all good writers—cannot stay the course. They cannot force themselves through those despairing moments of grind in the long distance race before you get your second wind and they cannot face responsibility. Here again journalism is the refuge. Even *Principia Ethica* would allow one to lower one's standards in the *Sunday Times* or *New Statesman*, where one is writing not sub specie aeternitatis, but for a short week-end. And in any case the responsibility is not so much yours as the editor's. Journalism is the opiate of the artist; eventually it poisons his mind and his art.

Off and on over the years I saw a good deal of Desmond, walking and talking with him at all hours of day and night, watching him try to write and even occasionally working with him. I am sure that his psychology as a writer was more or less that analysed by me in the previous paragraphs. One can only add that the charm of the dead cannot be reproduced second-hand in words. One can only record the fact that Desmond was the most charming of men, the most amusing companion, and finally had about him in friendship the honesty and faithfulness which I associate with old sheep dogs.

When I had written this, I remembered that Virginia had once in her diaries, when after being ill she was for a time only able to write her novel for an hour a day, amused herself by writing short accounts of her friends' characters. I turned up what she had written about Desmond and this is what she said in January 1919:

How many friends have I got? There's Lytton, Desmond, Saxon: they belong to the Cambridge stage of life; very intellectual . . . I can't put them in order, for there are too many. Ka and Rupert and Duncan, for example, all come rather later . . . Desmond has *not* rung up. That is quite a good preface to the description of his character. The difficulty which faces one in writing of Desmond is that one is almost forced to describe an Irishman. How he misses trains, seems born without a rudder to drift wherever the current is strongest; how he keeps hoping and planning, and shuffles along, paying his way by talking so enchantingly that editors forgive and shopmen give him credit and at least one distinguished peer leaves him a thousand in his will . . . Where was I? Desmond, and how I find him sympathetic compared with Stracheys. It is true; I'm not sure he hasn't the nicest nature of any of us —the nature one would soonest have chosen for one's own. I don't think that he possesses any faults as a friend, save that his friendship is so often sunk under a cloud of vagueness, a sort of drifting vapour composed of times and seasons separates us and effectively prevents us from meeting. Perhaps such indolence implies a slackness of fibre in his affections too—but I scarcely feel that. It arises rather from the consciousness which I find imaginative and attractive that things don't altogether *matter*.

Somehow he is fundamentally sceptical. Yet which of us, after all, takes more trouble to do the sort of kindness that comes his way? Who is more tolerant, more appreciative, more understanding of human nature? It goes without saying that he is not an heroic character. He finds pleasure too pleasant, cushions too soft, dallying too seductive and then as I sometimes feel now, he has ceased to be ambitious. His 'great work' (it may be philosophy or biography now, and is certainly to be begun, after a series of long walks, this very spring) only takes shape, I believe, in that hour between tea and dinner, when so many things appear not only possible, but achieved. Comes the daylight, and Desmond is contented to begin his article; and plies his pen with a half humorous half melancholy recognition that such is his appointed life. Yet it is true, and no one can deny it, that he has the floating elements of something brilliant, beautiful—some book of stories, reflection, studies, scattered about in him, for they show themselves indisputably in his talk. I'm told he wants power; that these fragments never combine into an argument; that the disconnection of talk is kind to them; but in a book they would drift hopelessly apart. Consciousness of this, no doubt, led him in his one finished book to drudge and sweat until his fragments were clamped together in an indissoluble stodge. I can see myself, however, going through his desk one of these days, shaking out unfinished pages from between sheets of blotting paper, and deposits of old bills, and making up a short book of table talk, which shall appear as a proof to the younger generation that Desmond was the most gifted of us all. But why did he never do anything? they will ask.

There is something of Desmond in Bernard in *The Waves*.
' "Had I been born," said Bernard, "not knowing that one

word follows another I might have been, who knows, perhaps anything. As it is, finding sequences everywhere, I cannot bear the pressure of solitude. When I cannot see words curling like rings of smoke around me I am in darkness—I am nothing. When I am alone I fall into lethargy, and say to myself dismally as I poke the cinders through the bars, Mrs. Moffat will come. She will come and sweep it all up." ' That was true of Desmond; he had a tremendous zest for life and friends and phrases and also that streak of melancholia when he fell into despair alone in front of the dying fire. Then he wrinkled his forehead and groaned 'O God! God!', and left it in despair for one of the innumerable Mrs. Moffats to sweep it all up. Of course, one of them came, for in 999,999 cases out of a million there is a Mrs. Moffat to sweep it all up for the Desmonds of this world. His wife Molly was one of them all her life; but an incompetent Mrs. Moffat, for she was much too charming, amusing, hesitant, and unsure of herself to be any good at sweeping up anything. She was one of those people whose minds go blank the moment they are faced by the slightest crisis; her vagueness and fluttering indecision must have been perpetually nourished by a lifetime of waiting for Desmond to return to dinner to which he had forgotten that he had invited several friends. The way that Molly's mind refused to work is shown by the following affectionate memory of her. One week-end she and W. B. Yeats were both staying at Garsington. On Saturday night after dinner the poet, as his way was, got off on one of his, to me boring, disquisitions about spirits, second sight, and mediums. He suddenly turned to Molly and said that he was sure that she was psychic and she must let him try to get her to 'see' things. Much against her will Molly at last gave in and said flutteringly that she could try. There were I suppose some ten or twelve people sitting around in the drawing-room, and poor Molly was seated in a chair next to Yeats who performed the usual ceremony of mumbo jumbo. There was a moment of complete silence, and then Yeats said: 'And now what do ye see, my dear?' Molly's mind went absolutely blank; she saw nothing and could not even think of anything which she might see. Yeats became agitated. 'Come now, my dear, come now, ye must see something.' A long paralysing silence, and then Molly said miserably: 'Yes, I think I do see something—a frog.' Yeats was outraged.

To return for a moment to Desmond. Bernard has something of Desmond in him, even in the last speech where he sits alone in the restaurant and talks about phrases. But Bernard is not Desmond; none of Virginia's characters are drawn completely or photographically from life. The final heroic charge against death, 'unvanquished and unyielding', was not in Desmond. The last time I saw him, not long before he died, I walked away with him from the house in Gordon Square where we had had a Memoir Club meeting. It was 11 o'clock and a cold autumn night. He was suffering terribly from asthma and was racked by a sudden fit of it as we turned out of the Square. I made him wait while I ran off to find him a taxi. When I put him into the taxi, he looked, not like an affable hawk or even a dishevelled fledgling, but like a battered, shattered, dying rook. At the corner of Gordon Square I suddenly saw him again as a young man walking with me on the hills above Hunter's Inn in Devonshire when we were on an Easter 'reading party' with Moore and Lytton. There are few things more terrible than such sudden visions of one's friends in youth and vigour through the miseries of age and illness. I left Desmond sitting in the taxi, affectionate, dejected, unheroic, because so obviously broken and beaten by asthma and by life; but brave in not complaining and not pretending and in still, when he could, making his joke and his phrase.

I have been led to say this about Desmond because I was

discussing the effect of journalism on the would-be serious writer. In the two years and four months between my resignation from the Ceylon Civil Service in April, 1912, and the outbreak of war in August, 1914, I had chosen my profession. I had become a writer of books, earning from them an average of £6 per annum, and a freelance journalist with a completely unknown earning capacity and future before me. Then the shot was fired in Sarajevo which destroyed the civilization and the way of life which I had known in the first 34 years of my life.

The author and G. E. Moore at Asham House, 1914

Part Three

THE 1914 WAR

O N Saturday, August 1, 1914, in the afternoon I bicycled from Asham to Seaford to bathe in the sea, as I did on many fine days that summer. It was a hot day and I swam out to a diving raft moored some little distance from the shore. I dived a long dive into the sea and came up against a large man with a large red face who was swimming out from the beach. I apologized and he said to me, almost casually: 'Do you know it's war?' We swam side by side for a bit and he told me that he was a London policeman on two weeks holiday, and, although he had had only a few days of his holiday, he had that morning had a telegram recalling him to duty in London. 'It's war,' he said again dejectedly, as we swam towards the beach; 'otherwise they wouldn't have recalled me.' That was how I first learnt that war was inevitable and that 19th-century civilization was ending. On Sunday, August 2, and Monday, August 3, I walked to Lewes and back 8 miles after tea to hear what the news might be, for it was still 19th-century civilization for us at Asham with no car, no buses, no telephone, and no newspaper unless one walked into Lewes to get one. The spectacle of the outbreak of war and the death of civilization as seen by me in Lewes was depressing. I stood about with some 20 or 30 other depressed persons outside the Post Office where short notices were posted up from time to time or at the railway station hoping to get somehow or other news of something definite. It came at last—we were at war, and I walked back the 4 miles to Asham.

It was, I think, the day that war broke out that Virginia and I walked from Asham to what is now Peacehaven and Telscombe Cliffs on the coast road between Newhaven and Brighton. The walk there and back was six or seven miles, beginning in the Ouse valley across the river, up through Southease on to the downs and then over the top of the down to the sea. That day now 50 years ago we passed, a quarter of a mile from Asham, Itford Farm, the house standing much as it did 500 years before and looking on to a valley which, except for the railway line, had changed little since 1414. In Southease we passed the church which stood there unchanged for 700 years, the farm which was unchanged since the 18th century, the rectory hidden by trees, and two or three cottages. After Southease across the down, the fields of stubble or uncut corn in the hollows, the shepherd and his great flock of sheep and his dog on the top or on the slopes, and no sign of human habitation all the way to the sea, except that one could just see a mile or more away above Piddinghoe a building known locally as Mad Misery Barn, a name which I always thought must be a corruption of Me Miserere. And when one got to the coast road overlooking the sea there were visible, looking east and west and north, only three or four houses, a few cottages, a largish farm house, and the Post Office which supplied teas as well as stamps.

In the tea room we found, to our surprise and slight annoyance, Jack Pollock (the son of old Sir Fred),[1] who had

[1] Sir Frederick Pollock, Eton and Trinity College, Cambridge, died at the age of 92 in 1937. He was an Apostle and I therefore got to know him when I was an undergraduate, but he was also a friend of the Stephen family. He was a strange, tough and stringy man of great and universal learning. He was Second Classic at Cambridge, Fellow of Trinity, Professor of Jurisprudence, a K.C., an authority on the history of law. When Virginia published a novel, she often received from him a letter of somewhat pedantic appreciation, pointing out minute errors about anything ranging from literature to seismology or

been a young Fellow of Trinity when I was up at Cambridge, and Prince and Princess Bariatinsky. Jack Pollock some years later married the princess and still later, when old Sir Fred died, succeeded to the baronetcy. I do not know what that strange party was doing at Telscombe Cliffs greeting the great war with tea and cakes. But our meeting now in memory seems to me an appropriate part of the unreality, the dreamlike catastrophe of those August days of 1914.

I have described the walk in some detail because when I look back to it, I see that part of the civilization which the war destroyed was the environment, the country and the country life, through which Virginia and I walked to the sea that day. Before the end of the war a company bought a stretch of land near Telscombe Cliffs Post Office and offered it for sale in building plots. They called it Anzac Cove, and, when this did not succeed, Anzac Cove was rechristened Peacehaven. Acre plots of land began to be sold and a rash of bungalows, houses, shops, shacks, chicken runs, huts, and dog kennels began to spread over Peacehaven and Telscombe Cliffs. It soon covered practically all the land between Newhaven and Brighton, smothering the fields and the downs, and beyond Brighton to Worthing and Littlehampton so that the south coast of England has become an almost unbroken chain of suburbs. This development seems to be, as I said, part of the destruction of the civilization, the way of life, which existed in Sussex and vast stretches of England before 1914. There were tremendous evils in that way of life and much of the civilization deserved destruction. But I don't see any point in destroying unless you put some-

---

ornithology. The last time I saw him was at a party on the stage of Sadler's Wells Theatre—he must have been about 90. His toughness was shown by the fact that, at about the same age, he was knocked down by a boy on a bicycle. I was told that the nonagenarian was unhurt; it was the boy who died.

thing rather better in the place of what you destroy. I can
see nothing whatever to be said for Anzac Cove and Peacehaven, and for what they have put in place of what they
destroyed around the Post Office and tea room at Telscombe
Cliffs. No sane man would walk to Peacehaven from Asham
today for on the way he would see lovely downs spattered
with ugly buildings and, when he got there, he would find
all round him, as far as the eye can see, miles of disorderly
ugliness, shoddiness, and squalor. If one has to choose
between the sheep and sheepdog, not to speak of the shepherd, of 1914 and the respectable devotees of T.V., football
pools, and bingo who flock into the hideous houses which in
1963 are flung together higgledy piggledy in Peacehaven,
then I am not sure that one should not prefer the civilization
of the sheep.

And now I must face the task of dealing with our life
during the four years of war. Our life during those four years
was dominated not only by the war, but also by Virginia's
illness, and I must therefore begin with the illness. In the
first chapter of this book I have given some account of the
nature and symptoms of the neurasthenia, as the doctors
called it, from which she suffered. As I explained there, I
had had no experience of insanity or mental illness and it
took me some time before I realized the seriousness of her
symptoms and the razor edge of sanity upon which her mind
was often balanced. I was already troubled and apprehensive
when we returned from our honeymoon in the autumn of
1912. All through the first seven months of 1913 I became
more and more concerned, for the danger symptoms or
signals became more and more serious. In January and
February she was finishing *The Voyage Out*, writing every
day with a kind of tortured intensity. I did not know then
what over the years we learnt bitterly by experience, that the
weeks or months in which she finished a book would always

The author and Adrian Stephen at Asham House, 1914

be a terrific mental and nervous strain upon her and bring her to the verge of a mental breakdown. It was not merely the strain of the mental intensity with which she always wrote, the artistic integrity and ruthlessness which made her drive herself remorselessly towards perfection. She also suffered from what most people would say was a weakness or fault of character, but which was intricately entangled with her mental instability, an almost pathological hypersensitiveness to criticism, so that she suffered an ever increasingly agonizing nervous apprehension as she got nearer and nearer to the end of her book and the throwing of it and of herself to the critics.

I have never kept a proper diary recording events and comment upon events, but for the last 50 years or more I have kept a skeleton diary in which I enter in a few lines a bare account of what I do each day. Very occasionally in times of crisis, when I want to make the record unintelligible to anyone but myself, I make my entries in cypher mainly composed of a mixture of Sinhalese and Tamil letters. My diary of the year 1913 shows very clearly the rapid progress of Virginia's illness and of my apprehension. From January to August I noted almost daily the state of her health, whether she could work, how she slept, whether she had sensations of headache; and in August I began to keep the diary in cypher.

The diary shows that after she finished the book and I had taken it to the publisher in March, she was continually suffering from bouts of intense worry and insomnia, and every now and again from the headache which was the danger signal of something worse. From time to time Sir George Savage was consulted, and some time in the spring it was at last definitely decided that it would not be safe for her to have a child. We spent most of our time in London in Cliffords Inn, but sometimes went for week-ends and holidays to Asham. In the first two weeks of July I became more and more alarmed. The symptoms of headache increased, she could not sleep, she would hardly eat anything. She could not work and became terribly depressed, and what was most alarming, she refused to admit that she was ill and blamed herself for her condition. I knew now that this irrational sense of guilt had been a symptom of her previous breakdown and had led to her jumping out of a window in an attempt to commit suicide. I realized in the first week of July when we were at Asham that one had to face the danger of suicide. I had undertaken to go to and speak at a Fabian Conference in Keswick on July 22 and Virginia insisted that I should go and that she was well enough to come with me. We went and it was the beginning of a nightmare which lasted for several months, one of those appalling nightmares which, because they belong to the world of reality and yet seem to be overlaid with unreality, have the double horror of the collapse of one's everyday life and, at the same time, of the most fantastic and devastating dream.

As soon as we got to the hotel at Keswick, Virginia became worse and went to bed and she remained in bed for the greater part of the two days of the conference. When we got back to London, I took her to see Sir George Savage. He said she must go at once to a nursing home in Twickenham and stay there for some weeks, remaining in bed. She had been to this nursing home several times before when there had been serious threatenings of breakdown. It was kept by a Miss Jean Thomas, who made a speciality of taking nerve or mental patients. She was somewhat emotional and adored Virginia, a combination which had its disadvantages, but old Savage thought well of her and Virginia liked her up to a point and was willing to go to her for a week or two.

It was at the interview with Savage that he made her a promise which led to catastrophe; he said that if she would agree to go to the nursing home for a week or two and rest

absolutely in bed under Jean's directions, she could go away
for a holiday in Somerset with me in August. We had more
than once stayed at an inn in the little village of Holford in
the Quantocks and we had planned to go and stay there for
some weeks in August. Virginia went into Jean's nursing
home on July 25 and she stayed there until August 11. She
appeared to be a good deal better and on August 11 we went
down to Asham meaning to stay there until August 23 when
we proposed to go to Holford. The nightmare closed in upon
us again during those twelve days. It became clear that she
was no better. She was terribly worried, full of delusions
about her own mind, sleepless, eating hardly anything. I
became convinced that at any moment she might fall into
complete despair and try to kill herself; what would the
position be if we were alone in a small inn in an isolated
Somerset village? To go off there with her in her present state
seemed to me to make a catastrophe almost inevitable.

On August 22 we went up to London on our way to Holford and stayed the night in Gordon Square with Vanessa.
In the afternoon I went to Savage, explained the situation,
and said that in my opinion it was terribly risky to take
Virginia in her present state of mind to a small inn in the
country. He rather pooh-poohed the danger and said that he
thought that in any case we must go, for if she was in the
state described by me, suddenly to tell her that she was not
well enough to go away would throw her into despair and
she would immediately try to kill herself. I had lost all confidence in old Savage and felt that I was in a hopeless
quandary. When I got back to Gordon Square, I discussed
the whole situation with Vanessa and with Roger, who
happened to be there. They agreed with me that it was
extremely dangerous to take Virginia to Holford. Roger
suggested that he should take me at once to Dr. Henry Head,
a brilliant physician whom he knew well, and see what he

would say. Head was a well-known consultant, a neurologist and an F.R.S. He was himself an intellectual and would understand a person like Virginia better than a man like Savage. We rang him up and he agreed to see me at once. I explained the situation and what I thought Virginia's mental condition was. He said that it was terribly risky to take her to Holford, but, as she had been told by Savage that she could go there, it would be still more disastrous suddenly to tell her that she was not well enough to go away. If we did that, she would almost certainly try to kill herself. I had better go with her as arranged next day to Holford and, of course, keep a continual and unobtrusive watch over her. It was possible that if I could get her to rest and eat there, she would begin slowly to mend. If I found that she got worse and more depressed, I must somehow or other get a friend to come down and stay as a second line of defence against an attempt at suicide. If then she got still worse and I felt that the situation was getting out of control, I must bring her back to town and try to induce her to come and see him (Head). I should write to him from time to time and keep him informed of how things were going on.

We went down to Holford on August 23. Fifty years ago it was a remote, lovely little village at the foot of the Quantock hills. It contained the pleasant Alfoxton or Alfoxden House in which William and Dorothy Wordsworth lived in 1797 and 1798. And only a few miles away in the village of Nether Stowey is the house where Coleridge lived. Walking on the top of the Quantocks above Holford with Wordsworth he began to compose *The Ancient Mariner*, and Dorothy's entry in her Journal for March 22 and 23 are:

22nd.—I spent the morning in starching and hanging out linen; walked through the wood in the evening, very cold.

2 3rd.—Coleridge dined with us. He brought the ballad finished. We walked with him to the Miner's house. A beautiful evening, very starry, the horned moon.

In 1913 the horned moon above Holford Coombe was the same as Dorothy had seen in 1798 and I don't think that really there had been much change in Nether Stowey and Holford and the Coombe since the February night when the Wordsworths and Coleridge walked to the Miner's house. Certainly if they had walked into the Plough Inn and joined us at dinner, they would have found it much the same as they had seen it 115 years before.

It was primitive but extraordinarily pleasant. The people who kept it—I have forgotten their name—were pure Holford country folk. I knew them well as I had stayed there before. As the days went by, they saw what state Virginia was in and they behaved with the greatest kindness, sensitiveness, and consideration. I don't suppose that today there is anywhere in Britain an inn such as the Plough was in 1913. The food was delicious, the most English of English food which could hold its own with the best cuisine of the world, but which people who for the past 150 years have despised all English cooking have never heard of. Nothing could be better than the bread, butter, cream, and eggs and bacon of the Somersetshire breakfast with which you began your morning. The beef, mutton, and lamb were always magnificent and perfectly cooked; enormous hams, cured by themselves and hanging from the rafters in the kitchen, were so perfect that for years we used to have them sent to us from time to time and find them as good as or better than the peach-fed Virginian hams which one used to buy for vast sums from Fortnum and Mason. As for the drink that they offered you, I do not say that you could compare it with, say, Ch. Margaux or La Romanée-Conti or Deidesheimer

Kieselberg Riesling Trockenbeerenauslese, but they gave you beer and cider which only a narrow minded, finicky drinker would fail to find delicious.

For the first week at Holford Virginia was very up and down. She insisted that she was perfectly well; she slept badly; it was with the greatest difficulty that she could be persuaded to eat; she certainly suffered from various delusions, for instance that people laughed at her. I had veronal tablets and I gave her one when she could not sleep. After the first seven days she was definitely worse—more depressed. The strain for one person to look after her was considerable, for I had to be on the alert continually, day and night, and yet, if possible, not give her the feeling of being watched. I had arranged with Ka Cox (who later married Will Arnold-Forster), a great friend of both of us, that, if I found it absolutely necessary, I would wire to her to come and join us. After the first week I came to the conclusion that it was not safe for one person alone to look after Virginia and I wired to Ka. She arrived on September 2. She was extremely good, but nothing could really be done. We lived the quietest possible life, walking a bit and reading. Things grew steadily worse and it became impossible to get Virginia to eat or to try to rest—the only things which might have done her good. After a few days both Ka and I agreed that it was not safe to go on at Holford and that I must, somehow or other, induce Virginia to come up to London and see a doctor.

What happened then shows that the working of the human mind, ill or well, insane or sane, is extraordinary and unpredictable. I went to Virginia and said that I thought we should not go on any longer in Holford; that I thought she was ill and so did her doctor and we were convinced that if she ate well and tried to rest she would soon recover as she had several times before; that she was convinced that she was not ill, that her condition was due to her own faults, and that eating and resting made her worse. I suggested that we should return to London at once, go to another doctor—any doctor whom she should choose; she should put her case to him and I would put mine; if he said that she was not ill, I would accept his verdict and would not worry her again about eating or resting or going to a nursing home; but if he said she was ill, then she would accept his verdict and undergo what treatment he might prescribe.

At first Virginia objected to the whole idea, but after some argument she agreed. When I asked her what doctor she would go to, she amazed me by saying at once that she would go to Head. It seemed to me at the time a kind of miracle. It was to Head that I wanted her to go, but I had always anticipated insuperable difficulties to getting her agreement to consult him. She could not possibly have known that *I* had consulted him, and, had she known, in her then state of mind, it would naturally have influenced her against him. When she said that she would go to Head, I felt for a moment as if she had read my thoughts, had taken the thought out of my mind. I do not think that she did this in any sense of thought reading. We often knew instinctively what the other was thinking, as is so often the case when two people live together continually and intimately. But I have never felt that this is in any strict sense of the words thought transference. We thought so often about the same things at the same time, even without talking about them, and therefore often at a particular moment we could guess what at that precise moment was in the other's mind. It is probable that what influenced her to choose Head was that Roger used to talk about him as not only an intelligent doctor, but also an intelligent man—and the two things do not necessarily go together.

I wired to Head for an appointment and on Monday afternoon, September 8, we took the train from Bridgwater to London. The journey had that terrible quality of the most real of real life and at the same time of a horrible dream, a nightmare. Virginia was in the blackest despair and there was, I knew, danger that she might at any moment try to kill herself by jumping out of the train. However, we reached London in safety and went to spend the night in Brunswick Square. Next day we went to see Head in the afternoon. I gave my account of what had happened and Virginia gave hers. He told her that she was completely mistaken about her own condition; she was ill, ill like a person who had a cold or typhoid fever; but if she took his advice and did what he prescribed, her symptoms would go and she would be quite well again, able to think and write and read; she must go to a nursing home and stay in bed for a few weeks, resting and eating.

We returned to Brunswick Square and then a catastrophe happened. Vanessa came and talked to Virginia, who seemed to become more cheerful. Savage had not known that we were seeing Head and a rather awkward situation had arisen about that. Head asked me to see Savage and explain how it had come about that I had brought Virginia to see him; he wanted me to arrange for him to have a consultation with Savage next day. I went off to Savage, leaving Ka with Virginia. I was with Savage at 6.30 when I got a telephone message from Ka to say that Virginia had fallen into a deep sleep. I hurried back to Brunswick Square and found that Virginia was lying on her bed breathing heavily and unconscious. She had taken the veronal tablets from my box and swallowed a very large dose. I telephoned to Head and he came, bringing a nurse. Luckily Geoffrey Keynes, Maynard's brother, now Sir Geoffrey, then a young surgeon, was staying in the house. He and I got into his car and drove off as fast as we could to his hospital to get a stomach pump. The drive, like everything else during those days, had the nightmare feeling about it. It was a beautiful sunny day; we drove full speed through the traffic, Geoffrey shouting to policemen that he was a surgeon 'urgent, urgent!' and they passed us through as if we were a fire engine. I do not know what time it was when we got back to Brunswick Square, but Head, Geoffrey, and the nurse were hard at work until nearly 1 o'clock in the morning. Head returned at 9 next morning (Wednesday) and said that Virginia was practically out of danger. She did not recover consciousness until the Thursday morning.

The responsibility for the catastrophe was in no way Ka's; it was mine. At Holford I had always kept my case containing the veronal locked. In the turmoil of arriving and settling in at Brunswick Square and then going to Head, I must have forgotten to lock it. When I went to Savage, Virginia lay down on her bed and Ka quite rightly left her so that she might if possible get some sleep. My case was in the room and she must have found that it was unlocked and have taken the veronal. I suppose, as a truthful autobiographer, I ought to record two psychological bad marks against myself in connection with this catastrophe. Though I was the cause of it, I did not at the time and have not since felt the misery and remorse that many people would think I ought to feel. This was due partly to the general fact, recorded by me in *Sowing* (pp. 15-16, 21-22),that I seem to be without a sense of sin and to be unable to feel remorse for something which has been done and cannot be undone—I seem to be mentally and morally unable to cry over spilt milk. In this particular case I felt that it was almost impossible sooner or later not to make a mistake of the kind. For the previous two months I had had to be on the watch day and night to prevent a disaster of this kind. No person by himself could really do this, and even after Ka came and we were two, it was not enough. This is shown by the fact that after the catastrophe, we had for weeks four trained nurses, so that there were always two in the room with Virginia day and night. The second psychological black mark—probably not unconnected with the first—is that, after that appalling day and night, when I went to bed at 1 in the morning, I immediately fell into a profound and peaceful sleep and did not wake up until seven hours later. This again confirms what I said in *Growing* (p. 228) that the only really bad sleepless night I can remember to have had in my life was in the village of Kataragama in Ceylon.

As soon as Virginia regained consciousness, I was faced with the problem of what to do. In those days, if anyone was in Virginia's mental state, dangerously suicidal, it was customary to certify them. The procedure took place before a magistrate who, on a doctor's certificate, made an order for the reception and detention of the person either in an asylum or in a nursing home authorized to take certified patients. Doctors were naturally unwilling to take the risk of leaving a suicidal patient uncertified in a private house. I was against certification, but agreed to go and see some mental homes which took certified patients. I think I went to see two or three which Head or Savage recommended. They seemed to me to be dreadful, large gloomy buildings enclosed by high walls, dismal trees, and despair. I told the doctors that I was prepared to do anything required by them if they would agree to her not being certified. They agreed not to certify her, provided I could arrange for her to go into the country accompanied by me and two (at one time four) nurses. This meant that it was impossible to take her to Asham, because it could not accommodate two or four nurses and was in any case too remote.

George Duckworth came to our rescue and offered to lend me his country house, Dalingridge Place. George was Virginia's half-brother, being a son of her mother by her first husband, Herbert Duckworth. He was a man of the world or at any rate what I think a man of the world in excelsis should be. As a young man he was, it was said, an Adonis worshipped by all the great and non-great ladies. He was still terribly good looking at the age of 45. A very good cricketer, Eton and Trinity College, Cambridge; he knew everyone who mattered; was a friend and private secretary of Austen Chamberlain, and landed in the comfortable job of Secretary to the Royal Commission on Historical Monuments and a knighthood. Married to Lady Margaret Herbert, he built himself a large house, Dalingridge Place, near East Grinstead, which had every modern convenience for a gentleman's residence including some highland cattle. He was an extremely kind man and, I think, very fond of Vanessa and Virginia. He had at that time a London house as well as Dalingridge, but Dalingridge was in full working order with cook, parlourmaid, housemaids, and gardeners. So all we had to do was to go down there and settle in.

There were many things to clear up in London, for we still had Cliffords Inn and all our possessions were there. There was a great deal of packing which, at the best of times, is one of the dreariest of occupations, and it was not until September 20 that we got away to Dalingridge. I took four mental nurses with us and Ka came and stayed for a few days. For the next two months—until November 18—we lived at Dalingridge.

I do not know what the present state of knowledge with regard to nervous and mental diseases is in the year 1963; in 1913 it was desperately meagre. After the catastrophe I practically gave up Savage as a serious doctor (though I still consulted him formally in order not to hurt or offend him) and went to Maurice Craig, the leading Harley Street specialist in nervous and mental diseases. He was a much younger and a more intelligent man and doctor than Savage, and he not only took charge of the case during its acute stage over the next two years, he also, for the rest of Virginia's life, remained the mental specialist to whom we went for advice when we wanted it. Over the years I consulted five neurologists or mental specialists, all at the head of their profession: Sir George Savage, Henry Head, Sir Maurice Craig, Maurice Wright, and T. B. Hyslop. They were all men of the highest principle and good will; they were all (or had been) brilliant doctors; I have no doubt that they knew as much about the human mind and its illnesses as any of their contemporaries. It may sound arrogant on my part when I say that it seemed to me that what they knew amounted to practically nothing. They had not the slightest idea of the nature or the cause of Virginia's mental state, which resulted in her suddenly or gradually losing touch with the real world, so that she lived in a world of delusions and became a danger to herself and other people. Not knowing how or why this had happened to her, naturally they had no real or scientific knowledge of how to cure her. All they could say was that she was suffering from neurasthenia and that, if she could be induced or compelled to rest and eat and if she could be prevented from committing suicide, she would recover.

The course of Virginia's illness vitally affected the course of our lives, and therefore from the autobiographical point of view I feel that I should deal with it in detail; but I also think that it ought to be of great intrinsic interest to describe the impact of illness or insanity upon such a remarkable mind as Virginia's. Her mental breakdown lasted in an acute form from the summer of 1913 to the autumn of 1915, but it was not absolutely continuous. There were two insane stages, one lasting from the summer of 1913 to the summer of 1914 and the other from January, 1915, to the winter of 1915; there was an interlude of sanity between the summer of 1914 and January, 1915. There was one remarkable fact about the two insane stages which throws light upon the primitive and chaotic condition of medical knowledge about insanity in 1913. There was at that time apparently a type of insanity scientifically known as manic-depressive. People suffering from it had alternating attacks of violent excitement (manic) and acute depression (depressive). When I cross-examined Virginia's doctors, they said that she was suffering from neurasthenia, not from manic-depressive insanity, which was entirely different. But as far as symptoms were concerned, Virginia *was* suffering from manic-depressive insanity. In the first stage of the illness from 1914 practically every symptom was the exact opposite of those in the second stage in 1915. In the first stage she was in the depths of depression, would hardly eat or talk, was suicidal. In the second she was in a state of violent excitement and wild euphoria, talking incessantly for long periods of time. In the first stage she was violently opposed to the nurses and they had the greatest difficulty in getting her to do anything; she wanted me to be with her continually and for a week or two I was the only person able to get her to eat anything. In the second stage of violent excitement, she was violently hostile to me, would not talk to me or allow me to come into her room. She was occasionally violent with the nurses, but she tolerated them in a way which was the opposite of her behaviour to them in the first stage.

As a person with no medical training and with experience of only one case of mental illness, my opinion about the nature and symptoms of Virginia's case is probably of little value, but I watched and studied it intensively for months, and I have very little doubt that some of my conclusions were right. For instance, practically all Virginia's (insane) symptoms were exaggerations of psychological phenomena observable in a large number of people, and particularly in her, when perfectly sane. You can be quite sanely angry, but if you get so angry as completely to lose control of yourself, you may be insanely angry. Virginia's fits of violence against the nurses during both attacks were the result of insane anger of this kind. The same thing applied, I think, to the alternation between depression and excitement, the depressive-manic stages. Nearly everyone experiences this kind of alternation in ordinary sane life—and Virginia certainly did when she was quite well. When I was not in good spirits or grumpy as a child, my nurse used to say: 'You must have got out of your bed on the wrong side.' Everyone knows what getting out of bed on the wrong side means. You suddenly feel that the bottom has dropped out of your world and you have fallen into a pit of desolation, futility, and hopelessness, and it is when you yourself can see no reason for this misery and despair that they are at their worst. This mood again and again seems to follow or to be followed by a feeling of unusual well-being and happiness. You get out of bed on the right side and the day seems to be brighter, the sun warmer, the air more sparkling, the coffee more fragrant than it has been before. And there is no more a discernible reason for your happiness than there was for your depression.

My nurse, who had imbibed the traditional knowledge of the human mind that nearly all nurses have possessed since Odysseus's nurse Eurycleia 2800 years ago burst into tears when she recognized the scar on his leg, used to call out to me when I was boisterously and unreasonably happy: 'Now then, Master Leonard, now then, you know there'll be tears before evening.' Sunt lacrimae rerum, said Virgil in one of the most beautiful and untranslatable of Latin hexameters. There always were, as my nurse and Virgil said, lacrimae rerum, tears before evening. The use of the word rerum, in the plural, by Virgil shows that tears were the same 2000 years ago as they are today; 'tears for things', Virgil says, not for any particular thing—just tears before evening, as my nurse said.

In the first weeks at Dalingridge the most difficult and

distressing problem was to get Virginia to eat. If left to herself, she would have eaten nothing at all and would have gradually starved to death. Here again her psychology and behaviour were only a violent exaggeration of what they were when she was well and sane. When she was well, she was essentially a happy and gay person; she enjoyed the ordinary things of everyday life, and among them food and drink. Yet there was always something strange, something slightly irrational in her attitude towards food. It was extraordinarily difficult ever to get her to eat enough to keep her strong and well. Superficially I suppose it might have been said that she had a (quite unnecessary) fear of becoming fat; but there was something deeper than that, at the back of her mind or in the pit of her stomach a taboo against eating. Pervading her insanity generally there was always a sense of some guilt, the origin and exact nature of which I could never discover; but it was attached in some peculiar way particularly to food and eating. In the early acute, suicidal stage of the depression, she would sit for hours overwhelmed with hopeless melancholia, silent, making no response to anything said to her. When the time for a meal came, she would pay no attention whatsoever to the plate of food put before her and, if the nurses tried to get her to eat something, she became enraged. I could usually induce her to eat a certain amount, but it was a terrible process. Every meal took an hour or two; I had to sit by her side, put a spoon or fork in her hand, and every now and again ask her very quietly to eat and at the same time touch her arm or hand. Every five minutes or so she might automatically eat a spoonful.

This excruciating business of food, among other things, taught me a lesson about insanity which I found very difficult to learn—it is useless to argue with an insane person. What tends to break one down, to reduce one to gibbering despair when one is dealing with mental illness, is the terrible sanity of the insane. In ordinary life, as her writings, and particularly her essays, show, Virginia had an extraordinarily clear and logical mind; one of the most remarkable things about her was the rare combination of this strong intellect with a soaring imagination. There were moments or periods during her illness, particularly in the second excited stage, when she was what could be called 'raving mad' and her thoughts and speech became completely unco-ordinated, and she had no contact with reality. Except for these periods, she remained all through her illness, even when most insane, terribly sane in three-quarters of her mind. The point is that her insanity was in her premises, in her beliefs. She believed, for instance, that she was not ill, that her symptoms were due to her own 'faults'; she believed that she was hearing voices when the voices were her own imaginings; she heard the birds outside her window talking Greek; she believed that the doctors and nurses were in conspiracy against her. These beliefs were insane because they were in fact contradicted by reality. But given these beliefs as premises for conclusions and actions, all Virginia's actions and conclusions were logical and rational; and her power of arguing conclusively from false premises was terrific. It was therefore useless to attempt to argue with her: you could no more convince her that her premises were wrong than you can convince a man who believes he is Christ that he is mistaken. It was still more useless to argue with her about what you wanted her to do, e.g. eat her breakfast, because if her premises were true, she could prove and did prove conclusively to you that she ought not to eat her breakfast.

We lived at Dalingridge, as I said, until November 18. At one time we had four nurses, two on duty in the day, and two at night. For some time Virginia was extremely violent with the nurses, but after about a month she became slightly better and it was possible to have only two nurses. It was one of the most perfect autumns for weather that I can ever remember, the gentle, windless, cloudless days of an Indian summer. There is, I think, not much to be said for the country round East Grinstead and to live in a Gentleman's Residence and a large garden belonging to someone else with someone else's servants, but four mental nurses of one's own, is not a pleasant experience. But there was a lawn and terrace at Dalingridge from which one had a magnificent view over the Sussex weald to the downs, and one could see the gap where Lewes lay and one knew that just through the gap there were the watermeadows of the Ouse valley and, in the hollow below the hill under the elm trees, Asham. When Virginia became calmer, I used to play croquet with her on this terrace after tea, and in the warm, peaceful, soft and sunny evening a kind of peace descended upon us as we looked towards the long hazy line of downs and the gap where Lewes lay. Virginia was anxious that we should leave Dalingridge and go and live at Asham.

After much consultation with doctors it was decided that it would be safe to go to Asham with two nurses in the middle of November, and this we did. We settled down and lived at Asham until August, 1914; early in the year I gave up Cliffords Inn. Virginia very slowly got better. In January it was considered safe to have only one nurse, and finally towards the end of February the last nurse went. Not that Virginia was fully recovered. She was still liable to moments of excitement and it was always difficult to get her to eat enough; she read, but was not able to work. I occasionally went up for a night or two to London and I once stayed for a week with Lytton at Lockeridge near Marlborough. When I was away Vanessa or Ka came to Asham and stayed with Virginia. Then in April it was decided that it was advisable that she should have a change and that we could safely go to Cornwall.

We went to St. Ives and Carbis Bay for three weeks, staying in lodgings. It was in some ways a nerve-racking business: Virginia was not fully recovered; she was nervous of
being with strangers; her delusions persisted not very far
below the surface of her mind; there was still continual
trouble about food and sleep. But Cornwall and St. Ives had
a nostalgic romance for her as it had for all her family. It was
the romance of childhood which can give to places and
memories a brilliance and glory unfading even when age has
destroyed all our other illusions. Every summer when
Virginia was a child the family went and stayed in Talland
House, St. Ives, and their time there remained in her
memory as summer days of immaculate happiness. *To the
Lighthouse* is bathed in the light of this happiness and, whenever she returned to Cornwall, she recaptured some of it.
This happened to some extent in the weeks which we spent
in Cornwall that April; memory calmed the jangled mind
and nerves.

We returned to Asham on May 1 and for the next three
months lived as far as possible a vegetative life. That
Virginia was not fully recovered is shown by the fact that I
still kept a daily record of whether she had a good, fair, or
bad day and a good, fair, or bad night, whether she had had
to take aspirin or veronal at night, and of similar facts about
her health. She read, but did not write, and *The Voyage Out*
still remained unpublished in the hands of Duckworth. In
many ways 1914 and 1915 were years which we simply lost
out of our lives, for we lived them in the atmosphere of
catastrophe or impending catastrophe. I did a certain amount
of work. I did some reviewing for the *New Statesman*, the
New Weekly, the *Co-operative News*, and *The Times Literary
Supplement*, and I began to write a book about the Co-
operative Movement, which was commissioned by the Home
University Library and, after a curious business with

Williams & Norgate who commissioned it, was eventually published by Allen & Unwin under the title *Co-operation and the Future of Industry*. I seemed in process of becoming a kind of authority on the Movement, for I made a dash from Asham in July to Keswick for a night in order to open a discussion on the Co-operative Movement at a small Fabian Society conference. The Webbs were there and so was Bernard Shaw, who at one point gave me the only serious dressing down I ever had from him, my sin—a somewhat inadvertent sin—having been to use the word 'natives' of Indians.

Walter Lippmann, then unknown, but later in life one of the most famous of American columnists, was also at the conference. We travelled down together from Keswick to Euston. I only saw him once or twice in my life again and I do not think that I had a premonition of his future eminence. But I liked him very much as a man and felt him to be both intelligent and sensitive, and we talked almost without stopping through the long hours of the train journey. Almost at once our talk became much more intimate than is usual with a new and casual acquaintance, so that I remember some of it as vividly after 50 years as if it had happened only a year ago. In June I had reviewed Freud's *Psychopathology of Everyday Life* in *The New Weekly* and before writing it I read *The Interpretation of Dreams*, which had been published the previous year. I am, I think not unreasonably, rather proud of having in 1914 recognized and understood the greatness of Freud and the importance of what he was doing when this was by no means common.[1] Somehow or other Lippmann and

[1] People, among whom I include myself, so often quite honestly, but mistakenly, credit themselves with this kind of foresight that I turned up my review in order to see what in fact I had said about Freud. I quote the following, which is almost exactly what I would write about Freud today: 'One is tempted to say that he suffers from all the most brilliant defects of genius. Whether one believes in his

I got on to the subject of Freud, psychoanalysis, and insanity. There are few things more unexpected and more exciting than suddenly finding someone of intelligence and understanding who at once with complete frankness will go with one below what is the usual surface of conversation and discussion.

Virginia and I planned to go away for a month or more in August to the Cheviot country in Northumberland and we engaged rooms in the Cottage Hotel in Wooler. When the war broke out, we hesitated for a moment, but in the end decided to go. On August 7 we travelled up to Wooler and stayed there until September 4, when we moved on to Coldstream across the border. We stayed at Coldstream until September 15, when we returned to London. It was strange and rather disturbing to be away from everyone whom we knew in a small hotel in Northumberland during those first weeks of war. The air of Wooler was always thick with false rumours. I must have heard almost at its source one of the most famous of these false stories which spread like a con-

---

theories or not, one is forced to admit that he writes with great subtlety of mind, a broad and sweeping imagination more characteristic of the poet than the scientist or medical practitioner. This wide imaginative power accounts for his power of grasping in the midst of intricate analysis of details the bearing of those details on a much wider field of details . . . his works are often a series of brilliant and suggestive hints. And yet from another point of view this series of hints is subtly knit together into a whole in such a way that the full meaning of a passage in one book is often to be obtained only by reference to some passage in another book. No one is really competent to give a final judgment upon even the *Psychopathology of Everyday Life* who has not studied the *Interpretation of Dreams* and Freud's more distinctly pathological writings.' And after saying that many people will say of Freud's books: 'Very interesting but too far fetched', I say that one cannot discuss the justice of such a verdict in a short review, I can only state my opinion that 'there can be no doubt that there is a substantial amount of truth in the main thesis of Freud's book, and that truth is of great value'.

tagious disease over the whole country. For one evening a man came into the bar of the hotel and in some excitement told us all that he had just come by train from Newcastle, and, while he was waiting in the station, he saw trainload after trainload of Russian soldiers with fur hats and guns pass through on their way to the south and to France.

I am inclined to think that the Cheviots are the loveliest country in England. Mountains some distance away create in many places superb landscapes, as for instance in Greece or when you look to the Sierra Nevada across the great Spanish plain. But to live in mountains is like living with someone who always talks at the top of his, or it may be her, voice. For beauty in everyday life I prefer hills which only occasionally pretend to be mountains, for instance the South Downs of Sussex, or mountains like the Cheviots which usually pretend to be hills. The Cheviots never shout and never insist. They have a superb sweep, but there is an extraordinary stillness and peace in the beauty of their forms; and nowhere in the world is the light and colour of sky and earth more lovely than in this bit of England—due, perhaps, to its being such a narrow strip of land between two seas.

Early in September we moved on across the border and the Tweed to Coldstream. This is very different country from the Cheviots, but the border and Tweed valley are in their own peaceful way of great beauty. And I must recur to the great subject of food. We stayed in rooms kept by a woman appropriately called Miss Scott. The many English people who think that good cooking begins only on the other side of the English Channel will never believe that a meal at Miss Scott's could be compared with one in Touraine or Provence. But in its own very different way Miss Scott's cooking was perfect. I still remember the bread and scones, the porridge, the scotch broth, the trout, the mutton, the butter, milk, and cream. It deserved the three stars for cuisine which you will find appended in the Michelin Guide to many restaurants and to places like Montluçon and Vienne.

When we got back to London in the middle of September the problem arose of where we should live. Virginia had barely recovered and it was obvious that any strain, mental or physical, was dangerous to her. I was convinced that she could not possibly, in her present state, stand the strain of London life, but she herself was always in favour of living in London. We spent several weeks looking at houses in London, Hampstead, Richmond, and Twickenham and we also went down to Asham for a time. Eventually we took rooms at 17 The Green, Richmond, temporarily, meaning to find a house in Richmond. We moved in on October 16. In 1914, before the motor car had destroyed its beauty and peace, Richmond Green was a charming place to live in. No. 17 was an old substantial house on the east side; on the south was the lovely Maids of Honour Row and the old palace. We had a large, comfortable, well-proportioned room on the first floor overlooking the Green.

The house was kept and the rooms let to us by a Belgian woman, Mrs. le Grys. She was an extremely nice, plump, excitable flibbertigibbet, about 35 to 40 years old. You never knew what was going to happen next in her house. Mrs. le Grys had only one servant, a typical overworked 'skivvy' of 50 years ago, wild and grubby, perpetually slamming doors and dropping with a loud crash trays laden with plates, cups, and saucers. I remember two of Lizzy's feats. One morning when I was in my bath I heard cries on the landing: 'Fire! Fire!' Putting on a coat and pair of trousers, I went out and found smoke pouring out of a room on the floor above; a big screen in flames was flung out of the window on to the pavement in front of the house. Lizzy had put a large piece of newspaper 'to draw up the fire', the newspaper had 'caught', things on the mantelpiece had 'caught', the screen had 'caught', even the wallpaper had 'caught'. It was a miracle that the whole house hadn't 'caught'.

Having escaped death by fire, a few days later we barely escaped death by water, again thanks to Lizzy. We were awakened by a tremendous throbbing and thumping and drumming and the whole house began shaking; it sounded, as Virginia said, as if there were a motor omnibus on the roof trying to start. I jumped out of bed and rushed into the bathroom, which seemed to be the focus of the din. When I turned on the taps, steam burst forth in such volume that it seemed as if it must be the prelude to a volcanic eruption. In fact large pieces of pipe, rust, and dark red water erupted. Why the boiler in the basement did not blow up, I do not know, for Lizzy had contrived to light an enormous kitchen fire when there was no water in the pipes. After that Lizzy was given notice by Mrs. le Grys and departed. In a way I was sorry to see her go, to know that I should never again see her grubby face and wild distracted eye or hear her breaking the crockery. I like to contemplate people who are the perfect prototypes of their class, even when the class is that of the 19th-century lodging house skivvy. If there is the platonic idea of the damp soul of a housemaid laid up in heaven, it will be the image of poor Lizzy's soul.

We settled down in Richmond and it seemed as if things were going well. We decided to try to find a house in Richmond and towards the end of 1914 we went to see Hogarth House in Paradise Road and fell in love with it. It was very beautiful. In 1720 Lord Suffield had built a large country house in a good sized garden; in the 19th century it had been sold and divided into two houses, one still called Suffield House and the other Hogarth House. Every room except one was perfectly proportioned and pannelled; there was quite a good garden. There were the usual hitches, alarms and excursions, over the negotiations, but eventually early in 1915 I obtained a lease and we were to move in in March. Virginia's health seemed to have improved and she had begun to work and write again. I was doing a good deal of work for the *New Statesman* and had begun a book commissioned by the Fabian Society on international government. Then quite suddenly in the middle of February there was again catastrophe. Virginia had had some symptoms of headache and had not slept well, but this seemed no more serious than what had occasionally happened during the previous six months. But one morning she was having breakfast in bed and I was talking to her when without warning she became violently excited and distressed. She thought her mother was in the room and began to talk to her. It was the beginning of the terrifying second stage of her mental breakdown. It was, as I have said, completely different from, almost the exact opposite of, the first stage. I had to get nurses at once, and, although Mrs. le Grys behaved admirably, it was obvious that we could not turn her house into a mental hospital. It was necessary to get Hogarth House ready for us to move into immediately, to take our furniture which was being warehoused and put it into the house and find servants. Annie, the cook, and Lily, the house parlourmaid, whom we had had at Asham, agreed to come, and early in March we moved into Hogarth House with four mental nurses.

The first fortnight was indeed terrifying. For a time Virginia was very violent with the nurses. The violence then subsided a little, but she began to talk incessantly. It is difficult now to remember accurately how long the various stages lasted, but I think in this stage she talked almost without stopping for two or three days, paying no attention to anyone in the room or anything said to her. For about a day what she said was coherent; the sentences meant something, though it was nearly all wildly insane. Then gradually it became completely incoherent, a mere jumble of dissociated words. After another day the stream of words diminished and finally she fell into a coma. I had a Richmond doctor, one of the best G.P.'s I have ever known, and the mental specialist, Maurice Craig, came down several times from London. They assured me, even when she was completely unconscious in the coma, that she would recover. They were right. When she came out of the coma, she was exhausted. but much calmer; then very slowly she began to recover, The number of nurses was reduced to two and then to one, and towards the end of the summer we went down to stay at Asham with the one nurse. By the end of the year she was well enough to do without nurses.

Quite apart from Virginia's madness, life in Hogarth House during the first six months of 1915 acquired a curious atmosphere of wild unreality. Strange, ridiculous scenes took place. Here is one, a kind of tragicomedy inserted in the tragedy. In the previous year when we were at Asham, we had engaged a house parlourmaid called Lily. Lily was one of those persons for whom I feel the same kind of affection as I do for cats and dogs. She was an extremely nice character, but temperamentally born to certain disaster. She was not feeble-minded, but simple-minded and she found it almost impossible to refuse anyone anything. When we wanted a servant at Asham we went to a Lewes agency and they gave us Lily's name and a reference to a convent at Haywards Heath. We took up the reference and a nun came out to see us. She told us that Lily had been seduced and had had an illegitimate child. She was not a Roman Catholic, but the convent had taken her in and cared for her and the child. The nun said that she was in many ways a very nice girl, but weak; if we took her as servant, we ought to 'keep an eye on her'; she hoped that we would let the convent know how things went on, as they would look after the child.

People like Lily have characters which seem to me psychologically fascinating. She was pure English, in fact a regular Sussex country girl. In England and in Sussex villages, the young women, even when they have illegitimate children, never, of course, have tragic or complicated characters, though the author of *Tess of the D'Urbervilles* and *Jude the Obscure* was an English writer who thought otherwise. The squeegee of Church of England and the rural middle class, the Sunday school and the rector and the rector's wife, the squeegee of a religion and morality which have scarcely any standard of value except that of respectability or disreputability, had passed over and flattened poor Lily—she had passed from the category of respectability into that of disreputability; it and she were quite simple and that was the end of it. Unfortunately for her and for us it was not the end of it. If Lily had been born in the neighbourhood of Skvoreschniki instead of Haywards Heath, she would have fitted, without any alteration except of name, into a Dostoevsky novel. If you had called her Marya Timofyevna instead of Lily, you might have seen at once that she was just another Lebyadkin's sister or even a female village Myshkin. These 'sillies', as Tolstoy called them, are terribly simple and at the same time tragically complicated.[1] You could almost see this in Lily's face; she had a long, pale, weak, rather pretty, sad face. There was a gentleness in her voice and manners which was certainly unusual in country girls of her class in 1913. And in 1913 in Haywards Heath fate had marked her down for disaster no less certainly than it had marked down the House of Atreus for disaster nearly 3,000 years before in Mycenae.

This is how fate set to work in Hogarth House, Richmond.

[1] The strange psychology of the 'silly' is extraordinarily interesting. I wrote something about it in *Sowing*, pp. 71 and 137.

One night at 3 o'clock in the morning I was suddenly woken up by Annie, the cook, bursting into my bedroom and crying aloud: 'There is a soldier in the kitchen; there is a soldier in the kitchen—and Lily's there.' I went down to the kitchen in the basement and found that indeed a soldier—a sergeant —was there and Lily too in some disarray. When I opened the door, the sergeant dashed past me down the passage, through the door into the garden (by which he had apparently come into the house) and presumably over a wall into the street—leaving behind him in the kitchen his cane. I told Lily that she had better go up to bed and that I would talk to her in the morning. Our conversation in the morning was very distressing. It was a moment at which Virginia was still terribly ill; it was essential that she should be kept completely undisturbed and unexcited, and one could not risk her being startled by soldiers dashing about the house and garden in the early hours of the morning. I told this to Lily and she was miserably contrite, saying that she had no excuse and had behaved abominably and had no right to expect to be kept on. I said that I thought I had better think the whole thing over, and, unless she objected, I must let the nuns know what had happened and consult them, as when I had engaged her they had asked me to keep in touch with them and let them know how she went on. She agreed to this and in fact seemed to be eager that I should consult the nuns. So I wrote to the convent and one of the nuns immediately came to Richmond to see me. She had a talk with Lily and then asked me not to dismiss her as she was full of remorse and had, the nun said, 'learnt her lesson'.

I agreed to this and so Lily remained. But she was very depressed and I was hardly surprised when she came to me after a few weeks and said that she thought she should go and try to find another place. It was not because I had in any way reproached her after I had agreed to her remaining, she said, because I hadn't done so; it was that she reproached herself; 'Mrs. Woolf was so good in taking me and now I keep on feeling that I have done her harm and I shall never again be happy here; it's better that I should go at once.' I said that I should be sorry if she went and that before finally deciding she ought to consult the nuns, and this she did. The nun wrote to me that she was very sorry, but she thought that Lily had better go as she had worked herself up into such a state of contrition and unhappiness that she would never settle down again with us in Richmond. So Lily left. There is no doubt that she was tragically sensitive and in Haywards Heath born to disaster. Yes, if she had been born in Skvoreschniki, she might have been Lebyadkin's sister and I suppose that she would have been seduced and ruined by Stavrogin. Her ruin in Haywards Heath was different, being, as I have said, English and presided over by the Church of England, Roman Catholics, and rural middle class and regulated by me and the nun on the highest principles and with scrupulous decorum. Not that I think it made much difference to poor Lily. As far as I can remember, the nuns told me that they had found her another place, but that after a time they lost touch with her. We never saw or heard from her again. Her epitaph has been written by two poets, one of the 17th and the other of the 18th century. 'When lovely woman stoops to folly, and finds, too late, that men betray, what charm can soothe her melancholy?' 'There is no armour against fate.'

The year 1915 with its private nightmare dragged itself slowly to an end. Meanwhile the public nightmare of the war also dragged itself on, but became continually more oppressive and terrible. In the first year of the war I was so entangled in the labyrinth of Virginia's illness—the psychological struggle, the perpetual problems of nurses and doctors, the sense of shifting insecurity—that I do not think that I had time to consider my own personal relation to the war and the fighting. But as the year waned and the fighting waxed and Virginia gradually grew better, I was forced to consider my position. Of my five brothers the two youngest, Cecil and Philip, joined up from the first day of the war. They had a passion for horses and riding and had joined the Inns of Court regiment a year or two before 1914. They were actually in camp with the regiment somewhere near Dover when the war broke out and they went straight into the Hussars, being given commissions. Two other brothers, Harold and Edgar, joined up later and took commissions, one in the R.A.S.C. and the other in an infantry regiment. On the other hand many of my most intimate friends were Conscientious Objectors and claimed exemption before the Tribunals which were set up when conscription was introduced. Personally I was, in a sense, 'against the war': I thought, and still think, that it was a senseless and useless war for which the Austrian and German governments were mainly responsible, but which our government probably could have prevented and should never have become involved in. (In this it was unlike the war of 1939 which, as soon as Hitler came to power in Germany, was inevitable.) But I have never been a complete pacifist; once the war had broken out it seemed to me that the Germans must be resisted and I therefore could not be a Conscientious Objector.

My brothers, Cecil and Philip, were in 1915 in training with their regiment in Mayfield, north of Lewes, and they used to come over to Asham to see us from time to time. They were anxious that I should join up and they assured me that, if I did, they could get me into their regiment. I think that, if I had not been married or even if Virginia had been well, I should probably have joined up, because, though I hated the war, I felt and still feel an irresistible desire to experience everything. When it became clear that sooner or later there would be conscription, I decided to let things take their course; if I were called up and put into the army, I would try to get a commission in my brothers' regiment. But the prospect was terribly disturbing. Virginia's state was still precarious; it was only with the greatest difficulty and by incessant watchfulness that she could be induced to live the kind of life which would allow her recovery to continue and consolidate.

When I saw that I should very soon be called up, I went to Dr. Maurice Wright to consult him both as a doctor and a friend. He was the doctor to whom, when I returned on leave from Ceylon, I had gone to see whether he could cure me of my trembling hands.[1] He also knew everything about Virginia, for I had consulted him when she was at her worst. He was, moreover, an exceptionally nice and very intelligent man. I was surprised to find him in the uniform of a colonel or it may even have been a brigadier. He was in fact head of the R.A.M.C. district which included Richmond and Surrey. I explained the situation to him and told him that I had come to him, rather as a friend than a doctor, to hear what he felt about it. He said that he thought it might be disastrous to Virginia if I were called up; he did not think that I was medically the kind of person who ought to be a private in the army and, having treated me unsuccessfully for a nervous disease, he could conscientiously give me a certificate to produce at my medical examination. He gave me the following certificate, with which, to tell the truth, I did not and do not entirely (medically) agree:

Mr. L. S. Woolf has been known to me for some years and has been previously under my care. Mr. L. S. Woolf is in my opinion entirely unfit for Military Service and would inevitably break down under the conditions of

[1] See *Sowing*, pp. 100-101.

178

active service. Mr. L. S. Woolf has definite nervous dis-
abilities, and in addition an Inherited Nervous Tremor
which is quite uncontrollable.

In 1916 I was duly called up and on May 30, with this
certificate in my pocket, presented myself at Kingston
Barracks. It was a curious experience. When I was taken in
charge by a sergeant-major, thrust into a room with a dozen
other sacrificial victims, and told to strip, I was back in my
prep. school in the year 1892. We waited and waited for the
doctor, shivering with nervousness and the winds which
whistled through the continually opening and shutting door.
At last I was examined by a very young doctor. Being naked
I had left Dr. Wright's letter in my coat, but I thought it
advisable for the moment not to say anything—the less a
new boy says, the safer for him. I was so cold and shivering
by this time that the doctor could not well avoid noticing
that my hands trembled more than those of the average
private. He did not say anything to me, but took me off to a
small room in which was sitting a doctor in the uniform of a
captain. 'Here's a fellow with corea, Sir,' he said. I only just
stopped myself telling him that I was not suffering from St.
Vitus's dance. The captain made me hold out my trembling
hand and began to cross-examine me. I told him I had a
letter from Wright and he sent me to fetch it. Nothing was
said to me and then after waiting an hour or so, I was told to
go; eventually, much to my surprise, I was given exemption
from every form of military service. What was even more
surprising was that when I was called up again in the great
comb out of 1917, and thought that I should inevitably be
sent to scrub floors and tables, at the very least, I was again
given the same complete exemption.

We saw a good deal of my brothers Cecil and Philip
during the first part of the war, when their regiment was
stationed first at Mayfield and later at Colchester. It led to a

curious incident which showed the thoroughness of the security system. I must begin the story by saying that in 1915 we let Asham for a time to a friend who was in the Foreign Office and had a brother-in-law who had a commission in an infantry regiment. One morning in Richmond the bell rang and I was told a gentleman wished to see me. A large man came into my room and presented a document showing that he was a Scotland Yard detective. He very politely said that he had to ask me a few questions. He then cross-examined me for about 20 minutes regarding Philip and Cecil, their movements and our meetings during the last 12 months. In doing so, he showed me that during the past months detectives had shadowed them; he knew, for instance, that on a certain day some weeks previously they had come from Colchester and had lunched with us in Richmond. After the 20 minutes of this, he suddenly stopped, smiled, and said that he spent a great deal of his time investigating mare's nests—'and this is another', he said. From what he told me then 'confidentially' and from what I heard later I found that the mare's nest had arisen in the following way.

The brother-in-law of my lessee had gone down to Asham one day to stay for a week-end with his sister. One afternoon he went down through the fields meaning to cross the railway line to the river bank. In the 1914 war, unlike the 1939 war, the railway line between Lewes and Newhaven was guarded by sentries. Lieutenant X, as I will call him, was, of course, in uniform. He was stopped by a sentry and told that no one was allowed to cross the line. Lieutenant X pointed out that he was an officer and that the sentry had no right to stop him. The sentry demurred and the officer pushed past him and crossed the line. The sentry reported the matter and some weeks later a staff officer appeared and interrogated the shepherd and his wife, Mrs. Funnell.[1] He asked them who

---

[1] See Part 1, p. 59.

the officer was who had been staying at Asham. Apparently they did not know about Lieutenant X, but they had often seen Cecil and Philip in uniform when they came over from Mayfield to lunch with us. So they said that if it was an officer in uniform, he must have been one of Mr. Woolf's brothers. And that started the mare's nest.

The war brought tragedy to Cecil and Philip. Occasionally there grows up between brothers a David and Jonathan affection. From their earliest years, when they were four and five years old—they were the two youngest in the family of nine brothers and sisters—there was this relation, this deep affection, between them. Temperamentally they were very different. Cecil was fundamentally a scholar, a gentle and cynical conservative; he had an exceptionally good mind and did brilliantly at Cambridge, finally getting a fellowship at Trinity just before the war. He was a historian and won his fellowship with an extremely learned dissertation, which was published under the title *Bartolus of Sassoferrato, his Position in the History of Medieval Political Thought*. Philip was much gayer, but also with a distinct vein of scepticism and cynicism; he was an artist and temperamentally revolutionary. He went up to Sidney Sussex, Cambridge, after leaving St. Paul's, but he soon gave up Cambridge to become a painter, and he was at the Heatherley School of Art when the war broke out. In so far as it was possible they were inseparable and, as I said, joined the same regiment from the beginning of the war. Being cavalry, their regiment was for some time not sent to France, and, when they did go to France, they were dismounted and sent into the trenches as infantry. Cecil was killed and Philip severely wounded and it was appropriate that the death of the one and the wounds of the other were caused by the same shell. The episode was characteristic of the 1914 war.

The Hussars were in the trenches in Bourlon Wood. They

had the Irish Guards on their right and a line regiment on their left. It was one of the costly muddles and disasters of 1916. Like some others who went through the fighting of the 1914 war in France and Flanders, Philip very rarely spoke about his experiences, but he did once describe to me what happened to them in Bourlon Wood. They were forgotten, no orders coming to them all day. They were shelled mercilessly all day. Their left flank was uncovered, for the line regiment melted away in the afternoon. Bourlon Wood had been reduced to a cemetery of broken and blackened stumps of trees. The Irish Guards were still on their right, but a drunken Irish guardsman was staggering about in no man's land shouting and singing; though shells fell all round him he was unhit. Late in the afternoon, the strain began to tell on the men, and the major, as officers did in those days, left the trench and walked up and down in the open; this was supposed to inspire the men with confidence. A shell burst near the major and he was severely wounded. Philip and Cecil left the trench to bring him in, but a shell fell between them; it killed Cecil, and wounded Philip.

Philip was for a long time in hospital in Fishmongers Hall by London Bridge, and later in the country. He recovered and went back to the front and was in France until the end of the war. Only at the end when the German line broke were the Hussars mounted and, as cavalry, pursued the retreating Germans. In this pursuit Philip's regiment suffered heavy casualties and he himself had a very narrow escape from a booby trap, a mine laid for them by the Germans. The mine blew up in the middle of the regiment.

I do not think that Philip ever completely recovered from Cecil's death. He lived, no doubt, a happy life, for he married happily and had three children of whom he was extremely fond. But it was happiness with a reservation. After demobilization he trained as a farmer and for a short time went to

India as adviser on cattle-breeding to the Indian Government. Then Jimmy Rothschild, who had married one of our cousins, asked him to manage the Waddesdon estate. Philip did this for over 30 years, and, when he retired, bought a farm and farmed on his own in Somersetshire. After the death of his wife, and when he was in his seventies, he committed suicide. I think that he just came to the conclusion that life offered him no longer anything worth the living. The contemplation of his life and death fills me with melancholy. For he was a most charming and intelligent man; everyone who knew him agreed about this. He was also, as I said, by temperament a gay and happy person. He had the catholic curiosity of mind, the passionate interest in men, women, and animals, in literature and art, in truth, which is one of the most effective means of keeping a man's life alive, of preventing him in middle age beginning the slow descent to life of a sea-urchin or a cabbage. He did not, I must repeat, live an unhappy life, indeed it was in many ways happy, but he deserved to achieve so much more than he did in happiness and in other things. If the Everlasting *has* fixed his canon 'gainst self-slaughter, I think the Everlasting has in this made one of his many mistakes, but the thought that someone has been brought to the point of suicide fills me with melancholy and despair.

I must go back to our own life during the war. I soon became involved in activities which were directed towards understanding the causes of the 1914 war and of war in general and of finding ways, if possible, of making war less likely in the future. What started me on this was that in 1915 Sidney Webb asked me whether I would undertake a research into this vast question for the Fabian Society and write a report on it, which might or might not be published as a book. The report would, in accordance with the usual Fabian Society procedure, be made to a committee of which he would be chairman and of which Shaw would be a member. But the committee would be a mere formality; I should be completely free to proceed in my own way, say exactly what I liked, and, if the book were published, it would be over my name. The Society would pay me a fee of £100.

My friends, and Maynard especially, were discouraging; they thought that I should find the whole thing very boring and a waste of time. It is significant that all these highly intelligent people with whom I discussed the matter thought of the problem as simply and solely a question of arbitration —'I hear', one of them would say to me, 'that you're going to write a book on arbitration.' The main reason for this was that in the happy, innocent golden age before 1914 intelligent people did not worry themselves about international relations and the problem of preventing war—they left all that to professional politicians and diplomatists. There were, of course, wars, but they were either colonial wars, in which white men slaughtered yellow men, or brown men, or black men, or wars between second-rate white men or second-rate white men's states in the Balkans or South America. In 1914, although colonial warfare, like the sun, never set on the British Empire, and we had had a nasty time beating the Boers, it was 60 years since we had fought a European nation and 100 years since we had been involved in a world war. We had a vague memory that it was about 250 years since we had seen the face of a foreign soldier on English soil— didn't Van Tromp once sail up the Thames in 1652 or 1653?—and that it was 848 years since Englishmen had heard 'the drums and tramplings' of a conquest. There were at rare intervals what the newspapers called a crisis, e.g. when a French colonel occupied a patch of African desert claimed by Britain; but the crisis and the French soon gave way when they heard us singing in the music halls:

We don't want to fight, but, by Jingo, if we do,
We've got the men, we've got the ships, we've got the money too.

Another rather vague recollection we had was of Hague Conferences, called by a somewhat foolish Tsar in the cause of peace, and that the conference had been asked to consider 'limitation of armaments, arbitration, and laws of war'. There were two conferences and we seemed to remember that they had confined their discussion to the laws of war and to arbitration and the principal result was the establishment of a permanent court of international arbitration at the Hague. That was why there was this vague idea among my friends and many other apparently well-informed people that the prevention of war was to all intents and purposes a question of arbitration.

I have often irritated people by saying that an intelligent person can become what is called an 'authority' on most 'questions', 'problems', or 'subjects' by intensive study for two or three months. They thought me arrogant for saying so, or, if not arrogant, not serious. But it is true. The number and volume of relevant facts on any subject are not many or great and the number of good or important books on it are few. If you have a nose for relevant facts and the trails which lead to them—this is essential and half the battle—and if you know how to work with the laborious pertinacity of a mole and beaver, you can acquire in a few months all the knowledge necessary for a thorough understanding of the subject.

In 1915 I worked like a fanatical or dedicated mole on the sources of my subject, international relations, foreign affairs, the history of war and peace. By 1916 I had a profound knowledge of my subject; I was an authority. This is not retrospective vanity; I can give, at the risk of appearing vain and boastful, a little proof of it. Early in 1920, Massingham, a famous editor in those days, of the *Nation*, asked me whether I would take Brailsford's place, during his temporary absence, as leader writer on foreign affairs. I did this for three months, writing everything which the *Nation* published on foreign affairs. In the middle of October Massingham wrote to me: 'Brailsford is back from Russia, and will resume his work for the "Nation" next week, so I shall not call on you for a Leader or for Notes; but I want to say what a very high value I attach to your work for us. It has been faultless in manner and quality and of the greatest possible service. I do hope you will regard yourself as attached to the paper, and open to do work for it whenever there is special pressure in respect of foreign affairs.' And on July 23, when in fact I was writing for Massingham, Clifford Sharp wrote to me asking me to write an article on foreign affairs for the *New Statesman*. Journalistically at any rate I had become an authority.

By the middle of 1915 I had completed my report and it was published immediately as a supplement to the *New Statesman*. It began by dealing with the causes of war and then examined the nature, history, and records of international law, treaties, international conferences and congresses, arbitration and international tribunals. My conclusion was that the first step towards the prevention of war must be the creation of 'an international authority to prevent war' and I examined the minimum requirements for such a league of states if it was to have any chance of success. Webb and I then drew up a formal international treaty for the establishment of such a supernational authority for the prevention of war, based upon my conclusions; this too was published as a supplement to the *New Statesman*. This was the first detailed study of a League of Nations to be published, the first working out and description of the structure which the Allied governments would have to agree to give it if it was to have any chance of preventing war or of making war less probable. During my work on this I became more and more convinced that the problem of an international authority and the prevention of war was part of a much larger problem—international government. It was commonly said or assumed that international government did not exist and could not exist among sovereign independent states; but a very little investigation convinced me that this was not true and that a considerable field of human relations had been subjected to various forms of international government. But practically no books existed on the subject and no attention had been given to it. I told Sidney Webb that I thought that it would be well worth while doing some serious work on it as it ought to throw important light on the whole field of international relations, including a League to prevent war. Webb agreed and the Fabians gave me a fee of £100 to write a second report.

I did an immense amount of work on this. You could not become an authority on international government in 1915 by reading books, because the books did not exist[1]; you had to go to what are called original sources. I had therefore to read Blue Books and White Books and annual reports dealing with such vast international organizations as the Universal Postal Union or the International Institute of Agriculture,

[1] There were in fact only two books of any use, and one of these was simply a work of reference. One was an American book, *Public International Unions* by Professor Reinsch. The other was the Yearbook of L'Union des Associations Internationales, *Annuaires de la Vie Internationale*; this remarkable book was invaluable to me, because it contained a list of all international associations, from the great International Institute of Agriculture in Rome to the International Association for the Rational Destruction of Rats or the secret international conference of 89 white slave traffickers which met in Warsaw in 1913 to consider 'an international agreement as to the future conduct of the trade' and which ended in the arrest of all 89 representatives by the Warsaw police.

and I had many interviews with civil servants and others who attended the conferences or congresses of these unions or associations as national representatives. It was perhaps from these interviews that I learnt most; I remember, in particular, the fascinating account of the problems of international government in the Universal Postal Union which the Post Office civil servant who represented Britain at the Union's Congress gave to me. It was he who told me the wonderful story of the bibles in Persia, which is worth telling again.

It was the rule of the Union that each country retains the sums which it receives from postal matter despatched from it. This on the whole works out fairly, but in 1906 Persia brought to the notice of the Union a case of considerable hardship. Persia is inhabited mainly by Muhammadans, Great Britain by Christians. The Christians of Great Britain and the U.S.A. have a passion for sending bibles to the Persian Muhammadans, but the Persian never sends his Koran to Britain or America. There were no railways in Persia, and the Persian government had to provide every year at vast expense strings of camels to carry the hundreds of foreign bibles to its subjects. The British and American governments retained all the large sums paid by their Christian subjects for postage on these bibles; the Persian government got nothing, and as Persians write few letters and send fewer parcels to foreigners, the Persians were being ruined by the Holy Bible. The justice and eloquence of the Persian plea had its effect upon representatives of the other nations at the Postal Congress and a new Article was added to the Convention of 1906 authorizing Persia to levy a special duty on all printed matter sent by post into the country.

The two reports which I had written and our draft treaty were published by me in a book, *International Government*, in 1916. It had, I think, some effect; it was used extensively by the government committee which produced the British proposals for a League of Nations laid before the Peace Conference, and also by the British delegation to the Versailles Conference. My authority for this statement comes from Sir Sydney Waterlow, Philip Noel-Baker, who was secretary, and Lord Cecil, who was head of the League of Nations Section of the British Delegation. Sydney Waterlow was in the Foreign Office and in 1918 he was instructed to draw up a confidential paper on 'International Government under the League of Nations' for use by the British Delegation at Versailles. He gave me a copy. In the prefatory note he said: 'The facts contained in Part I are taken almost entirely from "International Government", by L. S. Woolf (1916). Where a mass of facts has been collected and sifted with great ability, as is the case with Mr. Woolf's work, it would be folly to attempt to do the work over again, especially as time presses. My detailed descriptions of the various existing organs of international government are therefore for the most part lifted almost verbatim, with slight abridgements, from Mr. Woolf's book.'

My work on this book led me by degrees into what are euphemistically called practical politics. Many people besides myself and the Fabians were early in the war convinced that it ought, if possible, to be transformed into a war to end war, and therefore it was essential that some sort of international authority—a League of Nations, as it soon began to be called—should be established after the war in order to settle international disputes, promote the growth of a system of international law, and so help to keep the peace. Various groups of people of varying political complexion in Britain and other countries were formed to study the problems connected with the idea and to get the wider public to support it. In Britain the most important of these groups was the Bryce group, under the chairmanship of Lord Bryce, and in the United States the League to Enforce Peace.[1]

Goldsworthy Lowes Dickinson—Goldie, as his friends always called him—was one of the most active and influential of these workers. Goldie was a good deal older than I—18 years older—but I had known him well since my Cambridge days for he was an Apostle and one of the most popular of dons at King's. He was, I think, one of the most charming of men; he belonged to Roger Fry's generation, and it is curious to recollect how many of that Cambridge generation were remarkable for a particular variety of great, gentle, slightly melancholy, male charm. Roger himself had it, but Goldie had it in excelsis. The extraordinary gentleness of thought, speech, manner was an integral part of it and so was the melancholy; these had their charm, but also their defects or dangers. Goldie wrote a number of books of great merit, notably *Letters from John Chinaman* and his books on war and peace; they were extremely good and brought him considerable reputation and influence, but to those who knew him intimately and affectionately they were disappointing, and the disappointment was not, it must be admitted, unexpected. There was a weakness, a looseness of fibre, in Goldie and in his thought and writing, which was subtly related to the gentleness and high-mindedness. He was very fond of Virginia and he came to see us or stay with us from time to time. Virginia too was very fond of him, though the thin vapour of gentle high-mindness sometimes irritated her; it was, no doubt, in such a moment of irritation that she wrote the following in her diary on December 28, 1935, an extract which some of his friends thought I was wrong to include in *A Writer's Diary* (p. 251):

[1] Nearly all these groups published schemes for a League and in 1917 I published a book, *The Framework of a Lasting Peace*, giving the text of eight such schemes.

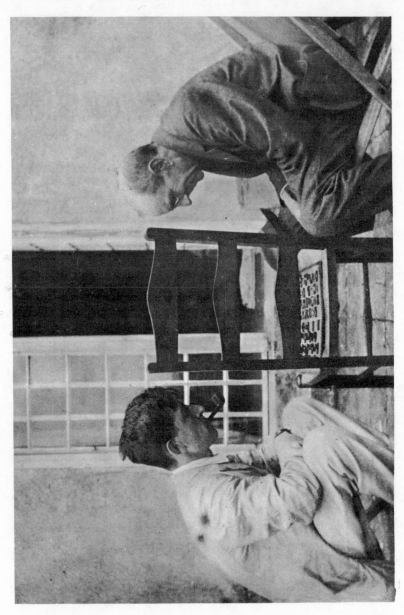

The author and G. Lowes Dickinson at Asham House, 1914

Goldie depresses me unspeakably. Always alone on a mountain top asking himself how to live, theorising about life; never living. Roger always down in the succulent valleys, living. But what a thin whistle of hot air Goldie lets out through his front teeth. Always live in the whole, life in the one: always Shelley and Goethe, and then he loses his hot water bottle; and never notices a face or a cat or a dog or a flower, except in the flow of the universal. This explains why his high-minded books are unreadable. Yet he was so charming intermittently.

Goldie was the most active member of the Bryce group. He, Sir W. H. Dickinson, M.P. (afterwards Lord Dickinson), J. A. Hobson, Raymond Unwin, H. N. Brailsford, and I were active in starting the League of Nations Society and were on its Executive Committee. It was a propaganda body, its object being to get the public to understand the necessity for a League and for its establishment in the peace treaty after the war. There was another organization, The League of Nations Association, formed about the same time and with much the same objects. But, as so often happens among the good and wise, the two organizations viewed each other with suspicion or misprision. The protagonists of the Association were Wickham Steed, Gilbert Murray, H. G. Wells, Lionel Curtis, and C. A. McCurdy, M.P. The Association thought us pacifist and pro-German, and we thought them much too violently the opposite. But as the end of the war and the making of a peace began to come in sight, it became obvious to us all and to both sides that it was absurd to have two rival organizations of this kind and that we ought to combine.

It was eventually decided that each of the two Executive Committees should appoint four representatives who should meet and try to work out a basis for agreement and amalgamation. The Society appointed as their representatives

Goldie, W. H. Dickinson, Hobson, and myself, the Association appointed McCurdy, Steed, Murray, and Wells. We very wisely decided to dine together and this we did two or three times. Over food and drink we found agreement on the terms of amalgamation and on the rules and objects of the new organization, which became the League of Nations Union.

At the first dinner I sat next to H. G. Wells, and we got on extremely well together, and this was the beginning of a friendship with him which was very pleasant and lasted until his death, though it was broken, as friendship with H.G. often was, by interludes of storm and stress. After the League of Nations Union business was over H.G. asked me to lunch at the Strand Palace Hotel, but when I met him there he whisked me off to Boulestin round the corner and I felt that he had promoted me. Over lunch he told me that he had come to the conclusion, as a result of the war and studying the League of Nations idea, that a history of the world should be written from a new angle, 'plainly for the general reader'. He thought it should be done to a certain extent co-operatively by a few people who looked at history and politics from the same angle. Would I co-operate? He proposed to take a room in the Central Hall and meet once a week with the following friends: Gilbert Murray, Lionel Curtis, J. A. Spender, editor of the *Westminster Gazette*, John Hilton, William Archer, and myself. Archer had agreed to act as a kind of secretary, but our meetings would be entirely informal and friendly tea parties. I accepted his invitation and for some months on Wednesday afternoons we had the most enjoyable meetings. Those who came were usually H.G., Archer, Gilbert Murray, and myself; at first occasionally Spender and Hilton turned up. H.G.'s original idea was that we should all take our part in writing the great work and I think that he even got to the point of apportioning provisionally periods to some of us. But very soon the whole thing degenerated or blossomed into a friendly and to me most enjoyable tea and talk. The history of the world faded further and further away and we discussed everything in the world except its history. Our first meeting was on October 30, 1918, and we still met occasionally in February, 1919, but then Wells got tired of it and told me that he was in fact writing the book on his own. I have as a memento of these many teas and talks a copy of *The Outline of History* inscribed to me by H.G.

I used to see H.G. from time to time and get affectionate cards from him and, when I edited the *International Review*, he very generously gave me *The Undying Fire* to serialize. But his temper was always uncertain for he was a terribly irritable little man, and you never knew when you might not unwittingly cause an explosion. I twice incurred his wrath. The first occasion was not very serious, but it was curious. Many Liberals and Labour people were greatly concerned at the atrocious proceedings in Ireland under the reciprocal violence of Black and Tans and rebels. But there were also some Conservatives who were horrified by the British government tolerating the behaviour of their forces, the Black and Tans, and one of these was Lord Henry Cavendish Bentinck, one of those curious Tory aristocrats who are always more liberal than the Liberals and continually vote against their own party. He was a brother of Ottoline Morrell's and I had met him at the Morrells' house. He formed a small society to agitate for 'peace with Ireland' and withdrawal of the Black and Tans. He asked me to join it and we used to meet, often in my office of the *International Review*. Except for Brailsford and, I think, Hobson, I cannot remember who were the other members. We were an ineffectual body but one day Henry Bentinck said that there was a young Conservative M.P. called Oswald Mosley, who had been in the 16th Lancers and had married Lord Curzon's daughter, but despite that was very advanced, was horrified by the Black and Tans, and would, if we approved, become treasurer of our society. We approved and at our next meeting Mosley appeared, a handsome young man in top hat and morning coat carrying a gold-headed walking stick. Mosley put new life into us and among other things it was decided that I should write to Wells and ask him to help further our objects. Back almost by return came a bitter, angry letter: the Irish were a set of nasty murderous thugs and they were getting all that they deserved.

H.G.'s second quarrel with me—I never really quarrelled with him—was more serious and more absurd. In 1932 I wrote in the *New Statesman* a review of his book *The Work, Wealth and Happiness of Mankind*; as with nearly everything he wrote, much of it was very good, and I gave it high praise. Unfortunately, I wrote among other things that some of the younger generation said that Mr. Wells was a thinker who could not think; in this, I went on, they are wrong, Mr. Wells thinks with his imagination. I immediately received a card from H.G., who was in the south of France, asking me to tell him who was the brilliant young critic who had said that he was 'a thinker who cannot think'. When I wrote the review, I remembered—or thought that I remembered—that A. L. Rowse had written the words in his book, *Politics and the Younger Generation*, which I had recently read. So when I got H.G.'s card I searched through Rowse's book, and to my astonishment could not find the quotation. I wrote to H.G. telling him this, namely that I had thought that I had read the words in Rowse's book, but that I was mistaken —the words were not in the book. H.G. exploded at once: 'It looks as though you wanted the thing said and hadn't the guts to say it as your own,' and I was told that I 'ought to do something in the way of public repudiation of that pseudo-quotation.' I wrote the following letter in reply:

19 March, 1932
Dear Wells,

I am not quite sure whether your card is serious or not. If you have seen my review, I cannot believe that it is. I read your book with the greatest admiration and said so quite clearly in my review. That the result should be your falling foul of me is only one more curious instance of the danger of praising an author's work. Why if I wanted to say that you are a thinker who cannot think, I 'should not have the guts' to do so, I cannot imagine. I am not conscious of being in the least afraid of expressing such opinions as I have in print.

I suggested to the editor that I should write a letter to the *New Statesman* explaining what I had done and your objection, though it seems to me that the result would only be to make you look slightly ridiculous, which personally I have not the least desire to do. The editor himself did not seem to be at all anxious to have the letter. However if you want me to do so, I will. Perhaps you will let me know?

Yours

Leonard Woolf

H.G. replied that it would not mend matters if I wrote a letter to the *New Statesman* in order to make him look slightly ridiculous, and he sent me the following draft of the letter which he required me to send:

In a review of *The Work, Wealth & Happiness of Mankind* in the N.S. of (date) I said (quote the passage under discussion). I made the statement in order to enhance the credit of Mr. Wells with your readers and as a delicately indirect way of expressing my own admiration for his work. There was no word of truth in that statement, objection has been made to it, and I tender my sincere apologies both to Mr. Wells and to the rising young economist to whom, in the first excitement of being challenged, I ascribed it.

He added that this was the simple, honest way out for me. 'What else, in the name of decency, *can* you do?'

I replied that 'I have the greatest admiration for you as a writer (and thinker), but I cannot agree to your writing the letters which I send to the papers'. I had therefore written my own letter, explaining what had happened and had sent it to the *New Statesman*. However the editor then received a telegram from H.G. asking him not to publish my letter and later on H.G. wrote to me that he had decided that the incident should terminate without publication. 'I was acutely hurt and exasperated by what I thought was a stroke of ungenerous and disingenuous detraction from you, because you have always been of importance in my mind. It seems you didn't mean it. I begin to think you didn't and anyhow we are too much in the same camp to knock the paint off each other in the sight of our enemies.'

Meanwhile there was a curious and, to me, amusing development. At that time I was editor of the *Political Quarterly* and some weeks before the storm with H.G. blew up, A. L. Rowse had submitted to me an article on the House of Lords. I had accepted it, but returned the MS. to him making suggestions for a few alterations. Now he returned the MS. to me and, when I read it, there (now crossed out) was the fatal sentence about H.G. I told Rowse what had happened and asked him whether he had any objection to my sending the sentence to H.G. and telling him how I had seen and forgotten it in Rowse's unpublished article. Rowse told me that H.G. had written to him from France and asked him to lunch in the following week—and it would be very awkward if he now found that it *was* Rowse who had said that he was a thinker who did not think.

So I never told H.G. and for a year or more he did not really forgive me. Then one day Mary Hutchinson rang me up and asked us to dine, but added that H.G. would be there and had we quarrelled and would I rather not meet him? I told her that he had quarrelled with me, but not I with him— and I always liked talking to him. We arrived before him and when he came and had shaken hands with Mary, he walked over to me, took my hand in his and patted it gently two or three times, looking at me with a slightly sheepish smile. It was our first meeting since the storm.

Meanwhile the war went on. Apart from Virginia's illness, the four years of the 1914 war were the most horrible period of my life. The five years of the 1939 war were more terrible and they brought the suicide of Virginia, but at least things moved and happened and one was kept keenly alive by the danger of death continually hanging just above one's head. The horror of the years 1914 to 1918 was that nothing seemed to happen, month after month and year after year, except the pitiless, useless slaughter in France. Often if one went for a walk on the downs above Asham one could hear the incessant pounding of the guns on the Flanders front. And even when one did not hear them it was as though the war itself was perpetually pounding dully on one's brain, while in Richmond and Sussex one was enmeshed in a cloud of boredom, and when one looked into the future, there was nothing there but an unending vista of the same boredom. When the telephone rang on December 2, 1917, and they told me that Cecil had been killed in France, in the dull, static greyness of one's days it was as if one had suddenly received a violent blow on the head.

There was indeed one lightening of the darkness. In the last two years of the war Virginia's health slowly but firmly improved. She was able once more to work and she wrote steadily at *Night and Day* so that she gave me the completed

MS. to read in March, 1919. Gradually too she was able, with cautious restraint, to live a social life. We began to see a large number of different people; among them were Philip and Ottoline Morrell, whom we got to know through Lytton. It was in 1917, I suppose, that we first went and stayed a week-end at Garsington. The house, Philip and Ottoline, the kaleidoscope of their friends and guests formed a framed picture of a society and life unlike any which I have ever met anywhere else in the real world; but in the world of fiction I recognized its counterpart, for the people in Crotchet Castle, Headlong Hall, Nightmare Abbey, and Gryll Grange would have felt quite at home and have fitted in beautifully at Garsington Manor. Garsington was a lovely Oxfordshire manor house with a lovely garden embellished with a swimming pool and peacocks. Ottoline was herself not unlike one of her own peacocks, drifting about the house and terraces in strange brightly-coloured shawls and other floating garments, her unskilfully dyed red hair, her head tilted to the sky at the same angle as the birds' and her odd nasal voice and neighing laugh always seeming as if they might at any moment rise into one of those shattering calls of the peacocks which woke me in the mornings at Garsington just as so often I had heard them blare in the jungles of Ceylon. She was, like the motley crowd which sat round her breakfast table or drifted about her garden, a fantastic hotchpotch.

Philip was a Liberal M.P., a supporter of Asquith as against Lloyd George, and politically and socially there was an aura of liberalism or even radicalism about him and Ottoline. They were leading members of that stage army of British progressives who can be relied upon to sign a letter to *The Times* supporting an unpopular cause or protesting against a pogrom or judicial murder. She was proud of having broken out of the ducal family and Welbeck, as a young woman, to study literature at Liverpool University under

Walter Raleigh. She became a patron of artists and writers, proletarians and Bohemians and underdogs. In Bedford Square or Garsington you would meet the Duchess of Portland, the immaculate Lord Henry, and Lord Berners (who had a piano or harpsichord in his car), but these aristocrats were heavily outnumbered by the underdogs and scallywags, penniless and, in the eyes of the Duchess, mannerless intellectuals or C.O.'s, like Gertler, John Rodke, and Middleton Murry.

I was, however, always fascinated to watch for the moment —not so very rare—when the aristocrat, which was only just below Ottoline's proletarian façade, would suddenly show itself and some scallywag would be put in his place by the great lady, the daughter[1] and sister of dukes. I have seen this happen when someone 'presumed' or went a little too far at Garsington, but it was still more amusing to see her absolute self confidence and unselfconsciousness in public. For instance, one summer evening when we had been to see her in Bedford Square, she walked back with us to Tavistock Square. Her appearance was more than usually fantastic and eccentric; her hat, hair, and clothes flopped and flapped around her; she looked like an enormous bird whose brightly and badly dyed plumage was in complete disarray and no longer fitted the body. Almost everyone turned to stare at her as she passed; and at one place, where the road was up, and men were working in a trench, they looked up at her, roared with laughter, and whistled and catcalled after her. She walked on absolutely oblivious and impervious.

The company of people whom one met at Garsington was, as I said, a strange hotchpotch. During the war there was a resident sediment of Conscientious Objectors, for Philip had a kind of farm and the Morrells, with their usual high-

[1] To be accurate, I think that Ottoline was only a grand-daughter and sister of Dukes of Portland.

minded generosity, took on to it a number of C.O.'s to whom the tribunals had given exemption from military service provided that they worked upon the land. The C.O.'s lived either in the house or in neighbouring cottages. There were, therefore, at meals a more or less resident population of Lytton, Gerald and Fredegond Shove, Clive Bell, Mark Gertler, and Frank Prewett, a poet. Superimposed upon this literary and artistic stratum was a drifting, irregular procession of incongruous figures from high society and high politics. At one week-end mixed in with the intellectual underworld were a beautiful and brainless deb and Lord Balniel, at the beginning of a political career which has resulted in his being a trustee of an incredible number of national art galleries and museums.

There were, too, frequent irruptions of the Asquith family. Margot, Lady Oxford, in particular used to appear suddenly at almost any time of the day or night. She was, as many reminiscences and her own autobiography show, a very English mixture of tomboy, enfant terrible, and great lady. What fascinated and eventually irritated or bored one was her indefatigable energy, her will which worked upon her environment like a psychological electric drill. It was quite impossible not to like her even when she was most intolerable—odi et amo. One afternoon at Garsington everyone, except Julian, Ottoline's daughter, and me, had gone off either to do their work or visit the Poet Laureate. I did not feel that I could bear the poetic pomposity of the Poet Laureate, so I stayed behind and played tennis with Julian. After a set or two she went indoors and I strolled about the garden. Suddenly Margot appeared. It was the moment of the great split in the Liberal Party between Lloyd George and Asquith, when L.G. had gone off with the swag and the two factions were locked in a deadly, catch-as-catch-can struggle. When Margot found that I was alone, I saw a

Sunday afternoon at Garsington
Above: Lytton Strachey and Yeats
Below: David Cecil, L. P. Hartley, Virginia, and Anthony Asquith

gleam in her eye which warned me to be careful. She began walking me up and down the lawn, she on my left with her right hand resting on my right shoulder. It was obvious that Margot wanted something and it was not long before she showed her hand (on my shoulder) and what was in her mind. 'I know you are a very great friend of Maynard Keynes' was the prologue to what was in the hand and the mind. I was told all the details of L.G.'s perfidy and dishonesty, of his complete lack of principles, and she insisted upon the importance of brilliant young men like Maynard not being cajoled by the abominable wizard. She hoped that I would tell him what she had told me and use my influence to guide his footsteps on the right path—into the Asquith camp. Maynard was much amused when I told him what she had said.

Margot, I think, admired and genuinely was fond of Virginia. But she was one of those people who quite naïvely are always trying to get something out of one. She once rang Virginia up and asked her to lunch with her 'entirely alone' in Bedford Square next Thursday—they would be quite alone as she wanted to talk to Virginia about an important matter. Virginia went on the Thursday to find a luncheon party of twelve people. Nothing was said about the important question until Virginia got up to go and then Margot said could she come next Monday to tea with us. She came to tea and explained that she admired Virginia's writing more than anyone's. 'What I want you to do, Virginia', she said, 'is to write my obituary in *The Times*—I am sure that, if you offer to do it, they will jump at it—and I feel I would die happy if I knew that my obituary in *The Times* was written by you.' Virginia said that she thought that Bruce Richmond was in charge of the obituaries and she did not think that he would welcome an offer from anyone to write one of them. She would not commit herself. 'Think it over, think it over,' were

Margot's final words. We often wondered whether she had asked Bruce Richmond to a solitary lunch (with ten other people) to discuss an important matter and had suggested that her obituary should be written by Virginia. If so, she was unsuccessful.

It would be unfair to Margot not to say that she was a giver as well as a taker. But her generosity was as peculiar as all her other actions. Just before the 1939 war she told Virginia that she had an original bronze reproduction of Houdon's famous statue of Voltaire. She explained that years ago she was walking in Paris with a friend of hers who was very much in love with her—though she was not in love with him. 'He took me into a shop selling antiquities and told me he wanted to give me a present; I must choose what I would most like to have in the shop. I decided to choose what seemed to me the most valuable and I took the Voltaire. And now, Virginia, I want to give it to you.' There seemed to be no reason and no explanation of why Margot should give Virginia the bronze Voltaire, and Virginia said that she really must not give it to her. But some time later, just after the beginning of the last war, when we were at Monks House, a Rolls drove up to the door and a chauffeur carried Voltaire into the house, a gift from her ladyship. The gift, the car, the chauffeur, the 100 miles journey to deliver the gift, the mystery of motive seemed to be characteristic of Margot.

The zenith of a Garsington week-end in late spring or early summer was Sunday afternoon; then, if the sun shone, a great convocation of young and old, of brilliant (and not so brilliant), of distinguished (and not so distinguished) men thronged the garden, strolling to and fro, sitting on chairs and seats, talking incessantly. It was not without significance that the company was almost entirely male. The only distinguished women whom I ever saw at Garsington were Margot, Katherine Mansfield, and Virginia; but there was always a galaxy of male stars, from ancient red giants like Yeats to new white dwarfs from Balliol and New College. The older generation would be there: Bertie Russell, Goldie Dickinson, Bridges, Lytton, Maynard; and then early in the afternoon there would be an irruption from Oxford of under-graduates or young dons. The Oxford generations of the nineteen tens and nineteen twenties produced a remarkable constellation of stars of the first magnitude and I much enjoyed seeing them twinkle in the Garsington garden. There for the first time I saw the young Aldous Huxley folding his long, grasshopper legs into a deckchair and listened en-tranced to a conversation which is unlike that of any other person that I have talked with. I could never grow tired of listening to the curious erudition, intense speculative curiosity, deep intelligence which, directed by a gentle wit and charming character, made conversation an art. And out of the Oxford colleges of those years came, besides Aldous, L. A. G. Strong, David Cecil, Maurice Bowra.

It was in Garsington too that we first came across Katherine Mansfield and Middleton Murry. When we first got to know them, they were living together and I suppose that it was shortly after this that they married. There was an atmosphere about them then of what I can only describe as the literary underworld, what our ancestors called Grub Street. There was also a queer air of conspiracy about them; it was as if you caught them every now and then exchanging a surreptitious wink or whisper: 'There you see, didn't I tell you how hostile the world is to us.' I never liked Murry; there was a strong Pecksniffian vein in him which irritated and revolted me.[1] He was always ready to weep loudly and

[1] I once reviewed in the *Nation* a book of his simply by mixing up indiscriminately quotations from the book and quotations from Pecksniff. I defied anyone to disentangle them, and I do not think anyone ever did—but the Murry-Pecksniff paragraphs made perfect sense.

generously over the woes of the world, but the eyes reminded me of the crocodile's.

Katherine was a very different person. I liked her, though I think she disliked me. She had a masklike face and she, more than Murry, seemed to be perpetually on her guard against a world which she assumed to be hostile. Very soon after we first met her she came and stayed an uneasy week-end with us at Asham. By nature, I think, she was gay, cynical, amoral, ribald, witty. When we first knew her, she was extraordinarily amusing. I don't think anyone has ever made me laugh more than she did in those days. She would sit very upright on the edge of a chair or sofa and tell at immense length a kind of saga, of her experiences as an actress or of how and why Koteliansky howled like a dog in the room at the top of the building in Southampton Row. There was not the shadow of a gleam of a smile on her mask of a face, and the extraordinary funniness of the story was increased by the flashes of her astringent wit. I think that in some abstruse way Murry corrupted and perverted and destroyed Katherine both as a person and a writer. She was a very serious writer, but her gifts were those of an intense realist, with a superb sense of ironic humour and fundamental cynicism. She got enmeshed in the sticky sentimentality of Murry and wrote against the grain of her own nature. At the bottom of her mind she knew this, I think, and it enraged her. And that was why she was so often enraged against Murry. To see them together, particularly in their own house in Hampstead, made one acutely uncomfortable, for Katherine seemed to be always irritated with Murry and enraged with Murry's brother, who lived with them and, according to Katherine, ate too much. Every now and then she would say sotto voce something bitter and biting about the one or the other.

The relation between Katherine and Virginia was ambivalent. Virginia's first impression of her in 1917, when she came and dined with us, was dismay—dismay at the cheap scent, the 'commonness'—'lines so hard and cheap'. But before the end of the evening she noted that 'when this diminishes, she is so intelligent and inscrutable that she repays friendship'. A curious friendship, with some deep roots, did spring up between them. When they did not meet, Katherine regarded Virginia with suspicion and hostility and Virginia was irritated and angered by this, and supercilious towards Katherine's cheap scent and cheap sentimentality. But when they met, all this as a rule fell away and there was a profound feeling and understanding between them. I can show it best by quoting what Virginia wrote in her diary about Katherine's death on January 16, 1923, for it is terrifyingly frank, not only about Katherine, but also about Virginia:

Katherine has been dead a week, and how far am I obeying her 'Do not quite forget Katherine' which I read in one of her old letters? Am I already forgetting her? It is strange to trace the progress of one's feelings. Nelly said in her sensational way at breakfast on Friday 'Mrs. Murry's dead! It says so in the paper.' At that one feels —what? A shock of relief?—a rival the less? Then confusion at feeling so little—then, gradually blankness and disappointment; then a depression which I could not rouse myself from all day. When I began to write, it seemed to me there was no point in writing. Katherine won't read it. Katherine's my rival no longer. More generously I felt, But though I can do this better than she could, where is she, who could do what I can't! Then as usual with me, visual impressions kept coming and coming before me—always of Katherine putting on a white wreath and leaving us, called away; made dignified, chosen. And then one pitied her. And one felt her reluctant to wear that wreath, which was an ice cold one. And she was only 33. And I could see her before me so exactly, and the room at Portland Villas. I go up. She gets up, very slowly, from her writing table. A glass of milk and a medicine bottle stood there. There were also piles of novels. Everything was very tidy, bright, and somehow like a doll's house. At once, or almost, we got out of shyness. She (it was summer) half lay on the sofa by the window. She had her look of a Japanese doll, with the fringe combed quite straight across the forehead. Sometimes we looked very steadfastly at each other, as though we had reached some durable relationship, independent of the changes of the body, through the eyes. Hers were beautiful eyes—rather dog-like, brown, very wide apart, with a steady slow rather faithful and sad expression. Her nose was sharp, a little vulgar. Her lips thin and hard. She wore short skirts and liked 'to have a line round her' she said. She looked very ill—very drawn, and moved languidly, drawing herself across the room like some suffering animal. I suppose I have written down some of the things we said. Most days I think we reached that kind of certainty—in talk about books, or rather about our writing, which I thought had something durable about it. And then she was inscrutable. Did she care for me? Sometimes she would say so—would kiss me—would look at me as if (is this sentiment?) her eyes would like always to be faithful. She would promise never never to forget. That was what we said at the end of our last talk. She would send me her diary to read and would write always. For our friendship was a real thing, we said, looking at each other quite straight. It would always go on whatever happened. What happened, I suppose, was faultfindings and perhaps gossip. She never answered my letter. Yet I still feel, somehow, that friendship persists. Still there are things about writing I think of and want to tell Katherine. If I had been in Paris and gone to her, she would have got up and in three minutes we should have been talking again. Only I could not take the step. The surroundings—Murry and so on—and the small lies and treacheries, the perpetual playing and teasing, or whatever it was, cut away much of the substance of friendship. One was too uncertain. And so one let it all go. Yet I certainly expected that we should meet again next summer and start fresh. And I was jealous of her writing—the only writing I have ever been jealous of. This made it harder to write to her; and I saw in it, perhaps from jealousy, all the qualities I disliked in her.

For two days I felt that I had grown middle-aged, and lost some spur to write. That feeling is going. I no longer keep seeing her with the wreath. I don't pity her so much. Yet I have the feeling that I shall think of her at intervals all through life. Probably we had something in common which I shall never find in anyone else. (This I say in so many words in 1919 again and again.) Moreover I like speculating about her character. I think I never gave her credit for all her physical suffering and the effect it must have had in embittering her.

As the war went on, I became more and more entangled in politics. The Russian revolution in 1917 was a tremendous event for me and for all those whose beliefs and hopes had been moulded in the revolutionary fires of liberty, equality, fraternity. I suppose everyone is born either a little revolutionary or a little anti-revolutionary, just as in the placid bourgeois English society of 1881 the poet remarked that

nature always does contrive
That every boy and every gal,

That's born into the world alive,
Is either a little Liberal,
Or else a little Conservative.

Born a year before the poet wrote *Iolanthe*, I was born a little
Liberal and also—though I did not realize it for some time
—a little revolutionary. I am on the side of Pericles and Tom
Paine; I am instinctively against all authoritarians, aristocrats, or oligarchs from Xerxes and Lycurgus to Edmund
Burke who held that 'a perfect democracy is the most shame-
less thing in the world' and 'nobility . . . the Corinthian
capital of polished society'. The psychology of the really
great revolutions, like those of 1789 and 1917, is curious. If
you are on the side of Pericles and Tom Paine, and alive
when society is shaken by one of these great political
cataclysms, you feel a sudden exhilarating release—the
feeling which the Conservative Wordsworth remembered to
have felt in 1789:

Bliss was it in that dawn to be alive,
But to be young was very heaven!

The release is something real—release from the tyrannies,
cruelties, injustices which principalities, power, the social
sclerosis of classes build up and so harden or ossify the
arteries of society.

I have described in the first volume of my autobiography
(*Sowing*, pp. 160-167) how as young men of 19 and 20 we
felt ourselves to be part of, active agents in, a great social
revolution:

We were not, as we are today, fighting with our backs
to the wall against a resurgence of barbarism and barbarians. We were not part of a negative movement of

destruction against the past. We were out to construct something new; we were in the van of the builders of a new society which should be free, rational, civilized, pursuing truth and beauty. It was all tremendously exhilarating.

The Dreyfus case, as I explained, seemed to us to be a turning point in this new struggle for liberty, equality, fraternity, and justice, and when at last the innocent man was reinstated, there was this tremendous feeling of release and exhilaration for those who stood on the side of truth and justice in this 'struggle between two standards of social and therefore of human value'.

The outbreak of the Russian revolution of 1917 produced the same feeling of liberation and exhilaration. In the long, grim history of despotisms the Tsarist régime of the 19th century must take a high place for savage, corrupt, and incompetent government. Even among the European royal families the Romanovs were distinguished for their unbalanced minds or feeble intellects, yet the Tsars exercised greater and more irresponsible power than even the German and Austrian Kaisers. Their ministers were second-rate men who ruled and were ruled by terror, for they administered a police state and were removed from office either by the whim of the Tsar or an assassin's bomb or bullet. The country was administered by an inefficient and frequently corrupt civil service, and the generals and admirals who mismanaged the army and navy were even worse than the civil servants. The horrifying barbarism of the aristocracy is shown by the fact that the mother of Turgenev, one of the most civilized and sophisticated of Russian writers—he died three years after I was born—had the right to flog her servants to death and exercised it. Though the government allowed Turgenev's mother freely to torture and kill her servants, he himself in

1852 was put under arrest for a month because he said publicly that 'Gogol was a great man'. The government attempted to rule by violence and terror, secret police and wholesale deportations to Siberia, the encouragement of anti-semitism and pogroms; they not unnaturally begat an oppo-sition which came to rely upon similar methods of murderous terrorism.

One had not to be very far on the Left to dislike Tsarism and to feel that the régime which was responsible for Turgenev's mother, Red Sunday of 1905,[1] Siberia, pogroms, and that last infirmity of ignoble minds, the 'Holy Monk' Rasputin, was indeed what was euphemistically called 'a blot on European civilization'. Even a Liberal British Prime Minister, Campbell-Bannerman, when the Tsar autocratic-ally dismissed the Duma, was moved publicly to say: 'The Duma is dead; long live the Duma.'

The first activity connected with the Russian revolution in which I took part was curious. Twelve prominent Labour and Trade Union leaders, among whom were Ramsay Macdonald, Robert Smillie, the Miners' President, and Philip Snowden, on behalf of the United Socialist Council, summoned to meet in Leeds on June 3, 1917,

Great Labour, Socialist *and* Democratic Convention
to hail the Russian Revolution
and to Organise *the* British Democracy
To follow Russia

To this Convention I was invited to go as a delegate, but I am now not quite sure what body I represented—it must have been, I think, either my local Labour Party or the

---

[1] January 22, 1905, a large body of strikers, led by the Govern-ment agent provocateur, Father Gapon, went to the Winter Palace in St. Petersburg to present a petition to the Tsar and were massacred by the Tsar's troops.

Fabian Society. At any rate on Saturday, June 2, I took the midnight train to Leeds. In the very early hours of a grey, chilly, windy summer morning, I came out of the Leeds central station in the distinguished company of Macdonald, Snowden, and other democrats. In the middle of the great war in all the large cities of England there were a number of violent and vociferous patriots who were always ready to throw stones at any democrat or socialist, or anyone who ventured to mention the League of Nations or, that dirtiest of all words, peace. Only a few weeks before I had been stoned in good company by a hostile crowd in Farringdon Street, a crowd of patriots who objected to us holding a Labour Party meeting in a hall there. Another crowd of hostile patriots soon surrounded us outside the Leeds railway station. They did not throw stones at us, but they booed us all the way to the Albert Hall where the Convention was held.

Labour conventions and conferences, on a large scale, are either very flat or very fizzy; the Leeds convention was one of the most enthusiastic and emotional that I have ever attended. All Labour people—indeed nearly all people in England—hated the Tsarist régime; they felt extremely uneasy when they remembered that they were fighting the war with that régime on their side, a war which we were fighting, according to President Wilson, because 'the world must be made safe for democracy'; and Mr. Asquith was telling us that

We are fighting for the moral forces of humanity. We are fighting for the respect for public law and for the right of public justice, which are the foundations of civilization.

The convention was a kind of public sigh of relief at the lifting of this incubus in eastern Europe. The ecstatic meeting passed four resolutions. It is worth recalling them from the ironical ebb and flow of time and events. Macdonald, who exactly 20 years later was to end his political career widely discredited as the rather pitiful prisoner of his aristocratic and Tory allies, moved the first resolution: 'Hail! The Russian Revolution.' At one time I knew Ramsay fairly well and later on shall have more to say about him; here it is sufficient to say that he was in his element in 1917, a period of his career in which he was a rebel and pacifist in the political wilderness, addressing this immense sympathetic audience in Leeds. For he was a fine figure of a man, with a handsome face to satisfy a maiden's or a hairdresser's dream, with a golden bell-like bull-like voice which said nothing at such inordinate length and so persuasively that he could always get a Labour audience shouting with enthusiasm—at least until August 23, 1931, when most Labour people thought he had deserted them for the Londonderrys and the Tories.

The second resolution, proposed by Snowden, pledged 'ourselves to work for . . . a peace without annexations or indemnities and based on the rights of nations to decide their own affairs'. The third resolution was on Civil Liberty, proposed by Ammon, a trade unionist Labour M.P., and Mrs. Despard. Mrs. Despard was a well known suffragette. A very frail elderly lady, she had, I think, only recently come out of gaol; she was given a tremendous reception by the meeting. Clio, the cynical Muse of History, who presumably knows both the future and the past, if she listened to our resolution, must have smiled grimly at the irony of facts. For this is what we voted unanimously:

This Conference calls upon the Government of Great Britain to place itself in accord with the democracy of Russia by proclaiming its adherence to and determination to carry into immediate effect a charter of liberties establishing complete political rights for all men and women, unrestricted freedom of the press, freedom of speech, a general amnesty for all political and religious prisoners, full rights of industrial and political association, and the release of labour from all forms of compulsion and restraint.

Another frail figure received an enthusiastic welcome when he supported the resolution in the precise, clipped, aristocratic voice which, I always think, Bertie Russell must have inherited from his 18th-century Whig ancestors. I wonder how many of us who cheered Bertie and the resolution remembered what we had voted for when the democracy of Russia was embodied in first Lenin, Trotsky, and Dzerzhinsky, and later Stalin. Finally in the fourth resolution we called upon 'the constituent bodies at once to establish in every town, urban and rural district, Councils of Workmen and Soldiers' Delegates for initiating and co-ordinating working-class activity'.

The only other thing that I remember about this conference is a speech by Tom Mann. He belonged to a generation of trade unionists which has now completely died out. He worked on a farm from the age of nine to the age of eleven, and from eleven to fourteen in the mines; he was a socialist and agitator and general secretary of the A.S.E. He excelled in the peculiar style of oratory which had developed in the working class and socialist movements of the continent and of Britain. The great exponents of it were the French. At big Labour or trade union conferences during the nineteen twenties there were usually foreign 'fraternal delegates' each of whom made a short speech. A Frenchman who often came as a delegate—I cannot remember his name—was an amazing orator. He was a short bearded man, unimpressive to look at; he would stand absolutely motionless on the rostrum, his right hand held out in front of him with the first finger pointing straight up to the roof. Then for five minutes a liquid fountain of words would issue from him ceaselessly, but rising a little and falling a little in a kind of rhythm, and one was hypnotized into the optical and oral delusion that this fountain of words was issuing not from his mouth, but from the tip of that first finger of his right hand. Nobody knew what he was saying—I don't know that he himself knew—but we were all carried away by it; it reminded me of a canary singing in a cage or even sometimes of a Chopin mazurka.

In June, 1918, I went to a great Labour Party Conference in the Central Hall, Westminster, at which the question of whether or not to continue the 'party truce' was discussed. Suddenly the proceedings were interrupted by a strange figure walking on to the platform and embracing the chairman. It was Kerensky who had fled from Russia after his government had been destroyed by the Bolshevik revolution of November, 1917. He spoke to us for five minutes and he was given an ovation. He was another of these orators whose words rose and fell in an inexhaustible, almost visible fountain of emotional sound. I do not think his Russian meant anything more than the French of the fraternal delegate or than the English of Tom Mann. For it was in this style of oratory that Tom Mann excelled.

Looking back to 1917 after nearly half a century, with the knowledge and even perhaps wisdom which half a century gives us, it is easy to deride our hopes and enthusiasm, our oratory and resolutions in the Leeds Albert Hall. To me personally the 46 years and my knowledge of what has happened in them have not brought me to repent or recant. I have always disliked and distrusted oratory and in the light of events I would wish to emend the wording of our resolutions. But if I could return to 1917 possessing the knowledge and experience of 1963 I would again welcome the Russian revolution and for the same reasons for which I originally welcomed it. Like the French revolution, it destroyed an ancient, malignant growth in European society, and this was essential for the future of European civilization. The intelligent revolutionary knows, however, that all revolutions must disappoint him. There is nothing more violent than violence and it is true that more often than not if you draw the sword you will perish by the sword. The violence of the great revolutions becomes more and more violent and the civilized men who made the violent revolution almost always perish by revolutionary violence until in the end power is safely in the hands of savage, ruthless, fanatical dictators, Marats and Robespierres, Dzerzhinskys and Stalins. Nevertheless the destruction of the ancien régime in France and of the Tsarist régime in Russia was essential—and indeed inevitable, in the sense that, if you go on pouring water into a glass after it is full, it is inevitable that the water will overflow. That is why, if I could return to 1789 and 1917, I would still be on the side of the revolution—though I have no doubt that I should have been guillotined by Marat and liquidated by Stalin.

The year 1917, historically so important, is also remembered by me personally and autobiographically for two reasons. I helped to found the 1917 Club and Virginia and I started The Hogarth Press. The 1917 Club was a strange phenomenon. I do not really like clubs. I have been a member of only three in London during my life, the Trade Union, the 1917, and the Athenaeum. Most are terribly respectable, with the kind of male pomposity and public school unreality which I find irritating. That is why for years I refused to join one and only late in life became a member of the Athenaeum. I rarely go to it, and when I do enter its famous doors it is usually to go to the lavatory on my way to somewhere else. Indeed it sometimes seems to me that I pay 22 guineas a year for the privilege and glory of using its distinguished urinals six or seven times in the year —which works out at the rather heavy cost of round about three guineas a time.

If the Athenaeum is the nadir of respectability, my other two clubs were the zenith of disreputability. The snobbery which induced me in old age to join the Athenaeum inversely induced me, when a callow labour neophyte, to join the Trade Union Club. I did not use even its lavatory. My memory is that it had a room or two on the first floor of a dingy building in Holborn, that I looked in once and was so depressed by its melancholy gloom and smell of stale beer that I never went there again.

I do not remember in whose brain the idea of a left wing club originated in 1917. I rather think it started in a conversation between Oliver Strachey, Lytton's brother, and me. At any rate in April we were sounding all kinds of people about the idea and found everywhere enthusiastic support for it. We got together a kind of informal committee which met for the first time on April 23 and continued to direct affairs until the first general meeting of the club on December 19. I have forgotten who all the people were who worked with us, but the following certainly were concerned in it with us: Ramsay Macdonald, J. A. Hobson, Mary Macarthur, a prominent woman trade unionist, and her husband, W. C. Anderson; H. N. Brailsford; Molly Hamilton (Mrs. M. A. Hamilton), who became a Labour M.P. and wrote the life of Macdonald; Emile Burns who became a communist. By July we were looking at houses in Long Acre and elsewhere and eventually we took the lease of a house in Gerrard Street, in those days the rather melancholy haunt of prostitutes daily from 2.30 p.m. onwards.

On December 19, as I said, we held the first general meeting; I was elected to the committee and remained a member of it for a good many years.

The membership of the club during its first years was a curious mixture. It was mainly political and the politicals were mainly Labour Party, from Ramsay downwards. But there was also an element of unadulterated culture, literary and artistic, and during the first two or three years of its existence it was much used by culture, particularly at tea time, so that if one dropped in about 4 o'clock and looked round its rooms, one would hardly have guessed that it was political. Virginia was often there and there was a strong contingent of Stracheys, including Lytton and a retinue of young women and young men who often accompanied him. Years later the stage must have invaded and captured the club, for, when I had long ceased to use it, I was asked, as a founder of it, to come to a dinner to celebrate its foundation. Ramsay Macdonald presided and I sat at the high table, as it were, with him and some other aging politicians, while the active members seemed to be mainly actors and actresses and musicians. In its beginnings the stage gave us, I think, only one member, Elsa Lanchester, and music only Cyril Scott.

It was at the club that I first got to know Ramsay Macdonald well, though during the war I also saw him a good deal in connection with the Union of Democratic Control. This therefore seems to be an appropriate place to say something about one of the most curious characters that I have known. When I first knew him, he was more or less in a political wilderness, partly because of his attitude towards the war and partly because he was not altogether trusted in his own party. He was M.P. for Leicester, but it must be remembered that he became chairman of the Parliamentary Labour Party only in 1922, five or six years after the time which I am writing about. In 1922 he had moved already to the right wing of the party, but in 1917 he was counted to be very much to the left, for he was a leader of the Independent Labour Party and the Union of Democratic Control.

I used to lunch with him now and again at the 1917 Club and was always amused to observe the acts which he would put on even for my benefit. For he was essentially an actor, the most egocentric and histrionic of men. I remember meeting him one Monday at the Club for lunch when he had come down straight from Lossiemouth and was going to the House in the afternoon for an important debate at which he was to make an important speech. We had met to discuss some political question connected, I think, with his speech.[1] Instead of getting down to business he gave me a long account of how he had spent the Sunday walking on the Scottish hills; it was the set sentimental speech in the mellifluous voice of the orator who wants to draw tears from your eyes before he moves on to the thunderous peroration. It was typical of Ramsay that he should address it to my stony and sceptical ears over the dreary rissoles of the 1917 Club. As we walked away he told me that he had influenza and that his temperature was 102, but that he must go and make his speech. I think it was in fact probably true that he had

[1] I think this is so because I remember a curious incident of that afternoon even today, 45 years later. For after lunch Ramsay and I had a discussion with Charles Trevelyan and E. D. Morel, of the U.D.C., and Camille Huysmans, the Belgian labour leader who subsequently became Prime Minister. After our talk we all walked away together accompanying Ramsay, I suppose, to the House. For I was walking ahead of the three others with Huysmans when in the middle of Trafalgar Square he told me that everyone in France realized that we were on the brink of military disaster, because Foch was completely incompetent being 'estropié à cause de prostate'. I had no idea what 'prostate' meant and made him explain. Huysmans knew everyone and was a highly intelligent man. I always remember his telling me this in Trafalgar Square because a few weeks later Foch routed the Germans.

travelled down in the night train from Scotland with a temperature of 102, had eaten his rissoles, had talked without stopping, and would go on and make his speech—all without turning a hair, for he had the kind of iron constitution which is the first and, when I think of the Prime Ministers I have known, perhaps the only necessary qualification or asset which a man must possess if he is to become Prime Minister.

I have never known a vainer and a more treacherous man than Ramsay. It was in 1916 that he asked me to come and see him one afternoon in his room in Lincoln's Inn Fields. He wanted me to write a regular article in the *Labour Leader* on the debates in parliament. I agreed to do it for a year. It was quite interesting, for I had a ticket for the Press Gallery in the House of Commons and only went to listen from time to time to important debates. After I had done it for some months, Ramsay asked me to come and see him again. He buttered me up for a bit, praising my articles, then he came round in a gyrating circle to the real point—couldn't I make it rather more *personal*, dealing with what the Labour M.P.'s actually said, and particularly the leaders—and he talked so much about himself that he left me in no doubt that by leaders he meant leader. When Ramsay talked about himself, he seemed to ooze vanity and it was to me very interesting to compare his attitude to these articles with that of another Labour leader who at that time was very well known. Near me in Richmond lived a Durham miner called Tom Richardson, who was M.P. for Whitehaven. Richardson himself was a pleasant man, but a typical rank and file miner Labour M.P. During parliamentary sessions he often had staying with him another miner M.P., Bob Smillie, President of the Miners' Federation of Great Britain. If there was any question or Bill important for Labour coming up in the Commons and I knew Smillie to be in Richmond, I used to go round in the evening to discuss it with him. He was the exact opposite of Ramsay. On the surface he was the dourest of Scots, with a granitic face, soul, and mind. Not only did he never use two words if one sufficed; he never used one word if silence sufficed. Beneath the granite he was the nicest and most simple and genuine of men. He was extremely intelligent. If the question or Bill was some labour problem which he knew about and I did not, he would explain it carefully to me; if it was something which I knew about and he did not, he would take any amount of trouble to pick my brains until he really understood it. This impersonal objectivity, this passionate pursuit of the thing rather than passionate concern with the self is even rarer with politicians than most people.

I once came across a curious case in which this pursuit of truth and knowledge was combined with ruthless egotism in a leading trade unionist. Years later when I was secretary of the Labour Party Advisory Committee on Imperial Questions the T.U.C. asked Charles Buxton, who was chairman, and me to meet the trade union delegates to an I.L.O. Conference and advise them about a draft treaty on forced labour which they would have to deal with at the conference. When the delegates turned out to be the great Ernest Bevin and the great J. H. Thomas, I felt a good deal of dismay as we sat down at the table to go through the treaty clause by clause. Bevin was a ruthless man who notoriously despised and distrusted intellectuals and Thomas despised them in a flamboyant way peculiar to himself. I suppose it took an hour or more to go through the draft treaty and I do not think that Thomas listened to a single word that was said. But Bevin amazed me. He was just like Smillie. He knew nothing about what is now called colonialism or the facts about forced labour in colonies and he saw that Buxton and I did. He picked our brains clause by clause and continually asked us what line we advised him to take over every detail. Like

Smillie, he was quick to see every point explained to him. But whereas when I left Smillie I always felt that, underneath the granite surface of the trade unionist, I had seen and felt a human being, when the door closed on Ernest Bevin, I felt that, having picked my brains, he would ruthlessly dismiss and, if necessary for his purposes, or perhaps even if unnecessary, destroy me. And there was nothing gentle or genteel about destruction by Ernest Bevin. I was present at the famous Labour Party Conference in the charming Brighton Regency Pavilion when Bevin battered George Lansbury to political death. I happened to be on Bevin's side in that particular dispute and Lansbury, with his slightly lachrymose, self-righteous righteousness which worked as persistently and noisily as an automatic drill, always tended to make me feel uncomfortable or irritable. But there was something indecent in the cruelty, the sadistic enjoyment with which Bevin destroyed the poor man.

To return to Ramsay, one of his most marked characteristics was tortuousness of mind. One never felt that one quite knew what he was really at, why he was doing or saying what he was doing or saying. This uncertainty was not peculiar to me; people who worked closely with him in the Cabinet or the House of Commons, like Sidney Webb and Arthur Ponsonby, always said the same—if you ever got a glimpse of what was really in his mind, it was so convoluted and equivocal that you felt that you had got inside a mental maze.

Here is a strange example of his methods. In 1924 I wrote a memorandum on some foreign affairs question—I no longer remember what it was all about—which was to be discussed at the next meeting of the Labour Party Advisory Committee on International Questions. About a week before the meeting I got a letter from him asking me whether I would come and have a talk with him about the memorandum one afternoon in his room in the House of Commons. He was at the time both Prime Minister and Foreign Secretary. I was an insignificant member of the Party; the memorandum was about a more or less insignificant subject; if passed by the committee, it would have merely gone up as a recommendation to the Executive Committee of the Party—and almost certainly have died the usual death there. But I found Ramsay with a copy of the memorandum on the table in front of him; he must have read it line by line and word by word, for it was covered with notes[1] which he had written on it in pencil. He then took me through the thing paragraph by paragraph by paragraph, arguing all the points minutely and carefully, and at the end he gave me his copy and asked me to consider what he had written there and what he had said. I was more than half an hour with him in the middle of an afternoon when parliament was sitting. He was at the time trying to combine the work of Prime Minister with the work of Foreign Secretary—an impossible job which no one dreamt of attempting again. Yet he must have given up at least an hour of his time to me and to this totally unimportant memorandum on a, for him, totally unimportant subject. I know that, as I sat opposite to him, I kept on thinking to myself: 'What on earth is going on in the tortuous maze of

[1] A curious thing happened with regard to these pencilled notes. The week after Ramsay gave them to me I reviewed a book on handwriting in which the author gave specimens of well known people's handwriting and explained how certain characteristics in the writing indicated certain characteristics in their psychology. One of the people he dealt with was Ramsay Macdonald and he maintained that a trait in Ramsay's character was shown by the fact that he made casual dots on the paper on which he was writing. I mentioned in my review that I had a document covered with Ramsay's handwriting in which there were no casual dots and that I did not think there was in his character the trait alleged by the expert. The expert asked to see my document and, as it was confidential, I allowed him to come to my office and look at it. He had to admit that there were no dots, but I do not think that he admitted being also wrong about Ramsay's character.

that mind?' I got, of course, a glimpse of his usual inordinate and jealous vanity; there was obviously some probably quite unimportant point in the memorandum on which, he felt, I ought to have consulted him, James Ramsay Macdonald, Prime Minister and Foreign Secretary. But there must have been, and I felt that there was, more to it than that. There was some inexplicable and for ever unascertainable worm in the labyrinth of his mind which caused him, with some satisfaction, to waste an hour of his time in a futile discussion with a futile intellectual over a futile memorandum.

Finally there was the curious streak of treachery in Ramsay. Some people in the Labour Party who knew him much better than I did, and therefore suffered much more from him, used to say that his instinct to double-cross and stab his friends in the back was derived from the traditional habit of the highland Scot to pursue secret feuds. I personally had a remarkable experience of this habit. In the last years of the war I got to know well Norman Angell and the group of young men—John Hilton, H. D. Henderson, and Harold Wright—who were tremendously influenced by his remarkable personality and his remarkable book, *The Great Illusion*. They ran a small monthly magazine, *War and Peace*, which propagated Angell's views; it was edited by Harold Wright and financed by the Rowntrees. They asked me to join the editorial board and, when Harold Wright was ill, I edited the paper for some months. When he recovered, he asked me what I thought of the paper and whether I had any ideas for its improvement. I said that I thought that, if Rowntree would finance it, it could be turned into an important international review[1] dealing with foreign affairs and problems of war and peace, with an advisory editorial board

[1] I proposed to publish the review at first in English, but with the hope that eventually it would be possible to publish it also in French and German.

consisting of all the leading socialists and trade unionists in Britain and on the Continent. I had discussed this idea with Camille Huysmans and some other continental socialists; they were all enthusiastically in favour of it, but there had seemed no possibility of financing it.

Harold asked me to put my scheme in writing so that he could put it before the Rowntrees. I did this and he and I had an interview with Arnold Rowntree and his business manager, Bonwick. The Rowntree Trust was willing to finance the review, provided that I would get the leading Labour and socialist people to join the board and would undertake to edit the review. As Harold was in favour of my doing this, I agreed. I went to Huysmans and he undertook to get all the continental leaders, and in this he was successful. I went to Ramsay Macdonald, Arthur Henderson, the Webbs, Smillie, and the other British leaders and they all agreed to join the board. The Webbs were particularly enthusiastic and had me to lunch to meet Branting, an influential Scandinavian socialist, and other foreign labour leaders to discuss details. I got the support and consent of everyone in writing except Ramsay's, though he had verbally agreed and told me that he thought well of the scheme. As he had not put anything in writing and July was waning with everyone soon going away for their holidays, I wrote him again. Two days later I lunched with him at the 1917 Club; the first thing which he said was that he had got my letter and would be delighted to join the board.

Two days later Arnold Rowntree asked me to come and see him. He told me that Ramsay had come up to him in the House and said that he understood that Rowntree was considering starting an international review supported by British and foreign labour leaders and edited by Leonard Woolf. He (Ramsay) would have nothing to do with it, and strongly advised Rowntree not to touch it; it was 'an absurd idea'. I told Rowntree what Ramsay had said to me two days before. Rowntree said that unless Ramsay gave it his unreserved support, they would not go on with the idea, as otherwise he would do everything to wreck it, and would probably succeed. I went off and rang up Ramsay, but could not get hold of him; so I wrote him a stiff letter asking him what the devil he meant by saying one thing to me and another to Rowntree. I got a wonderful letter back in which the worm coiled and uncoiled and coiled itself again until it was impossible to straighten anything out, but in the last sentence he did tell me to go ahead and God speed you. But I knew now that, whatever God might do, Ramsay was determined not to speed me—and Arnold Rowntree knew it too. He decided that, in the teeth of Ramsay's hostility, they would not go ahead with the original idea, but they asked me to edit the *International Review*, which they were prepared to start, a straightforward review on the lines originally sketched by me, but without any socialist and labour support; rather reluctantly I agreed. The question remains: why did Ramsay stab me in the back? No one could possibly know the convolutions in Ramsay's mind, not even, I think, Ramsay; but incredible though it may seem to be, I believe that one reason was that he himself edited an insignificant paper called the *Socialist Review*. My review could not conceivably have damaged his, but it was safer to stab it in the back before it was born. And yet to give him his due, Ramsay was so convoluted and ambivalent that I should not be at all surprised if he did not with a genuine tear in his eye and a little choke in his superb voice tell me to 'go ahead and God speed you' at the very moment that, with practised and unerring skill, he was putting his thin little knife into my back and into the *International Review* in the lobby of the House of Commons. One certainly gets a great deal more pleasure from contemplating the psychology of a man like Ramsay than pain from the way in which he treats one.

What with Ramsay and the *Labour Leader* and the abortive editorial committee for the *International Review*, not to speak of the Co-operative Movement, I had become very much mixed up with the whole Labour Movement, both on its political and its trade union and economic sides. To this in the last year of the war, owing to Sidney Webb, was added an entanglement with the Labour Party and its machine which lasted for over 20 years. Already in 1917 the feeling that the war must end sometime, if not soon, began to creep over us, and there was also a feeling that, if, as we were told, the war was to make the world safe for democracy, the Left and the Labour Party ought to have something to say about what kind of new world should rise out of the ruins of the old world and its great war. The structure of the Labour Party was primitive, and it was decided that Webb and Arthur Henderson should draft for it a new constitution which would enable the party to appeal both to the trade unions and to individuals, and organize them effectively into a political force capable of competing with the Conservative and Liberal Parties. When they had finished their work and the new constitution was ready to be put before a Labour Party Conference, Sidney asked me to come and see him.

He told me that they were instituting a system of advisory committees which was a new invention and which he thought should be of very great importance politically. Those who voted Conservative or Liberal and those whom they elected to the House of Commons were overwhelmingly middle class; if you took a cross-section of them, you would find it contained individuals working in every kind of profession and business, who by education and occupation could provide expert knowledge on every kind of political problem. The position of the Labour Party was entirely different. The

Labour electorate and the Labour M.P. were overwhelmingly working class and would remain so. By education and experience their knowledge was habitually limited to a narrow range of occupational and industrial conditions and problems. When the day came that 100, 200, or 300 Labour members were elected, the number among them who would have any real knowledge of finance, economics, education, international or imperial affairs would be dangerously small. Even on the Executive Committee, in which the policy of the Party on everything, from war and peace to income tax and infant schools, was determined, it was rare to find anyone with the elementary expert knowledge or experience necessary for advising or deciding. Webb proposed that the Executive Committee should set up four or five advisory committees consisting of experts appointed by the Executive and of any M.P.'s who wanted to join a committee. The advisory committee would be authorized to consider any question or problem connected with its terms of reference, and to send to the Executive reports and recommendations. Sidney asked me whether I would become secretary of the advisory committee dealing with international and imperial questions; he himself was going to be chairman, at least for a time. I agreed to do this.

The committee soon after the war split into two, one on international and the other on imperial questions, and I remained the secretary of both for over 20 years. For all that time we met once a week regularly upstairs in a committee room of the House of Commons, and a few persons on each committee did an immense amount of work. Many of these, who had remarkable expert knowledge and experience, were habitually disappointed by the results of their labours, but I think we did influence the Party's policy occasionally in important ways and—what was even more significant—a small number of Labour M.P.'s regularly attended our meetings and gradually became real experts on foreign or imperial affairs and policies. In many ways I much enjoyed the work, partly because I got to know a large number of different men and could observe intimately their relations to one another and sometimes their strange political and psychological antics; partly because I made many real and lifelong friends among them, and partly because I often got behind the scenes a fascinating view of that kaleidoscope of persons, politics, and policies which is a tiny corner in what we call history. Some of the details of this may be worth recounting, but I will not pursue them here, for they belong to the post-war world and therefore to my fourth volume if it should ever be written.

A few names should, however, be mentioned here. Charles Roden Buxton, a worthy member of the famous anti-slavery Buxton family, was chairman of both committees and did an enormous amount of work. Sir John Maynard succeeded Buxton as chairman of the Imperial Committee. He was a remarkable man; a retired Indian civil servant, he was the exact opposite of what many people would regard as the prototype of a high ranking Indian civilian; a first-rate administrator, he was a most intellectual progressive and progressive intellectual who devoted himself to promoting the prosperity and the freedom of what in those days were called 'subject peoples'. Two other ex-government servants, Norman Leys, who had been in the Kenya Health Service, and McGregor Ross, who had been head of the Kenya Public Works Department, devoted themselves to the cause of liberty, equality, and prosperity in Africa; Africans and African independence owe an immense debt to these two passionate, fanatical, and forgotten men. Drummond Shiels, who became Under-Secretary of State, and Arthur Creech Jones, who became Secretary of State for the Colonies, were also members to whom the new Africa and the new Asia owe a considerable debt. In international affairs an untiring worker was Phil Noel-Baker who crowned a distinguished political career by winning the Nobel Peace Prize in 1959. Finally in this list I mention with affection and respect Harry Snell, one of the Labour M.P.'s who learned much from the advisory committees. I got to know him well and was very fond of him. He began life as a farm worker and became a groom, a ferryman, and a public-house potman. He ended life as a peer and Deputy Leader of the House of Lords. But he remained always a countryman, the intelligent, wary, simple, kindly Harry Snell. When he was Deputy Leader of the House of Lords he came to me one day and said that a certain young hereditary peer, with Labour sympathies, had made rather a mess of his maiden speech, partly from nervousness at being kept on tenterhooks before he could catch the Lord Chancellor's eye, and partly perhaps because he had fortified himself against the nervousness. Snell thought him a youth of promise and asked me to get him to join one of the advisory committees, encourage him to take it seriously, and become a serious politician. We did this, and our pupil became, unaware of our guidance, a distinguished politician. What the ancestors of the peer and the potman would have thought of this I do not know. Even the House of Lords has seen some things change a little through the ages.

In 1916 and 1917 I suddenly found myself once more immersed in Ceylon affairs. In 1915 rioting broke out in Kandy and lasted for two days; after it had stopped in Kandy, it broke out in Colombo where it was extremely violent. There were many casualties and much damage to property. Five provinces were placed under martial law and the army restored order. Martial law continued for several months and large numbers of people were tried and sentenced by Courts Martial, the judges being military officers. 83 persons were condemned to death and 60 sentenced to life imprisonment. There is no doubt that many of these people were completely innocent of the offences with which they were charged. The Ceylon Government justified their actions by alleging that the riots were seditious. The Sinhalese maintained that there was no sedition at all or anywhere; no European was molested, no European property attacked; it was an exacerbated example of communal riots, indigenous in India and Ceylon. In this case economic questions had led to embittered feelings between the Buddhist Sinhalese and the Moslem Moormen which culminated in attacks by the Sinhalese upon the Moormen. The Government and the police had shown themselves weak and incompetent in the early stages and had so allowed the rioting to get out of hand.

The Sinhalese appointed two delegates to come to England and ask the British Government for an enquiry and revision of sentences: E. W. Perera, a Colombo advocate, and D. B. Jayatillaka (who later became Prime Minister of Ceylon and was knighted). They came to me and asked me to help them to get support for their demands. I went carefully into the evidence and came to the conclusion that the Sinhalese case was entirely correct and that there ought to be an enquiry and revision. For a year or more I worked closely with the two delegates and got to know them well. Jayatillaka was an exceptionally nice person and so was his wife; she used to come and dine with us and sing Sinhalese songs more beautifully than I had ever heard singing in Ceylon. The delegates and I did an immense amount of work in the press and House of Commons and at last in 1918 the Secretary of State for the Colonies agreed to receive a deputation on the subject.

Governments nearly always treat these kinds of deputation irritably and contemptuously, ignoring the evidence, particularly when the Government knows that it is in the

wrong, but on January 16, 1918, in the Colonial Office I got
a certain amount of cynical pleasure observing the antics of
myself and my fellow deputies on one side of the table and
of Under-Secretary of State for the Colonies, W. A. S.
Hewins, M.P., and his permanent officials on the other.
We were a motley gang, the Bishop of Lincoln, Gilbert
Murray, Sir J. Rolleston, and I supported the Sinhalese.
Sir V. Buxton introduced the deputation and I then made a
speech. I began by saying that I knew something about
Ceylon as I had been seven years in the Ceylon Civil Service.
Hewins looked me up and down and then turned and said
something, obviously a question, to his Permanent Under-
Secretary. He looked at me with some misprision. We all did
our best, but all we got from Mr. Hewins was the inevitable
and expected refusal. Who killed imperialism? I, said the
imperialist, with my imperialism—and my Hewinses and
my refusals.

And now I come to the fortuitous way in which we started
the Hogarth Press and became publishers. In the last two
years of the war Virginia's health became gradually more
stable. She was writing again strenuously and regularly. She
was at work on *Night and Day* and finished it at the end of
1918, and she also from time to time wrote short pieces like
The Mark on the Wall. In 1917 and 1918 there was not a
single month in which she did not have reviews in *The Times
Literary Supplement*; many of these were reprinted in *The
Common Reader* in 1925. She earned from these reviews
£95. 9s. 6d. in 1917 and £104. 5s. 6d. in 1918. The routine
of our life became pretty regular. We worked strenuously
during the week. In addition to my political activities I was
writing *Empire and Commerce in Africa*. Over the week-end
we usually went for what we called a treat. It was a mild
'treat', a bus to somewhere up the river and a walk and tea
in Hampton Court or Kingston perhaps. In those days—40

or 50 years ago—Richmond and Richmond Park, Ham, Kingston, Hampton Court were still very beautiful, and even on Saturdays and Sundays the beauty of trees and grass and river and willows was not yet obscured by hundreds of cars and thousands of people crawling like queues of blackbeetles and ants every week out of London in the morning, and having scattered their paper bags, ice-cream cartons, and beer bottles over the landscape, back again into London in the evening. Socially it was the prehistoric era in which one still had servants living in one's house. We had almost inherited from Roger Fry two: Nellie the cook, and Lottie the house-parlourmaid, who stayed with us for years. In 1917 they cost us in wages £76, 1s. 8d. Though we had two servants and two houses our expenditure in 1917 was under £700. And we saw and entertained a good many people. They came out to lunch or dinner with us at Richmond and often stayed the night.

I have never known anyone work with more intense, more indefatigable concentration than Virginia. This was particularly the case when she was writing a novel. The novel became part of her and she herself was absorbed into the novel. She wrote only in the morning from 10 to 1 and usually she typed out in the afternoon what she had written by hand in the morning, but all day long, when she was walking through London streets or on the Sussex downs or over the watermeadows or along the river Ouse, the book would be moving subconsciously in her mind or she herself would be moving in a dreamlike way through the book. It was this intense absorption which made writing so exhausting mentally for her, and all through her life she tried to keep two kinds of writing going simultaneously, fiction and criticism. After some weeks on a novel she would switch to criticism as a relief or rest, because, though she devoted great care and concentration to even a comparatively unimportant review, the part of her mind which she used for criticism or even biography was different from that which she used for her novels. The relief or relaxation which she obtained from this change in the angle of her mental vision was of the same kind as that obtained by a man whose work entails hard, concentrated thinking and who finds refreshment and relaxation for his mind in a hard, serious game of chess, because in the game he is using a different part of his mind and for a different purpose from what was required for his work.

As I have explained more than once in my autobiography, such wisdom as I possess is largely derived from the saws and sayings of my nurse who came from Somersetshire. One of the great truths which I learned from her was that all work and no play did irreparable harm to all humanity whom she and I recognized in a boy called Jack. The difficulty with Virginia was to find any play sufficiently absorbing to take her mind off her work. We were both interested in printing and had from time to time in a casual way talked about the possibility of learning to print. It struck me that it would be a good thing if Virginia had a manual occupation of this kind which, in say the afternoons, would take her mind completely off her work. Towards the end of 1916 we definitely decided that we would learn the art of printing. But that proved to be not at all an easy thing to do. The individual finds that very few actions are easy or simple for him, entangled as he is in the complicated machinery of life which, with him in it, is turned round and round and round by the colossal anonymous engine of 20th-century society. When we went to the St. Bride's school of printing down Bride Lane, Fleet Street, we learned that the social engine and machinery made it impossible to teach the art of printing to two middle-aged, middle-class persons. Printing could only be taught to trade union apprentices, the number of whom was strictly limited.

This seemed to end our career as printers before it could begin. But on March 23, 1917, we were walking one afternoon up Farringdon Street from Fleet Street to Holborn Viaduct when we passed the Excelsior Printing Supply Co. It was not a very large firm, but it sold every kind of printing machine and material, from a handpress and type to a composing stick. Nearly all the implements of printing are materially attractive and we stared through the window at them rather like two hungry children gazing at buns and cakes in a baker shop window. I do not know which of us first suggested that we should go inside and see whether we could buy a machine and type and teach ourselves. We went in and explained our desire and dilemma to a very sympathetic man in a brown overall. He was extremely encouraging. He could not only sell us a printing machine, type, chases, cases, and all the necessary implements, but also a 16-page pamphlet which would infallibly teach us how to print. There was no need to go to a school of printing or to become an apprentice; if we read his pamphlet and followed the instructions, we should soon find that we were competent printers. Before we left the shop we had bought a small handpress, some Old Face type, and all the necessary implements and materials for a sum of £19. 5s. 5d. The machine was small enough to stand on a kitchen table; it was an ordinary platen design; you worked it by pulling down the handle which brought the platen and paper up against the type in its chase. You could print one demy octavo page on it, and, I think, you could just squeeze in two crown octavo pages.

When the stuff was delivered to us in Richmond, we set it all up in the dining-room and started to teach ourselves to print. The Excelsior man proved to be right; by following the directions in the pamphlet we found that we could pretty soon set the type, lock it up in the chase, ink the rollers, and machine a fairly legible printed page. After a month we thought we had become sufficiently proficient to print a page of a book or pamphlet. We decided to print a paper-covered pamphlet containing a story by each of us and to try to sell it by subscription to a limited number of people whom we would circularize. Our idea was that, if this succeeded, we might go on to print and publish in the same way poems or other short works which the commercial publisher would not look at.

We set to work and printed a 32-page pamphlet, demy octavo, with the following title page:

Publication No. 1.

TWO STORIES
WRITTEN AND PRINTED
BY
VIRGINIA WOOLF
AND
L. S. WOOLF

HOGARTH PRESS
RICHMOND
1917

Virginia's story was *The Mark on the Wall* and mine was *Three Jews*. We even had the temerity to print four wood-cuts by Carrington. I must say, looking at a copy of this curious publication today, that the printing is rather credit-able for two persons who had taught themselves for a month in a dining-room. The setting, inking, impression are really not bad. What is quite wrong is the backing, for I had not yet realized that a page on one side of the sheet must be printed so that it falls exactly on the back of the page on the other side of the sheet.

We began to print *Two Stories* on May 3 in an edition of about 150 copies. We bound it ourselves by stitching it into paper covers. We took a good deal of trouble to find some rather unusual, gay Japanese paper for the covers. For many years we gave much time and care to finding beautiful, uncommon, and sometimes cheerful paper for binding our books, and, as the first publishers to do this, I think we started a fashion which many of the regular, old established publishers followed. We got papers from all over the place, including some brilliantly patterned from Czechoslovakia, and we also had some marbled covers made for us by Roger Fry's daughter in Paris. I bought a small quantity of Caslon Old Face Titling type and used it for printing the covers.

We printed a circular offering Publication No. 1 for 1s. 6d. net and explaining that we in The Hogarth Press proposed to print and publish in the same way from time to time paper-covered pamphlets or small books, printed entirely by our two selves, which would have little or no chance of being published by ordinary publishers. We invited people to become subscribers to the publications of The Hogarth Press, either A subscribers to whom all publications would automatically be sent, or B subscribers who would be notified of each publication as it appeared. We sent this notice to people whom we knew or who, we thought, might be interested in our publications. I do not know how many people we circularized, but we published in July and by the end of the month we had practically sold out the edition for we had sold 124 copies. (The total number finally sold was 134.) I still have a list of the 87 people who bought the 134 copies and all but five or six of them were friends or acquaintances. There are some rather unexpected names among them, e.g. Charles Trevelyan, M.P., Arthur Ponsonby, M.P., Mrs. Sidney Webb, and Mrs. Bernard Shaw. The total cost of production was £3. 7s. 0d., which

included the noble sum of 15s. to Carrington for the wood-
cuts, 12s. 6d. for paper, and 10s. for the cover paper. The
two authors were not paid any royalty. The total receipts
were £10. 8s. 0d., so that the net profit was £7. 1s. 0d.
Eventually 45 people became A subscribers and 43 B
subscribers. Among the A subscribers was one bookseller,
James Bain of what was then King William Street, Strand,
and except for him every copy of our first publications was
sold to private persons at the full published price. By 1923
the Press had developed to such an extent that we had become
more or less ordinary publishers, selling our books mainly to
booksellers at the usual discount, and we therefore gave up
the subscriber system altogether.

We so much enjoyed producing *Two Stories* and its sale
had been so successful (134 copies!) that we were induced to
go on to something more ambitious. Katherine Mansfield
and Murry were extremely interested in what we were doing,
and Katherine offered us for Publication No. 2 a long short
story which she had written, *Prelude*. When I look at my copy
of *Prelude* today, I am astonished at our courage and energy
in attempting it and producing it only a year after we had
started to teach ourselves to print. For we printed only in the
afternoon and even so not every afternoon; it is a 68-page
book and we printed and bound it entirely with our own
hands. The edition must have consisted of nearly 300 copies
for, when it went out of print, we had sold 257 copies.
Virginia did most of the setting and I did all the machining,
though I did set when there was nothing to machine.

I did not machine *Prelude* on our small handpress; in fact,
it would have taken much too long to do it page by page. I
machined it on a large platen machine which printed four
crown octavo pages at a time and which belonged to a
jobbing printer called McDermott. McDermott had a small
jobbing printing business in a street near The Green in

Richmond. I got to know him in a curious way and we became great friends. While printing *Two Stories*, I one afternoon, when I took a proof of a page, found that there was something wrong with it which I could not get right and could not understand. None of the letters printed completely black, there were tiny white dots everywhere. My pamphlet gave me no help. I had noticed McDermott's printing business; it was called The Prompt Press. (When I got to know McDermott, I sometimes thought that he had called it The Prompt Press on the principle of 'lucus a non lucendo'.) After struggling with my page for hours, I took a proof, walked down to McDermott's shop, and boldly— but rather tremulously—went in. I explained to McDermott that I was trying to teach myself to print and that I had got into an inexplicable difficulty. I showed him my speckled proof and asked him whether he could tell me what was wrong. 'Wrong?' he said; 'it isn't on its feet, that's all; it isn't on its feet.' He explained to me that, in locking up type in the chase, you might get the whole page infinitesimally not flat on the imposing surface—it would be 'off its feet' and would not print evenly.

This was the beginning of a friendship which lasted as long as we were in Richmond. McDermott had for years been a compositor in a very large London firm of printers. They had printed *The Spectator* and McDermott was never tired of telling me stories of the editor, St. Loe Strachey, Lytton's cousin, and what a fuss he made about the 'colour' —i.e. the inking—of the paper; it had to be very black indeed, too black for McDermott's liking. He had always had a longing for independence, for a small jobbing business of his own; he saved up for years, and late in life bought the business in the street near The Green. He began with an old fashioned Albion press, on which he printed posters, and two large platen machines, one worked by power and the other by treadle. Just before I got to know him he had bought and installed a very large rotary machine.

He was an extremely nice man and he was very much interested in our—to him—rather eccentric and amusing printing antics. He came and looked at our outfit and at what we were doing, and said that I could, if I liked, borrow the chases for his big treadle platen machine, lock up four pages of *Prelude* at a time, carry them down to The Prompt Press, and machine them myself on his machine. This I did, a pretty laborious business, but not quite as laborious as it would have been to print the 68 pages one by one. In the process I got to know McDermott and his business better and better. His large rotary press was really a white elephant; it was too large to be economical for the size of his business. It was continually going wrong; partly, I always suspected, because, having been a compositor all his life, he did not really understand machining and the kind of machine he had purchased. The result was that quite often, when I went down to print my own pages, I found him covered with oil and ink, pouring with sweat, and pouring a stream of the most hair raising language over his bloody machine. When that happened, instead of machining *Prelude* I spent the next few hours helping him to tinker at his bloody machine until I too was covered with oil and ink and pouring with sweat.

McDermott, I am sorry to say, produced one of the worst printed books ever published, certainly the worst ever published by The Hogarth Press. By 1919 we had become very friendly and he was eager that I should let him print a book for us. I had my doubts about this, because, though he was, of course, a first class compositor, he was a terribly impatient, slapdash worker, and in the other branches of printing was almost as much an amateur as I was. However, Virginia and I had discussed bringing out a book of her short stories and sketches, but had felt that it would be too much for us to print ourselves—and so, with considerable hesitation and certainly foolishly, I gave it to McDermott to print. It was bound in paper over boards with a woodcut design by Vanessa on the cover, and there were four woodcuts by her in the text. My greatest mistake was to allow him to provide the paper. He produced a nasty spongy antique wove and, ignorant as I was in those days about paper and printing, I had my doubts about it from the first. I went down and helped him to print the beastly thing. I have never seen a more desperate, ludicrous—but for me at the time tragic—scene than McDermott printing *Monday or Tuesday*. He insisted upon printing the woodcuts with the letterpress. The consequence was that, in order to get the right 'colour' for the illustrations, he had to get four or five times more ink on his rollers than was right for the type. His type was soon clogged with ink; but even that was not the worst: he got so much ink on the blocks and his paper was so soft and spongy that little fluffy bits of paper were torn off with the ink and stuck to the blocks and then to the rollers and finally to the type. We had to stop every few minutes and clean everything, but even so the pages were an appalling sight. We machined 1,000 copies, and at the end we sank down exhausted and speechless on the floor by the side of the machine, where we sat and silently drank beer until I was sufficiently revived to crawl battered and broken back to Hogarth House.

By having *Monday or Tuesday* printed for us by a commercial printer, we were, of course, abandoning the original idea of the Press, which was to print small books ourselves. In fact we had been already in 1919 forced fortuitously to take a similar step, the first step on the path which was to end in our becoming regular and professional publishers. In 1918 we printed two small books: *Poems* by T. S. Eliot and *Kew*

T. S. Eliot

Gardens by Virginia. Of Tom's *Poems* we printed rather fewer than 250 copies. We published it in May, 1919, price 2s. 6d. and it went out of print in the middle of 1920. Of *Kew Gardens* we printed about 170 copies (the total sold of the first edition was 148). We published it on May 12, 1919, at 2s. When we started printing and publishing with our Publication No. 1, we did not send out any review copies, but in the case of *Prelude*, Tom's *Poems*, and *Kew Gardens* we sent review copies to *The Times Literary Supplement*. By May 31 we had sold 49 copies of *Kew Gardens*. On Tuesday, May 27, we went to Asham and stayed there for a week, returning to Richmond on June 3rd. In the previous week a review of *Kew Gardens* had appeared in the *Literary Supplement* giving it tremendous praise. When we opened the front door of Hogarth House, we found the hall covered with envelopes and postcards containing orders from booksellers all over the country. It was impossible for us to start printing enough copies to meet these orders, so we went to a printer, Richard Madley, and got him to print a second edition of 500 copies, which cost us £8. 9s. 6d. It was sold out by the end of 1920 and we did not reprint.

The expansion of the Press into something which we had never intended or originally envisaged can be seen in the following list of books published by us in the first four years of its existence:

1917. L. and V. Woolf. *Two Stories*. Printed and bound by us.
1918. K. Mansfield. *Prelude*. Printed and bound by us.
1919. V. Woolf. *Kew Gardens*. 1st ed. printed and bound by us.
        T. S. Eliot. *Poems*. Printed and bound by us.
        J. Middleton Murry. *Critic in Judgment*. Printed for us.

1919.   Hope Mirrlees. *Paris*. Printed and bound by us.
1920.   E. M. Forster. *Story of the Siren*. Printed and bound
         by us.
         L. Pearsall Smith. *Stories from the Old Testament*.
         Printed for us.
         Gorky. *Reminiscences of Tolstoi*. Printed for us.

The publication of T. S. Eliot's *Poems* must be marked as
a red letter day for the Press and for us, although at the time
when I began to set the lines

> *The broad-backed hippopotamus*
> *Rests on his belly in the mud;*
> *Although he seems so firm to us*
> *He is merely flesh and blood.*

I could not, of course, foresee the remarkable future of the
author or the exact course of our long friendship with him.
I do not remember exactly how or when we first met Tom,
but it must, I think, have been in 1917, or even 1916. I
bought a copy of *Prufrock* when it was published by The
Egoist Ltd. in 1917, and it has the following inscription
written on the cover:

Inscribed for Leonard Woolf (my
            next   ⎫
                    ⎬ publisher)
            second ⎭
    with gratitude and affection
            T. S. Eliot

Tom showed us some of the poems which he had just written
and we printed seven of them and published them in the slim
paper covered book. It included three remarkable poems
which are still, I think, vintage Eliot: 'Sweeney among the

Nightingales', 'Mr. Eliot's Sunday Morning Service', and 'Whispers of Immortality'. Professional compositors, indeed all professional printers, do not attend to the sense of anything which they print—or so I was told by McDermott, who also one day said to me that of all the millions of lines which he had set in his time he doubted whether more than a few hundred were worth reading. But as an amateur printer and also the publisher of what I was printing, I found it impossible not to attend to the sense, and usually after setting a line and then seeing it appear again and again as I took it off the machine, I got terribly irritated by it. But I never tired and still do not tire of those lines which were a new note in poetry and came from the heart of the Eliot of those days (and sounded with even greater depth and volume in the next work of his which we published, the poem which had greater influence upon English poetry, indeed upon English literature, than any other in the 20th century, *The Waste Land*):

> The host with someone indistinct
> Converses at the door apart,
> The nightingales are singing near
> The Convent of the Sacred Heart,
>
> And sang within the bloody wood
> When Agamemnon cried aloud,
> And let their liquid siftings fall
> To stain the stiff dishonoured shroud.

When we first got to know Tom, we liked him very much, but we were both a little afraid of him. He was very precise, formal, cautious or even inhibited. One can feel this in the language of one of the first letters which he wrote to Virginia —in 1918—particularly in the first sentence:

Dear Mrs. Woolf,

Please pardon me for not having responded to your note immediately—on Mondays I never have a moment up till late at night. And I was not furthermore quite sure of being able to come, as I thought my wife might be arranging to return on Friday morning, but I now hear that she is coming tomorrow.

I shall look forward to Friday with great pleasure.

Sincerely yours

T. S. Eliot

Rather nervously after the war we asked Tom to come for a week-end to Monks House, and this broke the ice. The reserve, even the language thawed, and by 1922 it was Dear Virginia and Dear Leonard instead of Dear Mrs. Woolf and Dear Woolf. And the following is his letter accepting an invitation to tea, new style:

> Be sure that Possums can't refuse
> A tea with Mrs. Woolf on Tues.
> And eagerly if still alive,
> I'll come to Tea with you at five.
> I'd like to come at half past four,
> But have a business lunch before,
> And feel responsibility
> To do some work before my Tea.
> But please don't let the kettle wait
> And keep for me a cup and plate,
> And keep the water on the bile,
> A chair, and (as I hope) a Smile.

Or this in 1937:

Thank you, Virginia, I WILL come to Tea on Tuesday the 4th May at 4.30 and I hope that Leonard will perhaps

244

be in before I leave; anyway, it seems the only possibility between now and the end of May. But I don't see why you should be broadcasting without pay, unless you are appealing for a Good Cause (which is hard work at that): I should say that there was quite enough unpaid work to be had without adding broadcasting to it. To go to the Opera in a box is the only endurable way of going to the Opera: I have not been under such conditions for many a long year. Perhaps I shall go to Vienna and see if they have any cheap Opera there. I wish I might see you oftener, because as things are I seem to be degenerating into an Old Buffer. All my sports are getting to be Old Buffers' sports—e.g. I went to Wisbech last weekend, by way of the high table of Magdalene, to drink Port, and I have taken to the vice of Dining Clubs. It would not surprise me if I ended as a member of the Wine Committee of something or other; and this June I am to deliver the Prize Day Speech at Kingswood (Methodist) School. A respected citizen. And I have gone to live in Emperor's Gate. O dear. Am I a humbug? I envy you having finished an opus so recently as not to be expected to be working on a new one. I am trying to write a play, but it is very difficult, irritating when interrupted and tedious when not interrupted. O dear.

Your faithful

Tom

It was not until the end of 1922 that Tom gave us *The Waste Land* to read; we agreed to publish it; printed it ourselves and published it on September 12, 1923. That does not belong to this volume, but Tom was responsible for an interesting episode in our history as publishers which took place before the end of the war. He told us at the end of 1917 or the beginning of 1918 that Miss Harriet Weaver of *The Egoist*, which had published his *Prufrock*, was much concerned about a MS. by James Joyce which she had. Both she and he thought it was a remarkable work, but it was indecent and there were grave doubts whether it was publishable in England. He asked us whether we could perhaps consider it for The Hogarth Press or at any rate have a talk with Miss Weaver about it. This we agreed to do and on Sunday, April 14, 1918, Miss Weaver came to tea, bringing with her a large brown paper parcel containing the MS. of *Ulysses* by James Joyce—though not the whole of *Ulysses* because Joyce was still writing it. She left the MS. with us and we put this remarkable piece of dynamite into the top drawer of a cabinet in the sitting-room, telling her that we would read it and, if we thought well of it, see if we could get a printer to print it for us. The entry in my diary for the day is:

> Miss Weaver to tea about Joyce's book and the Egoist, a very mild blueeyed advanced spinster.

And this is Virginia's entry:

> But almost instantly Harriet Weaver appeared. Here our predictions were entirely at fault. I did my best to make her reveal herself in spite of her appearance, all that the editress of the Egoist ought to be, but she remained unalterably modest, judicious and decorous. Her neat mauve suit fitted both soul and body; her grey gloves laid straight by her plate symbolised domestic rectitude; her table manners were those of a well bred hen. We could get no talk to go. Possibly the poor woman was impeded by her sense that what she had in the brown paper parcel was quite out of keeping with her own contents. But then how did she ever come in contact with Joyce and the rest? Why does their filth seek exit from her mouth? Heaven

knows. She is incompetent from the business point of view and was uncertain what arrangements to make. We both looked at the MS. which seems an attempt to push the bounds of expression further on, but still all in the same direction. And so she went.

We read the MS. and decided that we would publish it if we could find a printer to print it. I showed it to William Maxwell of R. & R. Clark, Edinburgh, and to Clay, both very respectable printers of the highest rank. Neither of them would touch it and both of them said that no respectable printer would have anything to do with it, for the publisher and printer of it would certainly be prosecuted. All this took some time and it must have been in 1919 that we finally had to return the MS. to Miss Weaver.

The publication of Maxim Gorky's *Reminiscences of Leo Nicolayevitch Tolstoi* in 1920 was also another mile stone on the road of the Press towards ordinary, commercial publishing. I do not remember how we first came to know S. S. Koteliansky, always known as Kot, but I think that it must have been through Katherine Mansfield and Murry. In 1919 he came to us with a copy of the *Reminiscences*, just published in Moscow, which Gorky had sent to him, giving him the English translation rights. Kot suggested that he and I should translate it and The Hogarth Press publish it. We agreed to do this and thus began a collaboration between Kot and Virginia and me in translating Russian books. Our actual procedure in translating was that Kot did the first draft in handwriting, with generous space between the lines. and we then turned his extremely queer version into English. In order to make this easier and more accurate, we started to learn Russian and at one moment I had learned enough to be able to stumble through a newspaper or even Aksakov.

Gorky's book was a great success. We published it in

July and had to reprint it almost immediately, and in the first year we sold about 1,700 copies. It was reprinted many times and is still selling 40 years after publication. We serialized some of it in *The London Mercury*, and sold the American rights, so that at the end of 1920 Kot received nearly £50 which both he and we in those early days thought extremely satisfactory.

Kot was a fine translator from the Russian, and Lawrence and Katherine also at one time or another collaborated with him in translating. The translation of Bunin's *Gentleman from San Francisco*, a masterpiece or near-masterpiece, which he did with Lawrence and which we published in 1922, is magnificent. Gorky's *Reminiscences* is, I think, indisputably a miniature masterpiece of the purest water. Kot's English, which I had to turn into my English, was usually very strange, but it was also so vivid and individual that I was often tempted to leave it untouched. For instance, he wrote: 'She came into the room carrying in her arms a peeled-off little dog,' and on another occasion: 'she wore a haggish look'. If he was in doubt about a word, he sometimes looked it up in his dictionary and put all the variants into his translation, occasionally with curious results, e.g. 'he looked in the glass at his mug, dial, face'. One learned to the full Kot's iron integrity and intensity only by collaborating with him in a Russian translation. After I had turned his English into my English, we went through it sentence by sentence. Kot had a sensitive understanding of and feeling for language and literature, and also a strong subtle mind. He would pass no sentence until he was completely convinced that it gave the exact shade of meaning and feeling of the original, and we would sometimes be a quarter of an hour arguing over a single word.

The publication of Gorky was the beginning of our friendship with Kot which lasted 35 years, until his death in 1954.

He was a remarkable and a formidable man. Physically he was a Jew of the Trotsky type, with a pelt of thick black bristly hair going straight up into the air off his high forehead. His eyes, behind thick glasses, looked at, through, and over you, sad and desperate, and yet with resigned intensity. When he shook hands with you, you felt that all the smaller bones in your hand must certainly have been permanently crushed to a fine powder. The handshake, which always reminded me of the Commendatore taking Don Giovanni by the hand in the last Act of Mozart's opera, was merely an unconscious symptom of Kot's passionate and painful intensity and integrity. I always had a secret hope that this devastating handshake meant that Kot liked one, and that those whom he didn't like didn't get it, and so it was worth while enduring the pain, having experienced what, I felt, one would have experienced if Elijah, Isaiah, or Jeremiah had shaken hands with one. For if you knew Kot well, you knew what a major Hebrew prophet must have been like 3,000 years ago. If Jeremiah had been born in a ghetto village in the Ukraine in 1882, he would have been Kot. There are some Jews who, though their ancestors have lived for centuries in European ghettoes, are born with certain characteristics which the sun and sand of the desert beat into the bodies and minds of Semites. The heat of the desert burns their bodies until they are tempered like steel; it tempers their minds until they seem to be purified of all spiritual grit, leaving in mind and soul only pure, undiluted, austere, fanatical passion.

I am not saying that this is good or bad—I don't really know—but aesthetically it has a kind of austere beauty. In daily life it is also often extremely uncomfortable. Kot was not at all a comfortable man, but neither was Elijah nor Isaiah, I am quite sure. I have felt the same qualities of steely, repressed, purged passion, burnt into a Semite by sun and sand, in an ordinary Arab pearl diver from the Persian Gulf;

he stood on the shore in Ceylon looking down on his dead comrade—he had died when diving for pearls at the Ceylon pearl fishery—and he made a long speech to the dead man's brother. It was in Arabic and I did not understand a word, and yet I understood every word. It was Isaiah and Jeremiah and Job—and Kot.

Kot was born in a Jewish village and his family, before the 1914 war, was well off, his father owning a mill. The fortunes of the Koteliansky family in the Ukraine are part of the terrible story of misery, death, and destruction which have swept over Jew and Gentile in central and eastern Europe since 1914. For centuries no doubt Jews, like the Kotelianskys in eastern Europe, suffered spasmodically from pogroms. Every now and then deaths by violence here or a rape there reminded them of what some people would call realities; for them it was something which the experience of two millennia had taught them to expect from God and from Governments, but in between these visitations or realities Jehovah more or less honoured his promise to Abram.

After 1914 families like the Kotelianskys were ruthlessly wiped off the face of the earth. Their village suffered the tramplings of more than three conquests, it was fought over first by the Austrians and Russians, then by the White Guards and a 'brigand' called, I think, Petlura, and finally by the Red Army. The Kotelianskys were well liked even by their Christian neighbours, and, when anti-Semitic armies were known to be approaching, the old grandmother was hurried away by her Christian neighbours into the comparative safety of their village. She died in the midst of one of these removals, and by the end of the fighting, when the Red Army finally established itself, Kot's parents and most of his brothers and sisters and their families had been liquidated by one side or the other. One brother did escape and soon

In autumn

In winter

The road to Telscombe

In spring

In summer

after the war managed to reach Antwerp, and thence London and Canada.

Kot came to London with some kind of scholarship a few years before the 1914 war; he must have been nearly 30. In 1914 he met D. H. Lawrence on a walking tour in the Lakes and they took to each other at once. Kot's passionate approval of what he thought good, particularly in people; his intense hatred of what he thought bad; the directness and vehemence of his speech; his inability to tell a lie—all this strongly appealed to Lawrence. When Kot approved of anyone, he accepted him absolutely; he could do no wrong and Kot summed it up always by saying of him: 'He is a real person.' This ethical accolade was given by him to very few people. Lawrence, Katherine Mansfield, and Virginia were among the few who received it. When he said of someone: 'You see, he is a *real* person, yes, a *real* person,' you felt that you and he and that 'real person' had received some blessed vision or even sacrament of reality. Lawrence liked this kind of thing in Kot, just as he liked Kot's ruthless condemnation of people like Murry, and they became very fond of each other.

Kot's condemnations were terrific. If you said to him: 'Do you like such and such a book?' and he did not, he would say: 'It is hor-r-r-ible,' and the roll of his r's was like the roll of thunder on Mt. Sinai. Or he would say of someone of whom he disapproved: 'A swindler, just a swindler'—and you felt that his vehemence had blown away all screens, disguises, veils, and uncovered the nakedness of some wretched sinner.

Kot once told me a little story which gives the flavour of his character and of his relations with the Lawrence circle. He went to stay for a weekend with Lawrence and Frieda near Chesham. It was only the second time that he had met Frieda and only his third meeting with Lawrence. At lunch Frieda began lamenting how much she missed her children. (She had left her husband and children to marry Lawrence.)

251

Kot said: 'Frieda, you have left your children to marry Lawrence—and if you choose Lawrence, you must stop complaining about the children.' After lunch Frieda left them and Lawrence and Kot sat talking while outside the rain poured down in torrents. Suddenly the door opened and there stood a young woman with her skirt tucked up, in Wellington boots, soaking wet. She said: 'Lorenzo. Frieda has asked me to come and tell you that she will not come back.' 'Damn the woman,' shouted Lawrence in a fury, 'tell her I never want to see her again.' The young woman said nothing, but turned and went out into the rain.

The young woman was Katherine Mansfield, and it was the first time that Kot saw her. Later they became great friends. Katherine's feeling for him is clearly shown in her letters and journals; he was perhaps the only person whom she trusted and respected completely. And of Katherine Kot always said: 'She is a real person.' When I first knew Kot, he sat in a room at the top of a high building in Sicilian Avenue, and there sometimes when we were sitting talking and Katherine was there, she would say to him: 'Now, Kot, howl like a dog.' And Kot would howl like a dog with such canine verisimilitude, with so melancholy and penetrating a howl, that from far off, even as far off as Russell Square, would come the answering howl of real dogs. This accomplishment had been acquired by Kot in the following way. When a young man in the Ukraine he had fallen in love with a woman living in a village about five miles from his home. He used once a week to go and see her, and then had to walk back the five miles late at night. The darkness, loneliness, silence terrified him, and he taught himself to howl like a dog because then the dogs in distant villages howled back in answer to him, and he felt that at any rate he was not entirely alone in a dark and hostile world.

The world in which Kot lived remained for him a dark

and hostile world even in Acacia Road, St. John's Wood, where for many years he lived alone. I went to see him there a few days before his death. Owing to the war and the aftermath of war I had not seen him for a long time, but, although obviously ill, he was the same as he had always been. My hand was crushed in the iron hand of the Commendatore. His hair was grey, his body flagging, but the spirit of Elijah, Isaiah, and Jeremiah remains to the end indomitable. Yes, Kot was a real person.

It is perhaps worth while recording the finances of The Hogarth Press in the first four years of its existence, during which we published the nine books listed on pages 241 and 242. By the end of 1920 the total capital expenditure was £38. 8s. 3d., on the printing machine, type, accessories, and a paper cutting machine. The following shows the net profit on each of the eight books:

	£	s.	d.
Two Stories	7	1	0
Prelude	7	11	8
Kew Gardens	14	10	0
Eliot's *Poems*	9	6	10
Murry's *Critic in Judgment*	2	7	0
Forster's *Story of the Siren*	4	3	7
Mirrlees's *Paris*	8	2	9
Stories from the Old Testament	11	4	5
Gorky's *Reminiscences*	26	10	9

In the first four years, therefore, the total net profit was £90, but this was without any charge for rent and overheads. We usually paid the author 25 per cent. of the gross profits, and, where we printed the books ourselves, nothing was charged for printing and binding.

When the war ended, though the MS. of *Ulysses* was in

the cabinet in the drawing-room and I was on the point of buying McDermott's large platen printing machine from him for £70, we still had no idea of turning ourselves into an ordinary, commercial publishing business. But by 1924, if not indeed by 1922, we had, without realizing it, done so. For in 1922 we published Bunin's *Gentleman from San Francisco*, Dostoevsky's *Stavrogin's Confession*, Virginia's *Jacob's Room*, *The Autobiography of Countess Tolstoy*; in 1923 *Tolstoy's Love Letters*, Goldenweiser's *Talks with Tolstoy*, Roger Fry's *Sampler of Castile*, Stephen Reynolds's *Letters*, Forster's *Pharos & Pharillon*; in 1924 Freud's *Collected Papers* and the beginning of the Psycho-analytical Library, *Kenya* by Norman Leys, *The Rector's Daughter* by F. M. Mayor, Living Painters: *Duncan Grant, Seducers in Ecuador* by V. Sackville-West, *Early Impressions* by Leslie Stephen.

Ten years after we started printing *Two Stories* The Hogarth Press was a successful commercial publishing business. It remained for Virginia and me, and has always remained for me, a half-time occupation. I have little doubt that, if I had made it my full-time occupation, it would have become a bigger, fatter, and richer business. I have often heard it said by professional publishers and other people who know the book producing and book selling industry far better than I do that it would be quite impossible today to do what we did in 1917 to 1927, i.e. build up a successful publishing business from zero with no capital. Costs of production have increased to such an extent and publishing is so geared to large scale, best seller industry that today there is no place for the kind of books with which we began and which floated The Hogarth Press into prosperity. I see the added difficulties, but I am not convinced that the thing would not be possible in 1963. First, one would have to have, of course, the kind of luck which we had—to know or find a few writers, unknown but potentially of the first class. Secondly, one would have to start it, as we did, as a very part-time occupation, making one's living for the first years in other ways. Thirdly, one would have to refuse absolutely, as we did for many years, to publish anything unless we thought it worth publishing or the author worth publishing. I think that 'thirdly' is the most important of the three conditions of success. Most small publishers perish by trying to become too big too quickly. One reason why the Press survived was because for many years our object was, not to expand, but to keep it small. In business the road to bankruptcy is paved with what the accountant calls 'overheads' and too many publishers allow their 'overheads' to dictate to them the size of their business and the kind of books they publish. My theory was that the main object of a publisher, as business man, should be to keep his overheads as near to zero as possible, and, if he did that, he could forget about them and publish only what he wanted to publish. I still think that this had a good deal to do with the survival of The Hogarth Press.

The last year of the war was incredibly gloomy. Looking back on it I feel as if we lived in a perpetual fog. Only a few incidents emerge from the fog into my memory. Air raids became important. Bugles were blown and Virginia and I and Nellie, the cook, and Lottie, the housemaid, went down into the basement kitchen, and remained there while the anti-aircraft guns blazed away in Richmond Old Deer Park and sometimes the shrapnel fell rattling into the area.

One night when Desmond was staying with us there was one of the longest and most violent thunderstorms which I have ever lived through. It was impossible to sleep and Desmond and I sat talking and looking out of the window of his room on to the street. At about 3 o'clock in the morning a solitary horseman cantered down the empty street through the pouring rain while the lightning flashed and the thunder rolled around him.

At 11 in the morning of Monday, November 11, 1918, I was writing in my room in Richmond when the maroons, as they were called, were fired. From this we knew that the armistice had been signed and that the Great War had ended. Virginia celebrated the return of peace by going to the dentist in Harley Street and I restlessly followed her. We met in Wigmore Street and drifted to Trafalgar Square. The first hours of peace were terribly depressing. The Square, indeed all the streets, were solid with people, omnibuses, and vehicles of all kinds. A thin, fine, cold rain fell remorselessly upon us all. Some of us carried sodden flags, some of us staggered in and out of pubs, we wandered aimlessly in the rain and mud with no means of celebrating peace or expressing our emotions of relief and joy. Our emotions of joy and relief ebbed, our spirits flagged. All, or nearly all of us, decided at the same moment to go home, and at once it became impossible to go home, for the buses, the trains, the stations became a solid mass of people struggling to go home Eventually we managed to get to Waterloo and some two hours later Richmond.

On the first page of this book I recorded that the one thing which I remember in my return from Ceylon after seven years to Europe is the chocolate creams in Marseille. It is a strange fact—I have no doubt, discreditable to me, some unsavoury juggling between my scruffy ego and sluttish id—that one of the chief things which I remember as connected with the return from those terrible four years of war to peace is chocolate creams. A good many Belgian refugees in the first year of the war settled in Richmond and a large florid Belgian woman opened a kind of delicatessen shop (as they were called in those days) and tea-shop some way up the hill near Richmond Bridge. As the war went on delicatessen became very thin on the ground and chocolate creams vanished. Some months after armistice day, Virginia and I, walking up Richmond Hill, looked into the shop and there upon the counter were slabs of chocolate cream bars. When I was a child, you could buy large fat bars of chocolate cream which cost, I think, a halfpenny the bar. Some were made by Cadbury and some by Fry, and if you were an addict of Cadbury, you regarded the Fry eater as a drinker of Musigny Vieilles Vignes regards the drinker of Australian Burgundy. I belonged to the Cadbury school and have remained an addict of chocolate cream in bars ever since (though I have not seen any for years). The Belgian chocolate cream bars were un-English, being thin and continental, but when we saw them, the world seemed to change just a little and we dashed into the shop and each bought three bars which was the maximum that Madame X allowed each customer to buy. We carried them back to Hogarth House and ate them silently, almost reverently. The Great War was at last over.

INDEX

INDEX

INDEX

INDEX

INDEX